Presenting Disneyland

FORGOTTEN PHOTOGRAPHS FROM OPENING DAY

AARON H. GOLDBERG

Presenting Disneyland

FORGOTTEN PHOTOGRAPHS FROM OPENING DAY

AARON H. GOLDBERG

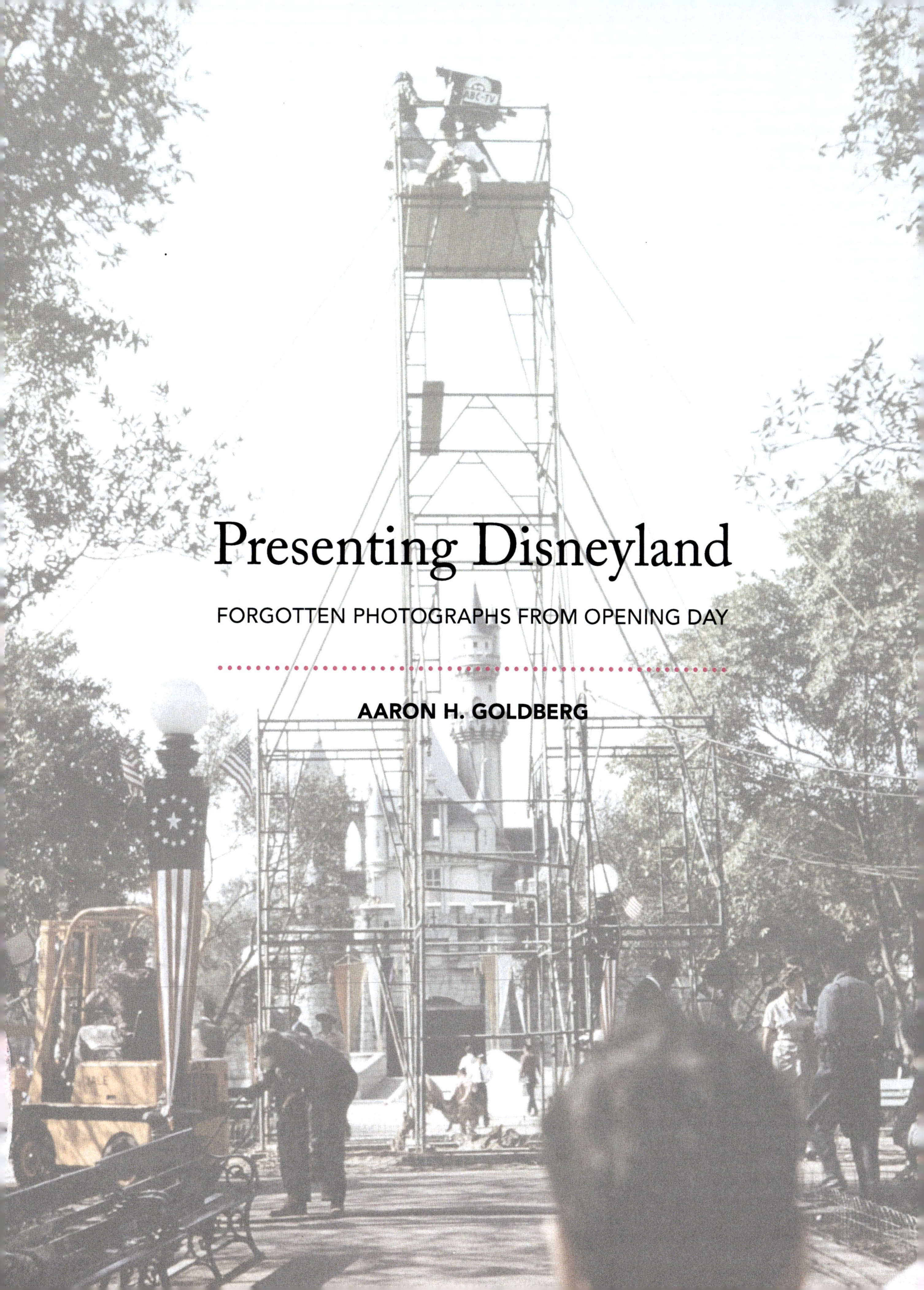

Presenting Disneyland
Forgotten Photos from Opening Day

Cover design by Rob Yeo Design
Interior layout and typesetting by Sue Balcer
Published by Quaker Scribe Publishing
Philadelphia, Pennsylvania
quakerscribe@gmail.com

First printing 2023

ISBN: 978-1-7336420-8-8
Library of Congress Control Number: 2023903724

Visit the author on the web: www.aaronhgoldberg.com
Follow Aaron H. Goldberg on Twitter & Instagram at @aaronhgoldberg

Contents

Foreword from Bob Gurr

As you begin your scan through what you might have thought was going to be a regular book, you'll find that Aaron's latest read is a bit different, as he presents newly discovered early Disneyland photographs. Pause first at a letterhead—Disneyland Inc. You have just received an invitation to be one of the first guests at a press preview and dedication of this crazy new 1955 park called Disneyland.

No doubt you have been following its progress, since October 1954, on a fascinating new TV show, also called Disneyland. You already know a lot about what you'd experience if you ever got the chance to visit there yourself someday. But look, you have been chosen to visit before actual opening day! You, yes you. "Oh, our whole family can go together. I can't wait to tell friends all about what we will see."

Alright, I fooled you. But hey, let's pretend we really were there on dedication day, and that we also took many pictures, which we are eager to show everyone in exactly the same way the newspapers would describe the following day—by reporting stories along with fresh photos.

Pretend a bit more; fantasy is perfectly normal. Rather than read this book like a book, enjoy the dedication of Disneyland vicariously. With your Mickey Mouse ears on, delight yourself now as is if you were actually there on July 17, 1955. Savor the photos and read the commentary from those journalists who were there with you that day.

Yes, I was there too, even before. Walt Disney had been gathering the most astonishing team of every skill and trade, beginning in 1952, to help him build his park, which he first dreamed of in 1938. In October of 1954, Walt hired me on as a car body stylist. He had created a little mechanical car, in need of a new body, to be used on a new amusement ride to be called Autopia.

Throughout 1954 and into 1955, the Walt Disney Productions Studio in Burbank, California was all abuzz with every kind of craftsperson imaginable. Along with everyone else, I was in an enchanted forest of future Imagineers. Walt handed me the Autopia car body design assignment. "And oh yes, engineer the car mechanical parts too. While you're at it, we need a parking lot train. Also, one of our sponsors, Carnation, wants a period ice cream truck."

Dedication day was when . . . eight months? I winced at how I was to design, help manufacture, deliver, and test four vehicle projects in time. That was normal; every person was doing many jobs all at the same time. Amazingly, we all made terrific progress, gradually doing additional work down in Anaheim at the park construction site.

Finally, it was dedication day. I'd gotten to bed by midnight the night before, and then back down to work by 8:00 am, just like every previous day for months. A three-hour round trip, no freeway, just dirt and gravel road construction to be gradually completed in time. The dedication was to be shown live on a ninety-minute national TV program. Now we had two gigantic projects under foot. TV crews, miles of cables, scaffolding and forklifts, cameras to be positioned. Disneyland was still a mad construction zone, hot asphalt paving still cooling, fresh paint still drying.

Showtime. Each of us had been given very specific orders, times, and locations. Mine seemed easy. Autopia ride operators would help me reposition nine Autopia cars from the ride to the backstage line up to await the start of the parade. While I was mingling in the crowd of Hollywood actors and various VIPs in front of City Hall, Walt introduced me to actress Gale Storm, along with her two little boys. Walt wanted to show her around to meet other guests and said "Bobby will watch your boys." As the parade started, Gale was in the front row, center Autopia sheriff's car, the boys with me on her right (see page 28!).

After our Autopia unit in the parade peeled off to return the cars to the ride, the boys were still with me—mom nowhere in sight. I was now assigned to help with the TV show broadcasting live from Autopia, which was swarming with those Hollywood actors. During the broadcast, the boys stayed with me in the car as I drove them round and round the ride track. At one point, they yelled "git him, git him," so I hit the car in front of us hard enough that it went up over a track curb. As we passed by, I saw the driver was a short Black man wearing an eye patch.

In the newspaper the following morning, I saw a photo of the man in the car. Oh no, it was Sammy Davis Jr. It seems the boys knew all the actors and had goaded me into doing the hit. For years after, I felt bad I would never have the chance to apologize to Mr. Davis—and tell him "the boys made me do it."

Today I still have vivid memories of Disneyland's dedication day. I trust you will feel your own nostalgia as you delight in enjoying Aaron Goldberg's *Presenting Disneyland*.

—Bob Gurr, Legendary Disney Imagineer

Bob's Bio:

Bob had a hand in designing most all of the attraction vehicles with wheels in the original Disneyland park, including:

- Autopia cars
- Haunted Mansion Doom Buggies
- Monorail
- Submarine Voyage
- Matterhorn Bobsleds
- Peoplemover
- Flying Saucers
- Main Street Omnibus
- Disneyland Fire Engine
- and many more . . .

Bob also developed the first realistic humanoid animatronic—Mr. Lincoln—for Great Moments with Mr. Lincoln. Bob received the prestigious Disney Legend Award in 2004, and his handprints adorn the Court of Legends at the Disney studios in Burbank. He has the distinct honor of having a window on Main Street, USA in both Disneyland and the Magic Kingdom. Apart from Disney, Bob designed the King Kong Encounter animatronic for Universal Studios Hollywood and the flying UFO for the opening ceremonies of the 1984 Olympic Games in Los Angeles; assisted Steven Spielberg in preproduction for the Jurassic Park T-Rex animatronic dinosaur; and designed effects for Michael Jackson's "Victory" tour, as well as countless other projects and attractions that have entertained us for years and will continue to live on for generations to come.

Introduction

On July 17, 1955, the world was officially introduced to Disneyland. Thousands became acquainted in person, while millions more watched on television at home. Today we are closer to Disneyland's one hundredth anniversary than to its opening day. In many respects a visit decades later is similar to the park's opening day. It can be exciting, crowded, magical, memorable, entertaining, and of course, an escape from your norm—just about everything Walt Disney hoped it would be.

At first glance the concept of Disneyland, or at least the story that has become the standard for how it all began, is a tale of a father and his two daughters looking for a place where they could engage in some sort of activity together. As Walt would often reminisce:

> *"Disneyland really began when my two daughters were very young. Saturday was always Daddy's Day, and I would take them to the merry-go-round, and sit on a bench eating peanuts, while they rode. And sitting there, alone, I felt there should be something built, some kind of family park where parents and children could have fun together."*

Depending upon who you ask or what you read, the catalyst for Disneyland may or may not have been entirely based on that anecdote. As newspaper archive research reveals, as early as 1932, Walt had some dreams percolating about a theme park enterprise to capitalize on the success of his studio and to fulfill the demand of the public's interest in Mickey Mouse.[1]

While conducting interviews for Disneyland's grand opening, Walt was often asked how long he had been dreaming about his Disneyland project. He routinely stated, "Since I moved out to the Burbank studio. That was about 1938. Originally, I planned to have it right at the studio. I got everything figured out except where to park the cars. Later I talked to the City of Los Angeles about putting it in Griffith Park, but that seemed too involved with red tape." As an aside, his daughter Diane was born in 1933 and his daughter Sharon was born in 1936.[2]

Ultimately, after several waves of success and struggle through the 1930s and 1940s, Walt was finally prepared to embark on his theme park conquest by the 1950s.

In July of 1951 Walt visited Tivoli Gardens in Denmark. His friend, and the eventual host of Disneyland's opening day festivities, Art Linkletter accompanied him on the trip. Walt was so impressed with what he experienced in Europe, he returned home fully committed to creating his own amusement enterprise, which was initially planned for sixteen acres in Burbank, California. He made headlines in September of 1952 when he announced his plan to open the park.[3]

Unfortunately, Burbank didn't share the same excitement as Walt did and the city rejected his plan. This rejection eventually brought the park to the 160 acres in Anaheim, California that debuted to the world as Disneyland in 1955.

Regardless of how or why Disneyland came to be, one thing is certain: Walt was ahead of his time with his theme park—on so many levels. He knew his marketplace, often predicting what his audience would desire even before they knew they were thirsting for it.

Walt Disney was a visionary. He opined and dreamt about the future. He also loved to reminisce and ruminate about the past. These attributes are on display throughout Disneyland and explicit in the words chosen for Disneyland's dedication:

"To All Who Come to This Happy Place, Welcome. Disneyland is your land. Here age relives fond memories of the past... and here youth may savor the challenge and promise of the future. Disneyland is dedicated to the ideals, the dreams, and the hard facts that have created America . . . with the hope that it will be a source of joy and inspiration to all the world. July 17, 1955."

I've often said Walt Disney was the world's biggest and most successful purveyor of nostalgia. Psychologists often call nostalgia "the memory of happiness," as it can be associated with happy memories from the past.

However, nostalgia is not just about happy memories; it can also be about longing for a time when things were simpler or for a time when we felt more connected to others. It can even operate as a source of comfort in times of sadness or distress.[4]

Swiss Psychologist Carl Jung saw nostalgia as a way of reconnecting with our past and understanding our present. He also saw nostalgia as a way to access the shared history and experience that we all have as human beings. (Bet you didn't expect to hear about Jung in a book about Disneyland!) There's something kind of Jungian about that Disneyland dedication, isn't there?

Today we know nostalgia is very powerful. In the not-so-distant past, it was often considered to be an overwhelmingly negative concept. For example, during World War I, nostalgia was associated with illness, as soldiers at war overseas became incredibly homesick.[5] Ironically, Walt spent some time away from his family due to World War I.

Today's research shows that nostalgia is actually very influential and positive for us. It can boost our mood, increase self-esteem, provide a sense of social support, and help with difficult life transitions and situations.[6] Research also shows that the more nostalgic one is, the more authentic one feels, which has positive consequences for psychological well-being.

Perhaps no place fosters nostalgia better than Disneyland, and this is possibly why many of the nearly 850 million people who have visited and experienced a day in the park have found it so meaningful and enjoyable.

So, with our theme park psychoanalysis complete, let's get a healthy dose of nostalgia from Disneyland without actually visiting. I'm excited and proud to present over 100 never before seen or published photos, in color no less, from Disneyland's opening day, July 17, 1955.

What you will see in the following pages is a visual history from a former Disney studio employee. His photos—actually, Kodak Kodachrome slides—were previously lost to the decades until I acquired them and had each slide professionally cleaned, restored, and digitized.

In an effort to properly complement these wonderful photographs with relevant content, rather than my own written commentary, I chose what I believe to be a more powerful companion: original quotes from Walt Disney, press clippings, and interviews from the months and days leading up to the park's opening and the few months after.

Here and there you will also find smatterings of historical information, facts, and notable tidbits. There are also a handful of photos that are not from opening day but from the days prior, along with a few from Christmas time,1955, and into the year 1956. I hope you enjoy *Presenting Disneyland* as much as I enjoyed putting it together.

Oh, and one last thing, a big thank you to retired Imagineers Tom K. Morris and Bob Gurr. Tom helped me identify several folks in the photos, and Bob was gracious enough to give us a few words about his opening day experience and contributions to Disneyland.

Aaron H. Goldberg
March 2023

Disneyland inc.

1313 HARBOR BLVD. ANAHEIM. CALIF. TELEPHONE: KEYSTONE 5-1181

June 30, 1955

Welcome to Disneyland!

May we extend to you a cordial invitation to attend the invitational press preview and dedication of Disneyland on Sunday, July 17th.

In order to plan this day for your complete enjoyment, we are anticipating your acceptance of the enclosed invitations. We have compiled the attached information to answer your questions about the day's events.

We are looking forward to the pleasure of having you join us for a memorable and happy time on July 17th.

Cordially yours,
DISNEYLAND, INC.

Jack C. Sayers

Jack C. Sayers
Customer Relations Director

DISNEYLAND PREVIEW INFORMATION

INVITATION TICKET. Please bring the enclosed invitations with you to Disneyland on Sunday, July 17th. The invitation will be honored at the admission gate and for all rides, exhibits and amusements in Disneyland.

WINDSHIELD STICKER
Please place the enclosed windshield sticker on the driver's side of the windshield. This sticker will help expedite your car through traffic in the vicinity of Disneyland and will also admit you quickly into Disneyland's parking area, which will be closed to the general public that day.

DIRECTIONS TO DISNEYLAND
Please note the reverse side of your invitation ticket with the map of Southern California's principal Freeways and roads leading to Disneyland. Directional signs, pointing the way to Disneyland, will be posted along the Santa Ana Freeway and on other key roads near Disneyland.

MAP OF DISNEYLAND
As you enter the Disneyland parking area, the attendant will give you a map of Disneyland, showing location of all major areas, rides, exhibits and facilities.

CLOSING TIME:

In order to prepare for the public opening at 10:00 a.m. the following morning (Monday, July 18th), Disneyland will be closed at 8:00 p.m. Admission gates will be closed at 7:30 p.m., so if you plan to visit Disneyland late in the day, please time your arrival before that hour.

DEDICATION AND OPENING CEREMONIES

Formal dedication ceremonies and special events will take place within Disneyland beginning at 4:30 p.m. These ceremonies will be telecast as a news event over the ABC-TV network between 4:30 and 6:00 p.m. During the telecast, Disneyland's admission gates will be temporarily closed between 4:20 p.m. and 5:30 p.m. If you wish to be present during the telecast, please plan to arrive at Disneyland by 4:15. At 4:00 p.m., Disneyland guides and attendants will clear certain areas within Disneyland in preparation for these ceremonies. May we ask you kind cooperation in moving to the areas designated by the guides and attendants at this time.

Public Relations Department
Disneyland, Inc.
Anaheim, California

"I could never convince the financiers that Disneyland was feasible, because dreams offer too little collateral."

—Walt Disney

Forgotten Photos
From Opening Day

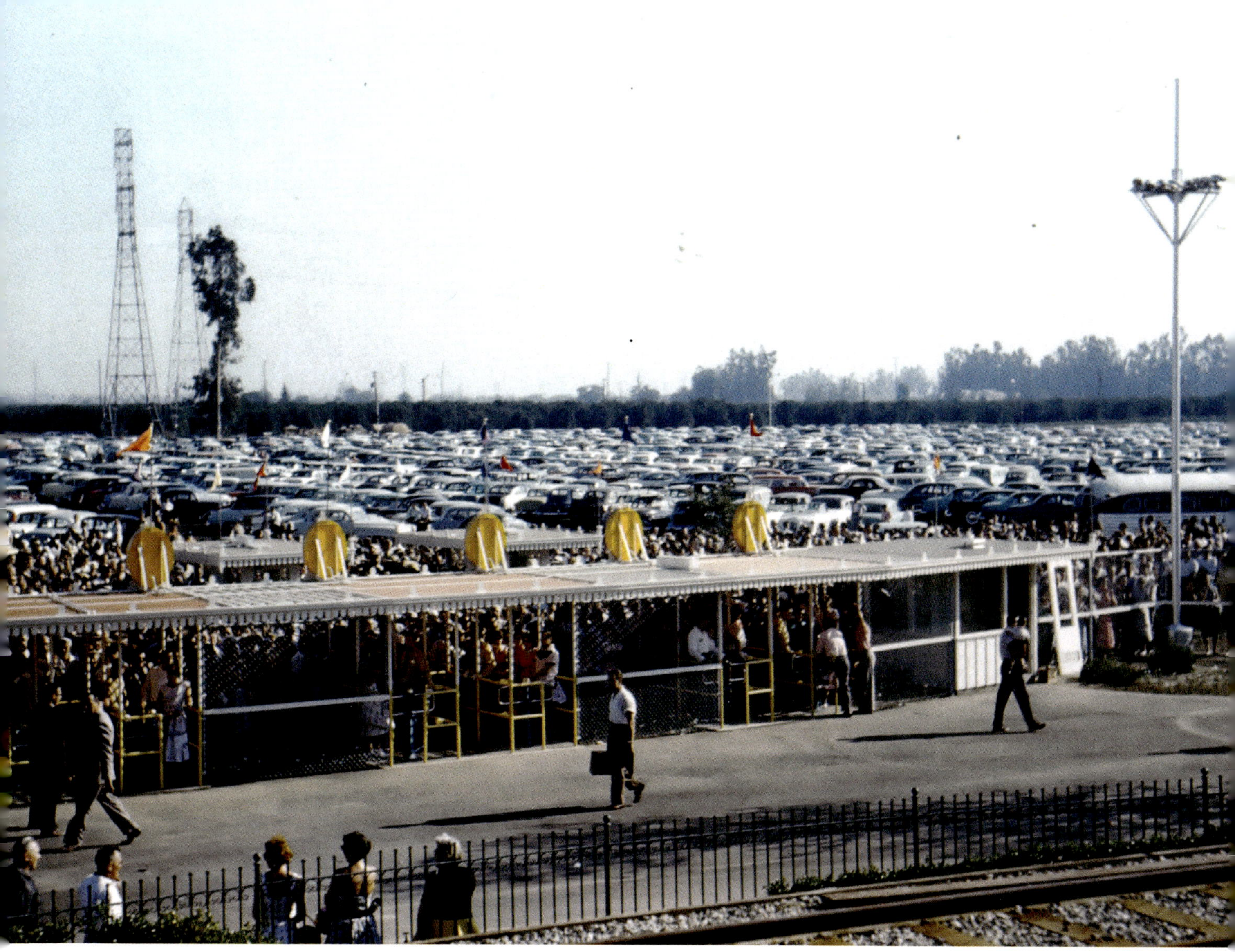

"The first year I leased out the parking concession, brought in the usual security guards—things like that. But soon I realized my mistake. I couldn't have outside help and still get over my idea of hospitality. So, we now recruit and train every one of our employees. I tell the security police, for instance, that they are never to consider themselves cops. They are there to help people. The visitors are our guests. It's like running a fine restaurant. Once you get the policy going, it grows."

— Walt Disney speaking about Disneyland from Walt Disney Productions Tencennial Press Clippings

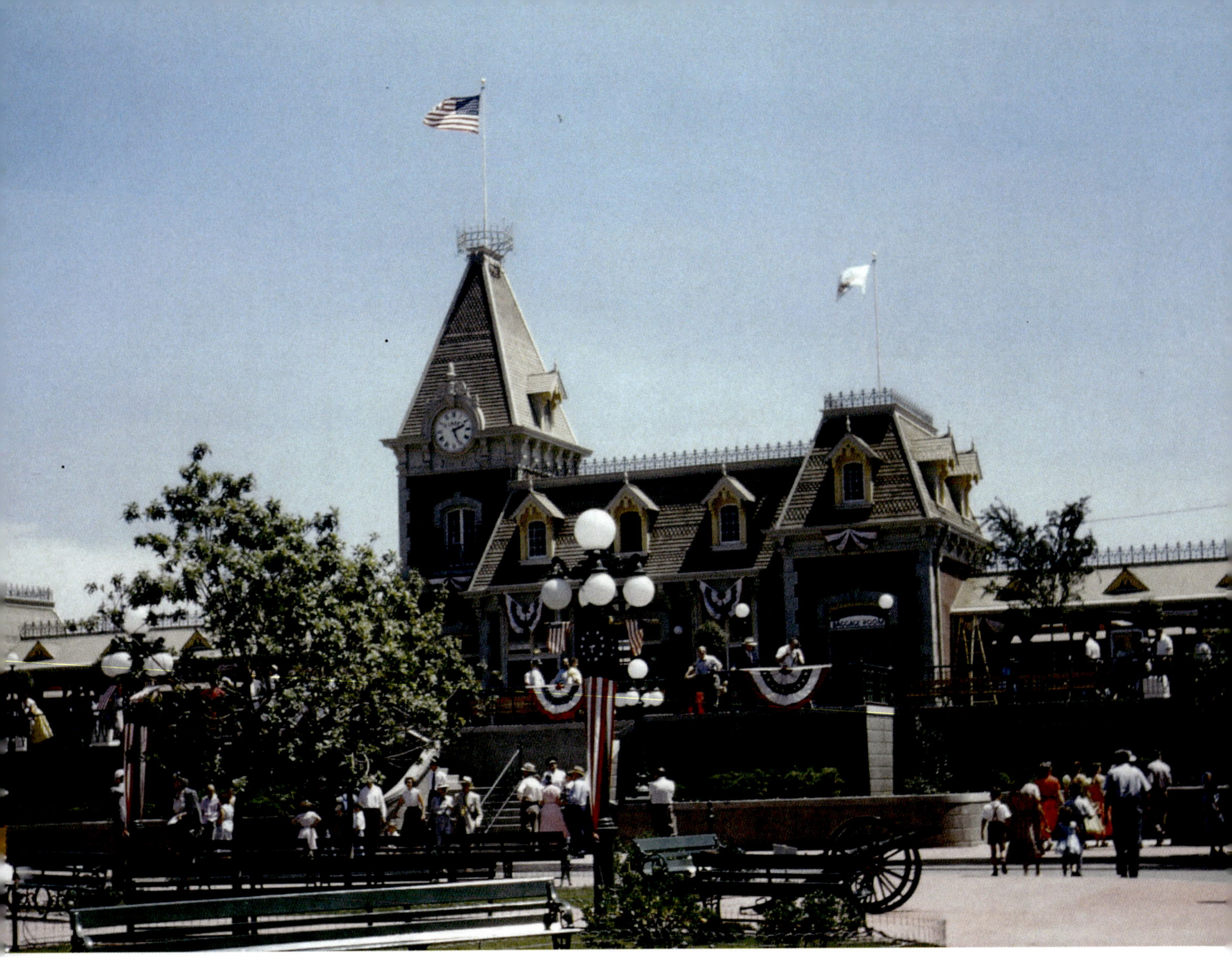

"Opening day admission price for adults is $1.00, tax included. For children, under 12, admission is 50 cents, tax free. Tickets may be purchased only at Disneyland. Your admission ticket entitles you to roam all the lands of Disneyland and view the many exhibits and free shows without any further charge. Disneyland's rides and other unique amusements are all popularly priced. Disneyland's parking area will accommodate 12,175 cars, for the convenience of visitors driving private vehicles. A nominal charge of 25 cents covers all-day parking."

The American Broadcast Company (ABC) had 29 television cameras set up throughout the park. Many of the cameras were borrowed from television stations across the country. Technicians laid over 85,000 feet of coaxial cable throughout the park and a production staff of nearly 70 people worked to broadcast Disneyland's debut around the country. Over 60 million people watched the festivities at home.

—***Long Beach Independent***, July 15, 1955

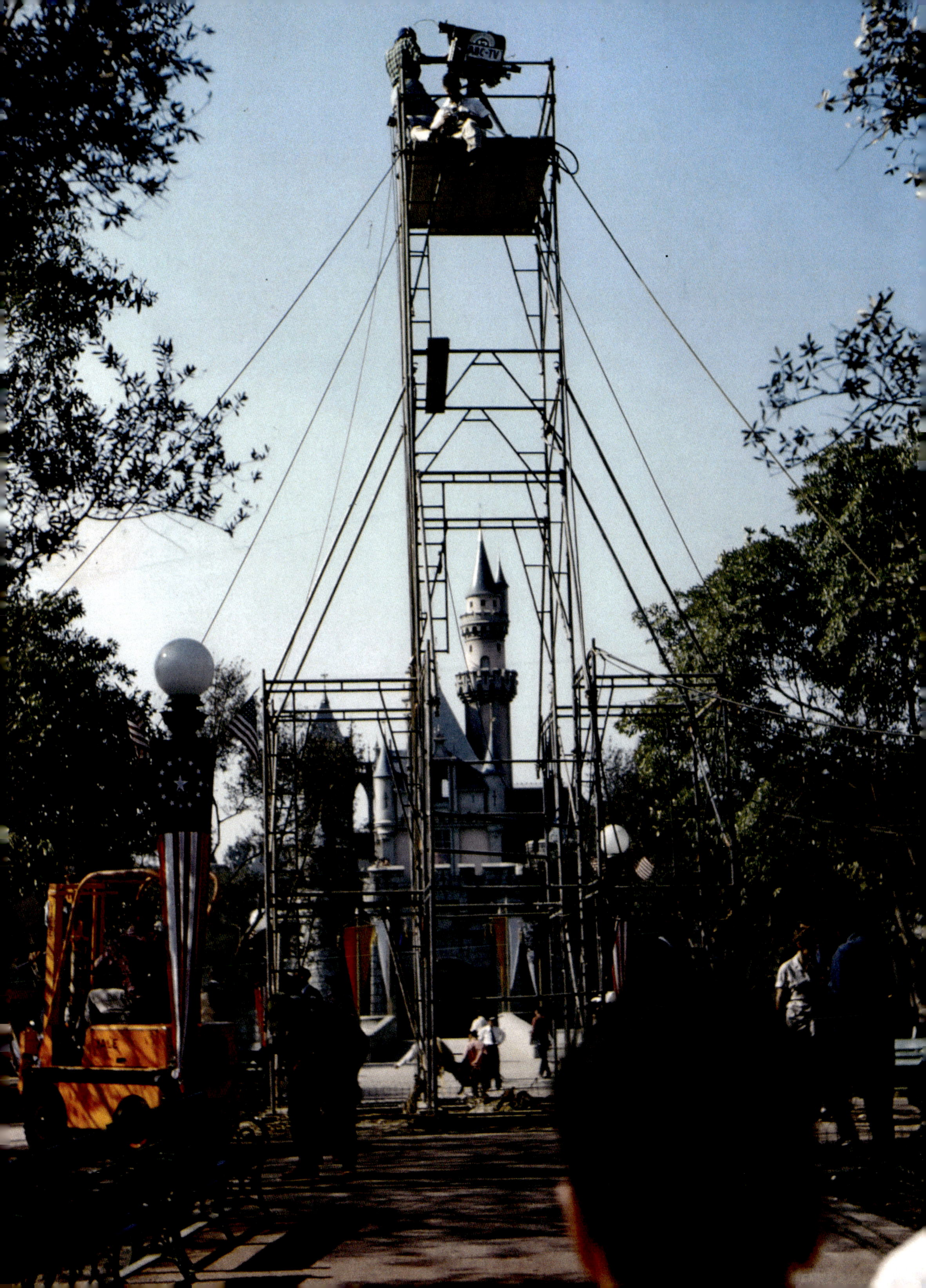
ABC-TV

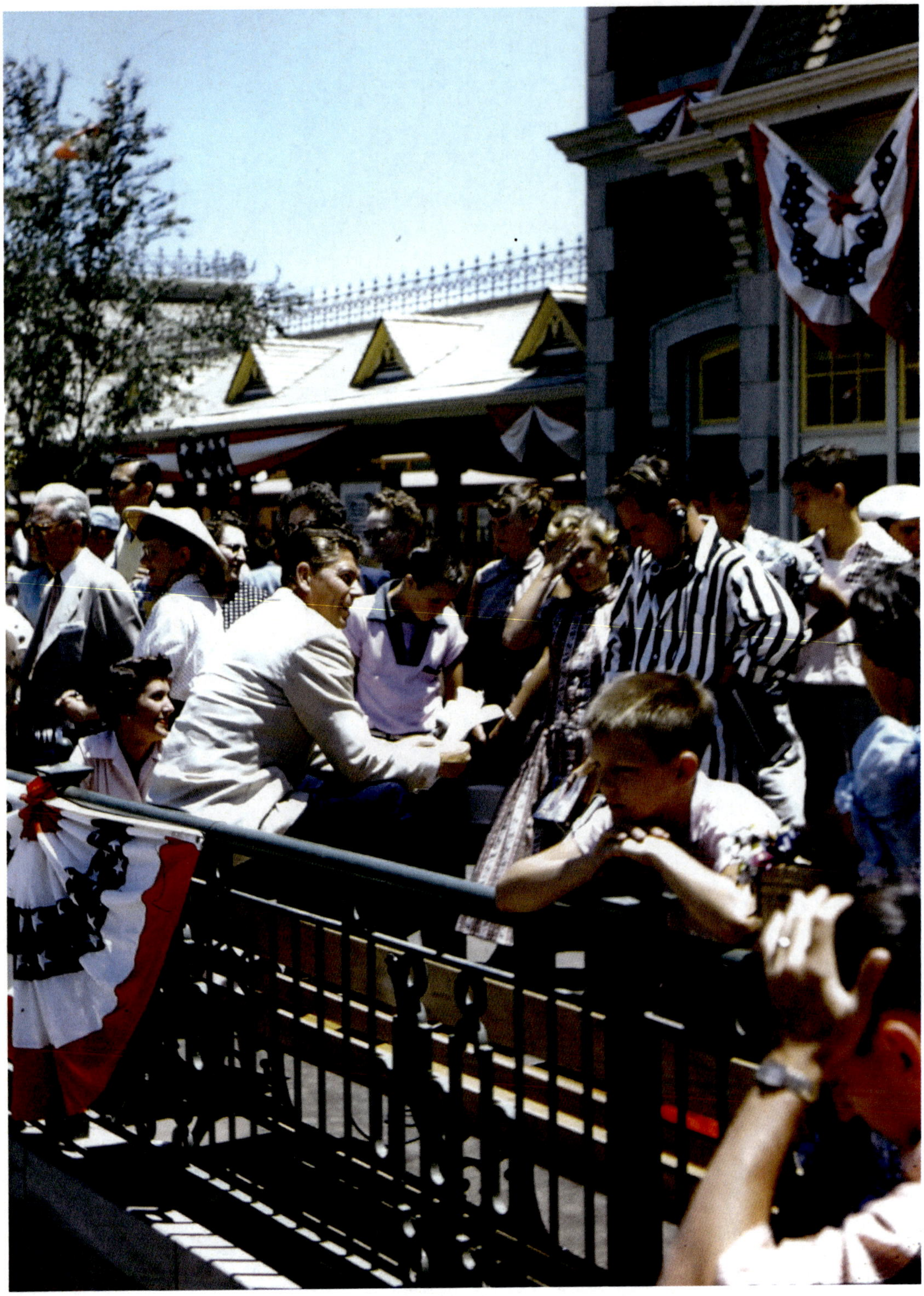

Long before he was governor of California and president of the United States, actor Ronald Reagan was a part of Disneyland's television debut, alongside Art Linkletter and Bob Cummings.

(Reagan's wife Nancy is seated beside him.)

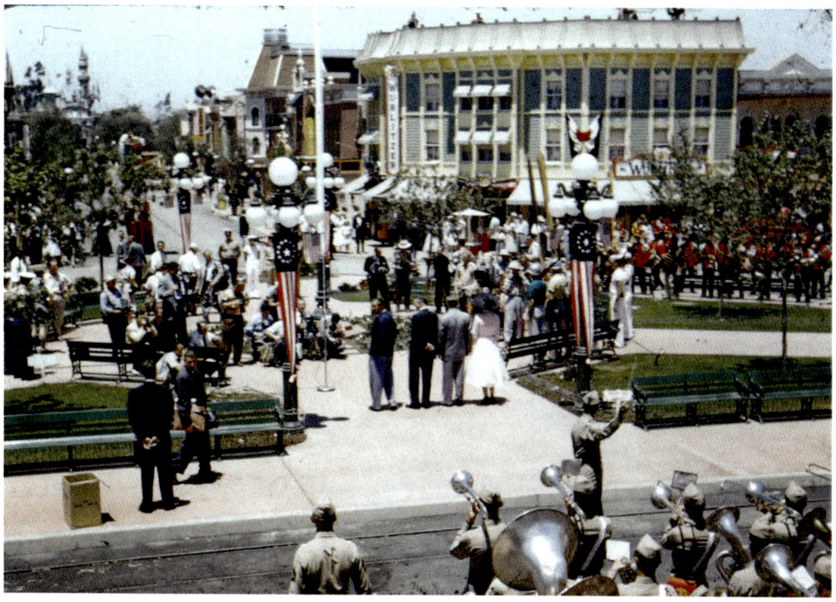

"It was a big flat grove as far as you could see, the land was covered with orange trees. No mountains or rivers or hills or space ships or jungles. Just flat land.

That was a year ago. Walt Disney, the man who is the creator of Mickey Mouse and all his older brothers and sisters in Fantasyland—had the idea of bringing Main Street, Fantasyland, Adventure and Tomorrowland—all of them—together in this very orange grove.

To do it he hired a lot of people. Needed was a landscape architect to choose all kinds of plants for special places and put them together to look well and grow healthy.

Disney hired the firm of Evans and Reeves and said, 'Here are things I want you to do: On Main Street and all around this part,' he pointed to the blueprint of the hub in Disneyland where all the entrances are to the different sections, 'everything is going to be scaled down in size so a child can see it without straining. Find trees and plants that are the right size, so that they will be sure to look as if they had always been here.'

'And, finally,' said Disney, 'you see all these castles and buildings in Disneyland?' The castle itself is 70 feet tall—the Landscape Architect could hardly help seeing it. 'Let the castle be glimpsed through the trees!'

The chief landscape architect hired a crew of 30 men to work days. Another crew of 10 men worked nights to take care of wiring the plants and watering what had been planted just to keep it growing.

There was no way of watering the plants and trees once they had been planted. An old-fashioned water wagon was used in the early part of the job to bring water to the thirsty plants. Later on, there was a giant sprinkler system. It has 1065 sprinklers, and they carried 5950 gallons of water a minute every time the water was turned on. Now water comes from wells on Disney's property.

Remember, it all started with an orange grove a year ago."

—***Long Beach Independent***, July 15, 1955

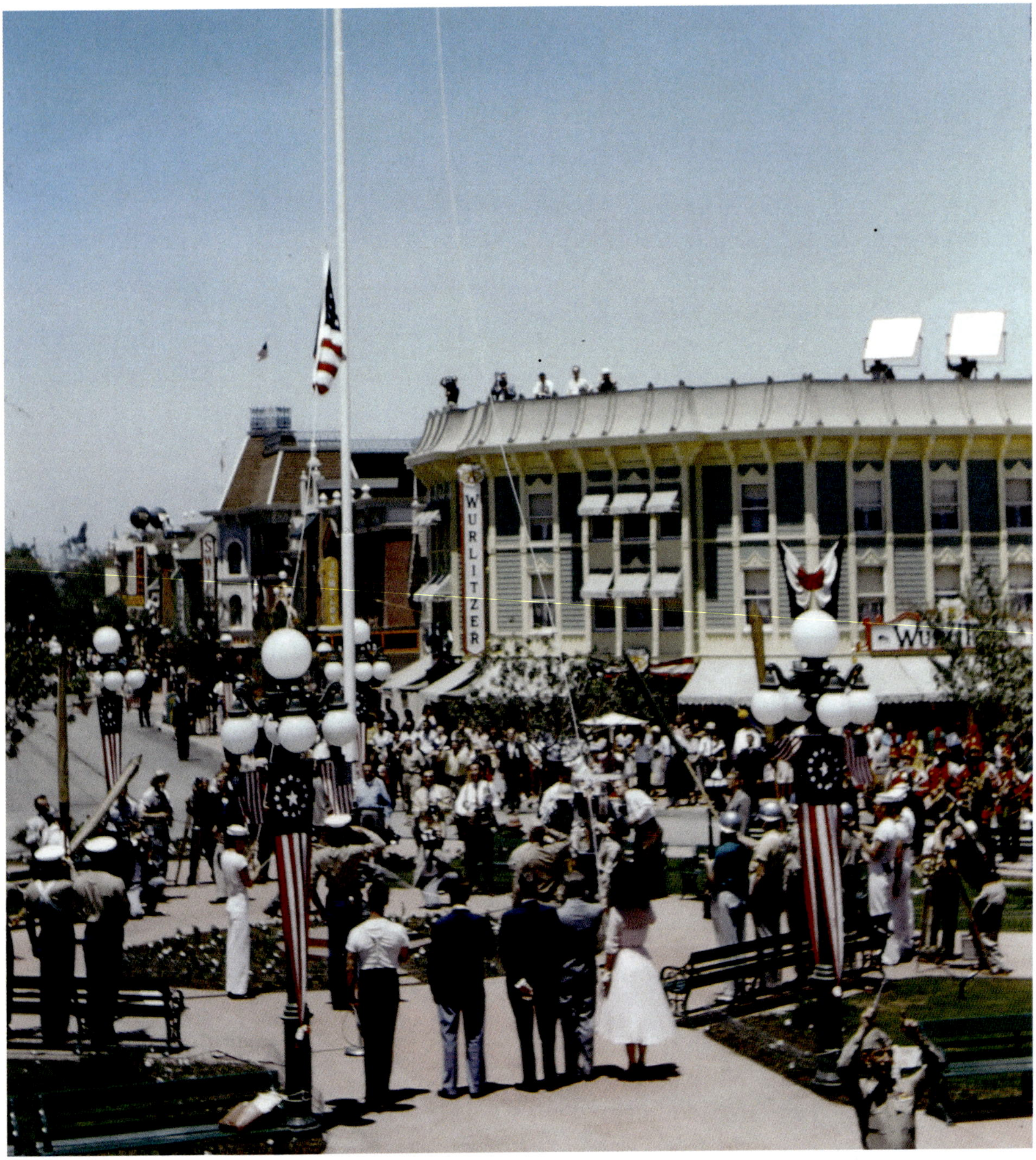

"When you're curious, you find lots of interesting things to do. And one thing it takes to accomplish something is courage. Take Disneyland for example. Almost everyone warned us that Disneyland would be a Hollywood spectacular—a spectacular failure. But they were thinking about an amusement park, we believed in our idea—a family park where parents and children could have fun—together."

—Walt Disney speaking about Disneyland from Walt Disney Productions Tencennial Press Clippings

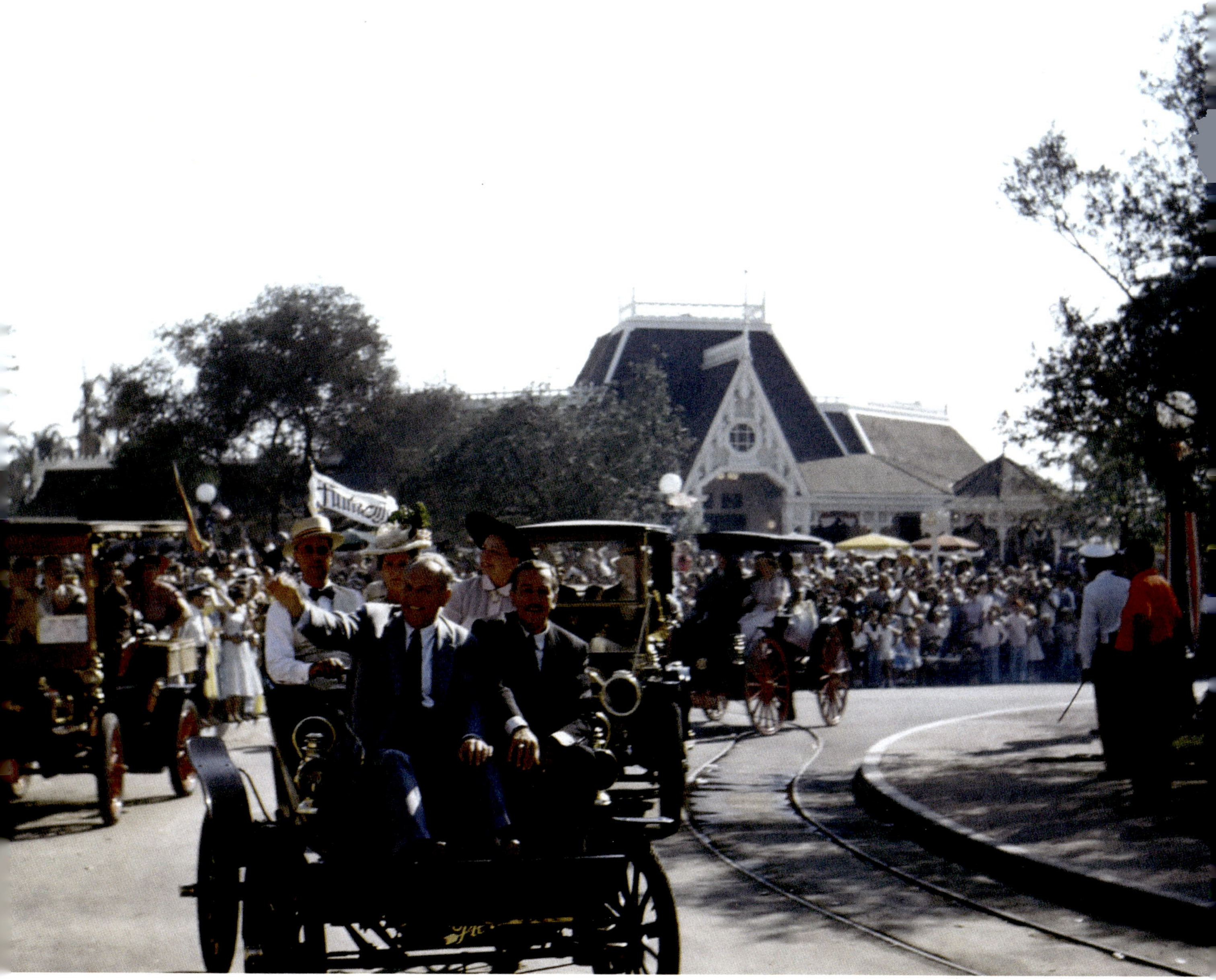

Walt Disney with the thirty-first governor of California, Goodwin Knight.

"Why be a governor or a senator when you can be king of Disneyland"

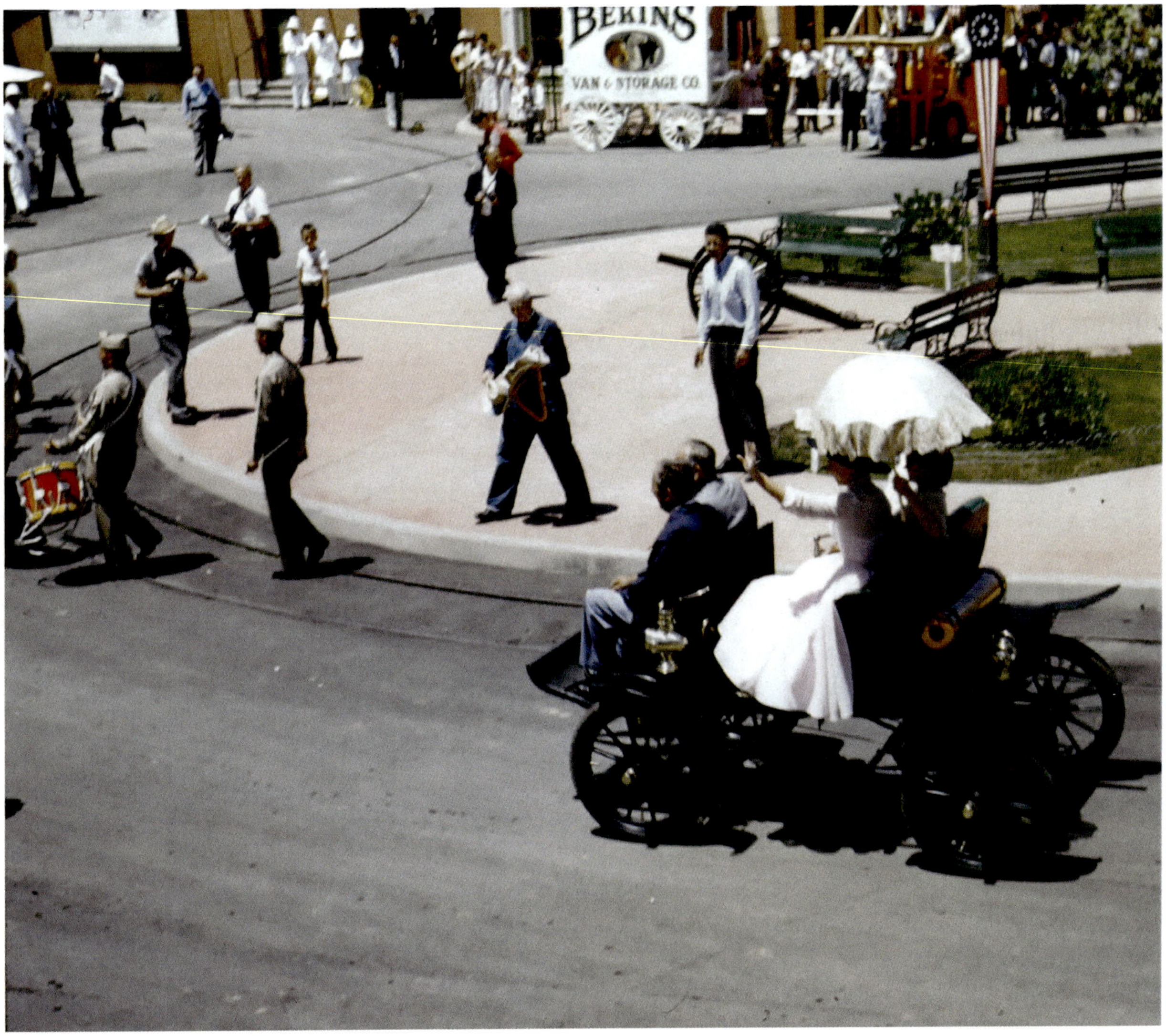

— Walt Disney speaking about Disneyland from Walt Disney Productions Tencennial Press Clippings

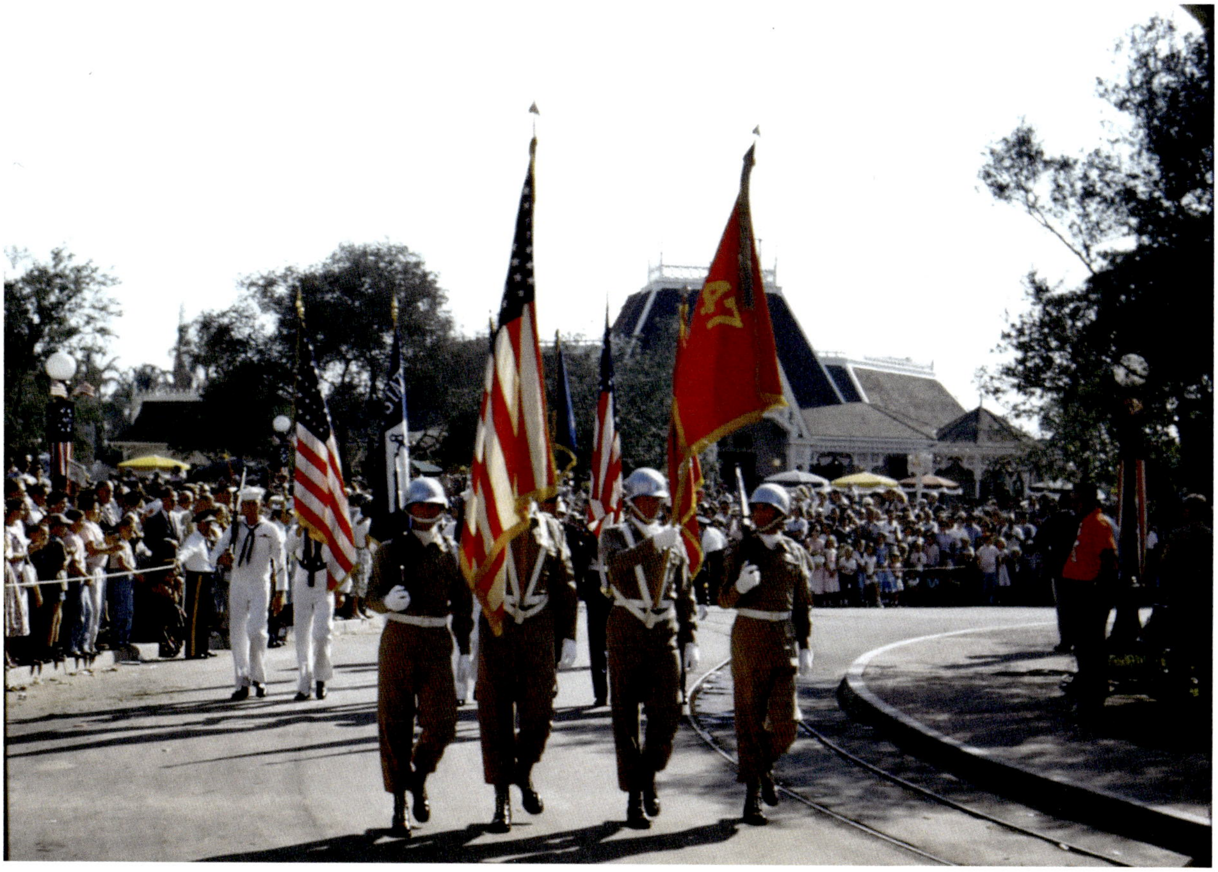

The United States Armed Forces were well represented on opening day. The 146th Fighter Interceptor Wing of the California Air National Guard did a flyover. On the ground the U.S. Marine Corps Band and Color Guard from San Diego proudly marched in the parade.

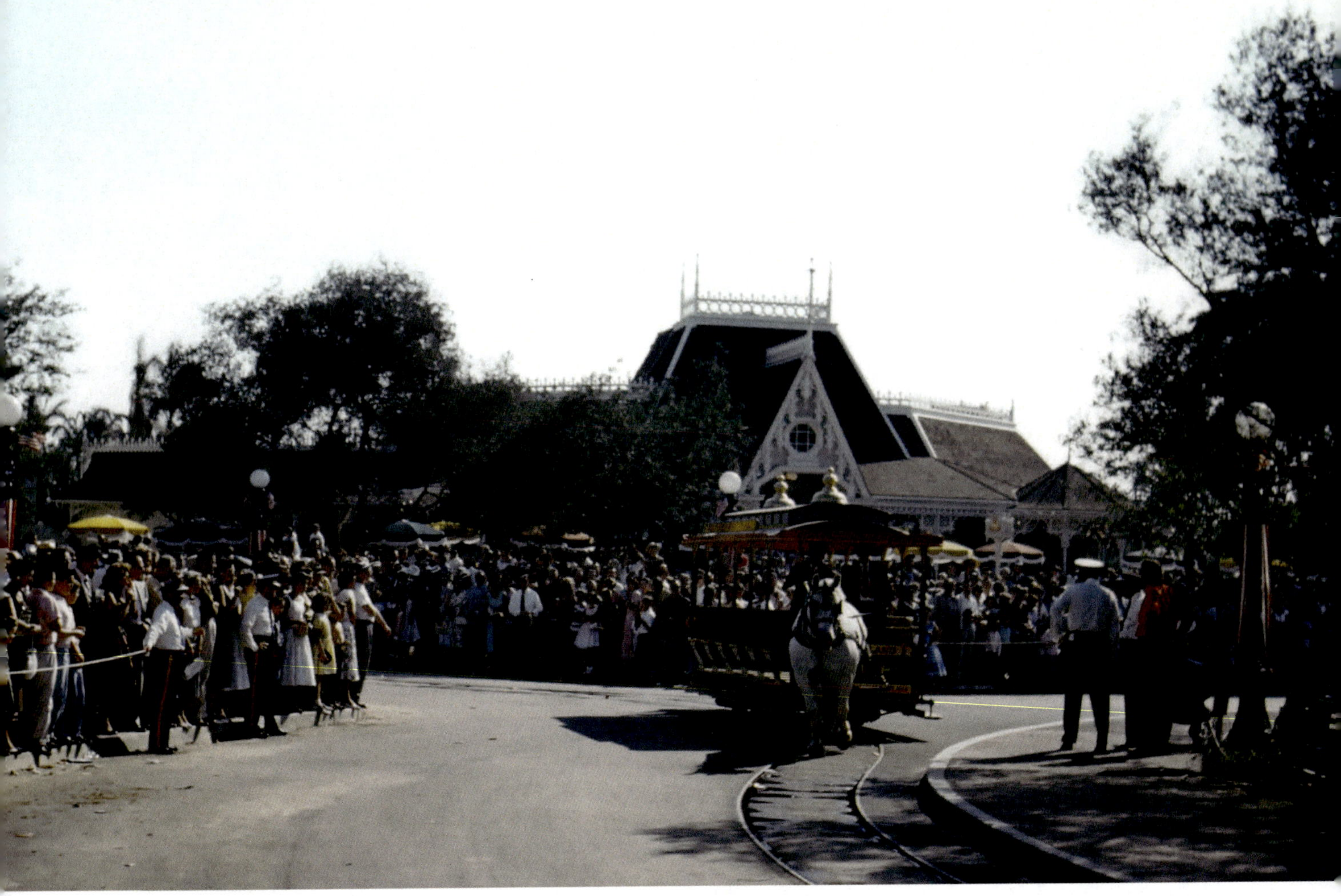

"The idea of Disneyland is a simple one. It will be a place for people to find happiness and knowledge. It will be a place for parents and children to share pleasant times in one another's company: A place for teacher and pupils to discover greater ways of understanding and educating. Here the older generation can recapture nostalgia of days gone by, and the younger generation can savor the challenge of the future. Here will be the wonders of nature and man for all to see and understand."

—Walt Disney's 1953 Disneyland Prospectus

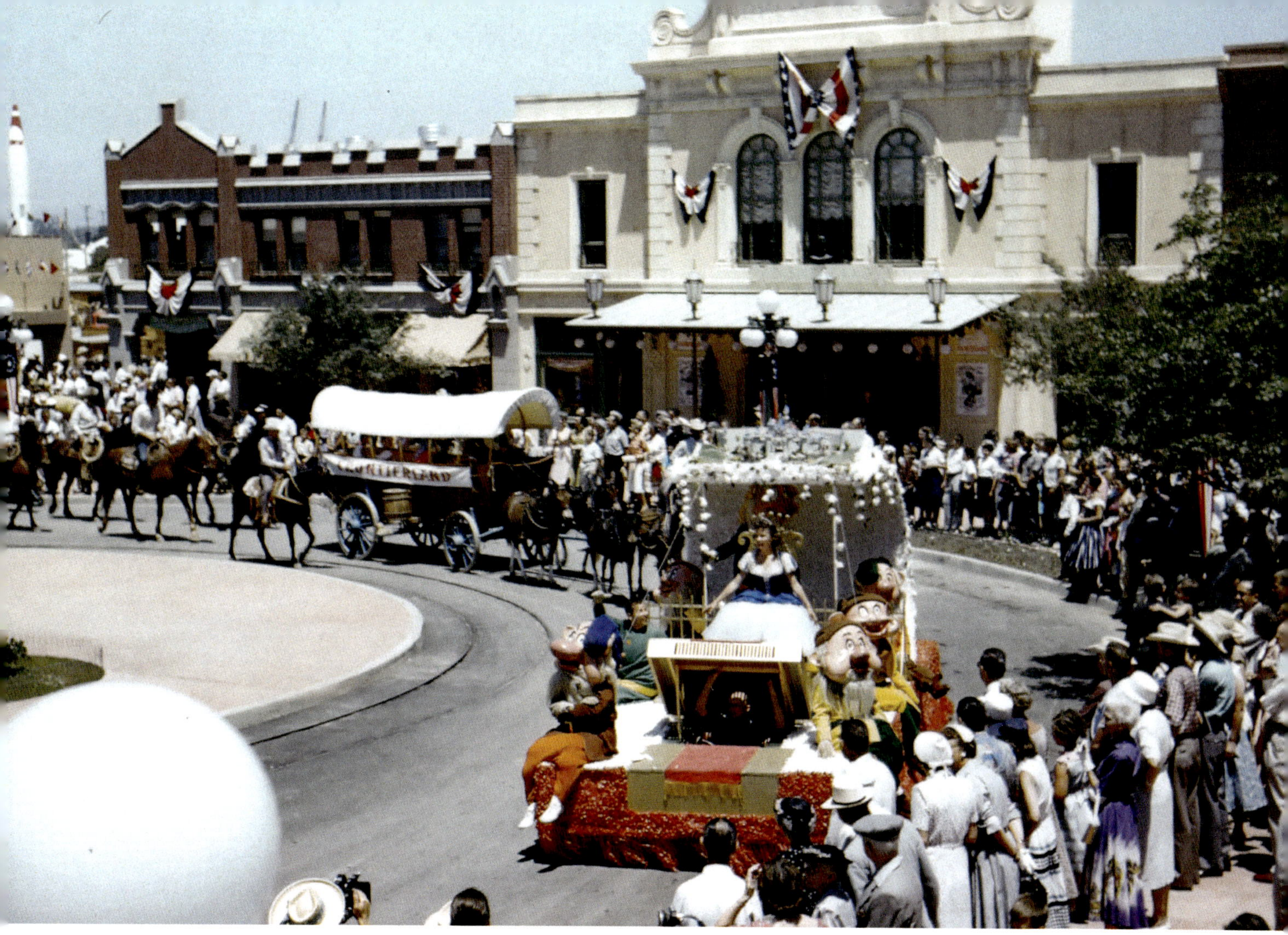

"Walt Disney is one step ahead of others in the motion picture industry. He is now engaged in a full-length feature picture that will take one year to complete at a cost of $500,000, 'Snow White and the Seven Dwarfs.' . . . A contract has been drawn up between Walt Disney and R.K.O. Distributing Company whereby arrangements have been completed for the use of Mickey Mouse characters for television. In your homes, therefore, when television entertainment is made possible in the near future, probably the first entertainment to be presented will be Walt Disney's comic characters."

—Kay Kamen, Disney's licensing and marketing maven, ***Montreal Gazette***, April 23, 1936.

Just what is Disneyland? 160 acres of happiness.

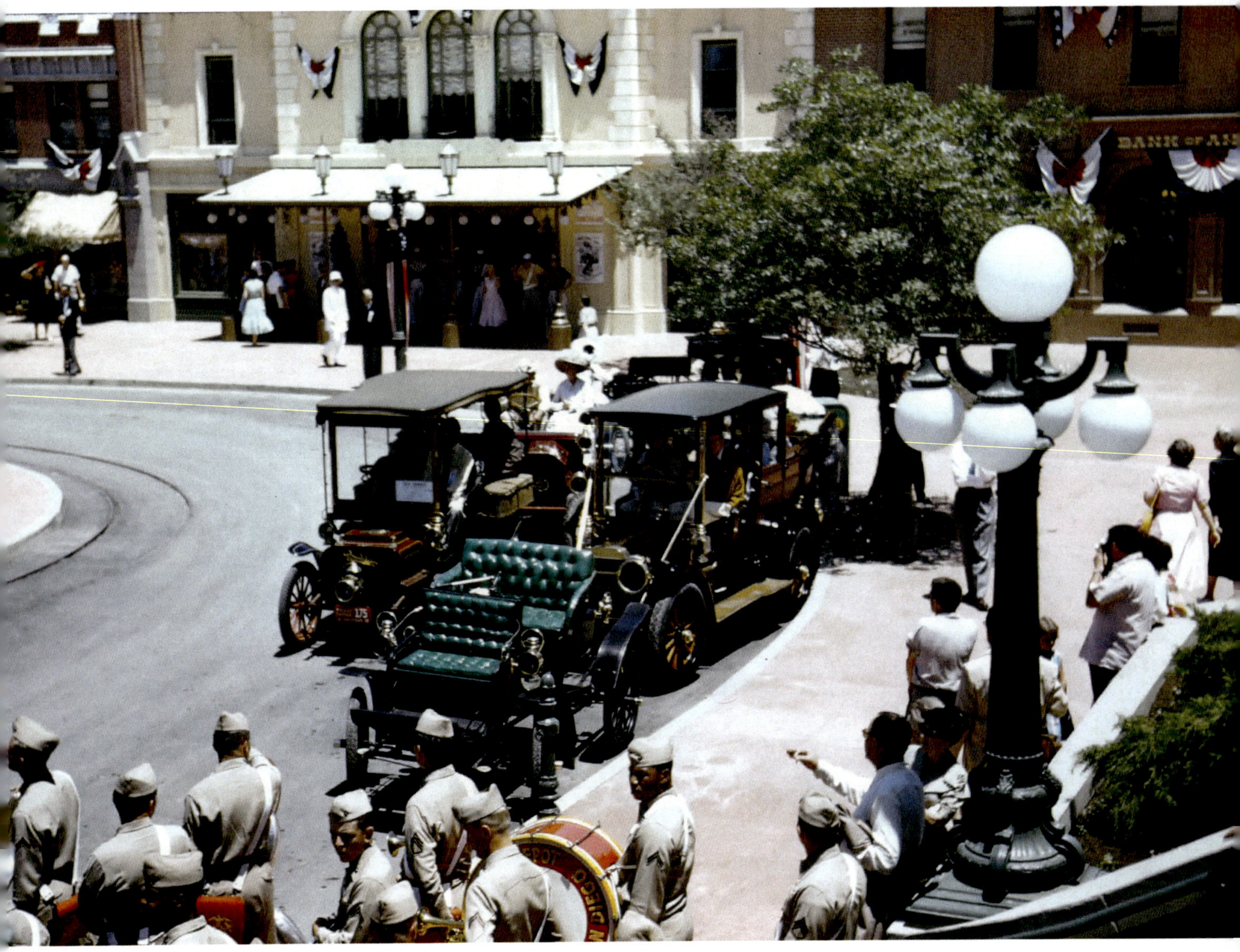

'It's a fabulous playground. Something of a fair, a city from the Arabian Nights, a metropolis of the future, a showpiece of magic and living facts, but above all, a place for people to find happiness and knowledge. It's something I dreamed up years ago."

– Walt Disney, ***Orlando Sentinel***, August 14, 1955

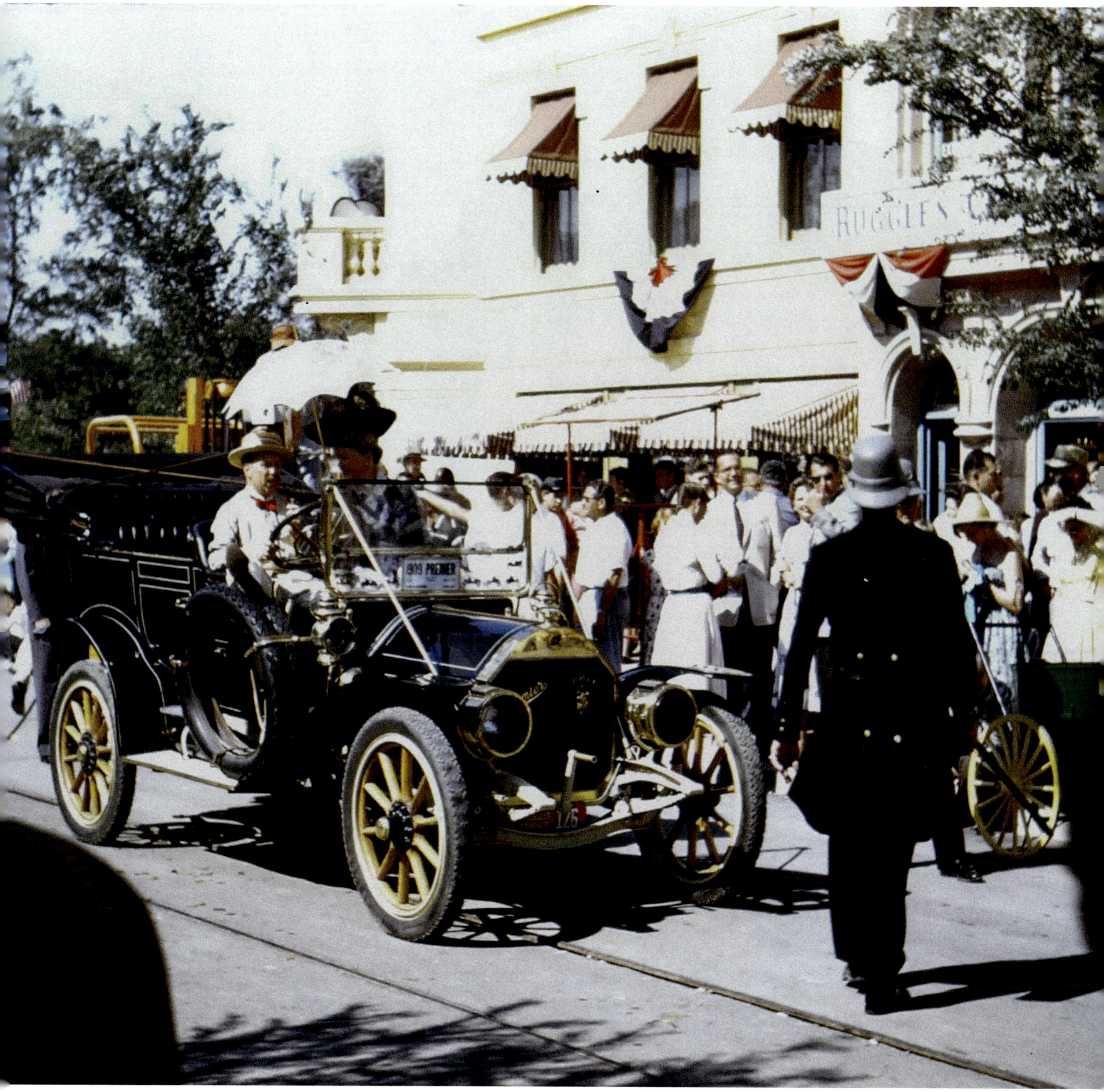

"I don't want the public to see the world they live in while they're in the park. I want them to feel they're in another world."

— Walt Disney speaking about Disneyland from Walt Disney Productions Tencennial Press Clippings

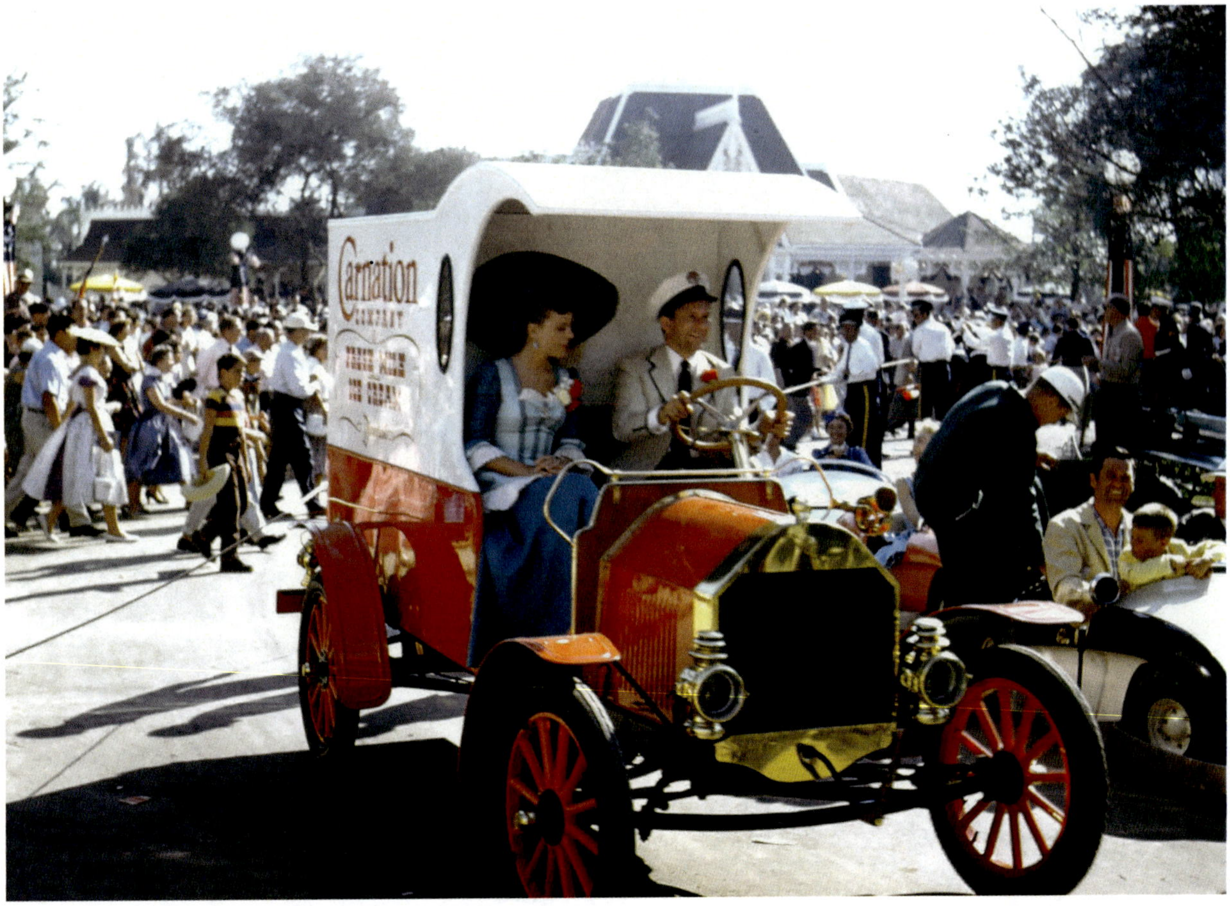

"Nostalgia is in store for those who remember happy hours spent in the corner sweet shop or ice cream parlor of the Gay Nineties when they visit the Carnation Ice Cream Parlor in Disneyland . . . Wire backed chairs and wire-framed tables, leather tufted seats and island benches around the columns have been faithfully reproduced. Even a marble counter top is installed at the soda fountain.

Beneath this 1890 counter will beat the heart of the latest 20th century fountain. This stainless-steel unit will give all an opportunity to compare the old and new. Instead of the proprietor packing ice with an ax handle or a ball bat and then sprinkling it with rock salt, the unit takes care of that with a refrigeration compartment with three separate temperature controls.

Carnation has exclusive rights on milk, ice cream and other dairy products in Disneyland and will serve all of the eating facilities in the park. An early model truck will service these customers. Scaled to five-eighths—a special panel body, brass headlights, radiator, high pressure tires, tufted leather upholstery, Carnations delivery truck will fit into Main Street bustle of horse-drawn drays and trolleys."

— ***Long Beach Independent***, July 15, 1955

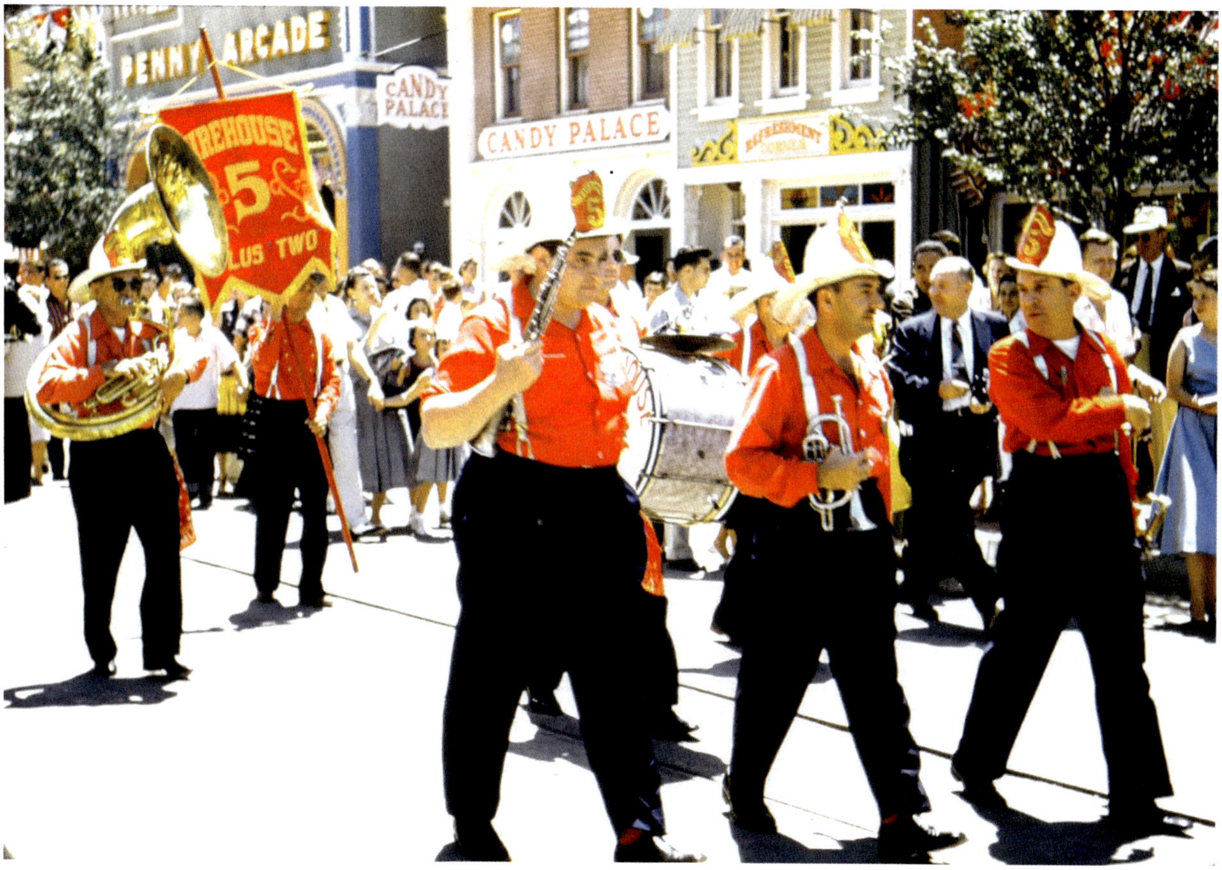

The Firehouse Five Plus Two Dixieland jazz group was composed of Disney studio personnel that evolved from bands created to play in camp shows during World War II. Led by Ward Kimball, the group appeared on television in "At Home with Donald Duck," "The Disneyland Tenth Anniversary Show," and "The Mickey Mouse Club," in the "Fun With Music Day" segment. Other members included George Probert, Frank Thomas, Harper Goff, and Eddie Forrest. They recorded and released albums under the Good Time Jazz Label.[7]

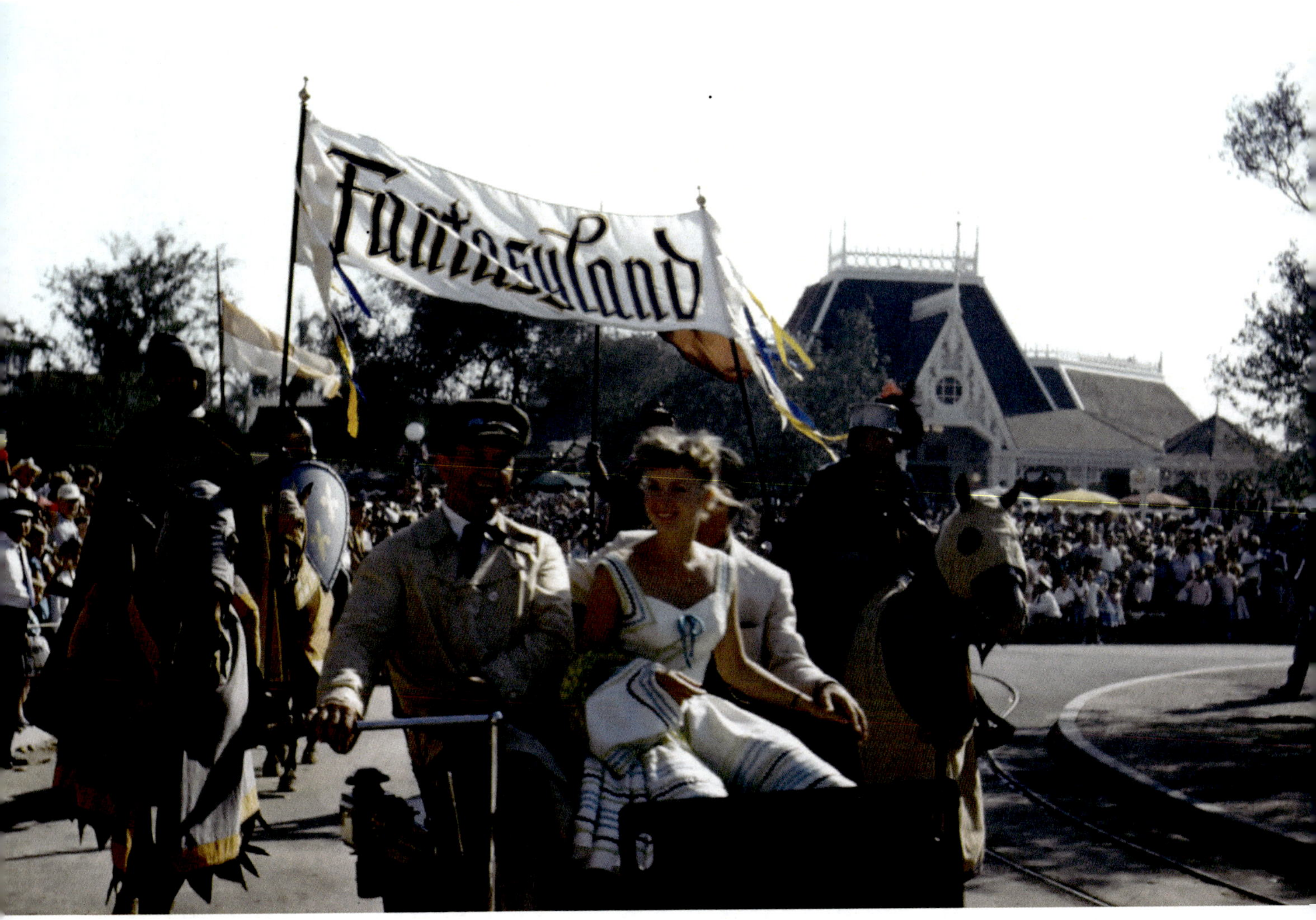

Both known for their talents in singing and acting, Debbie Reynolds and her husband, at the time, Eddie Fisher (seated behind her and holding her hand) were the parents of Princess Leia, aka Carrie Fisher.

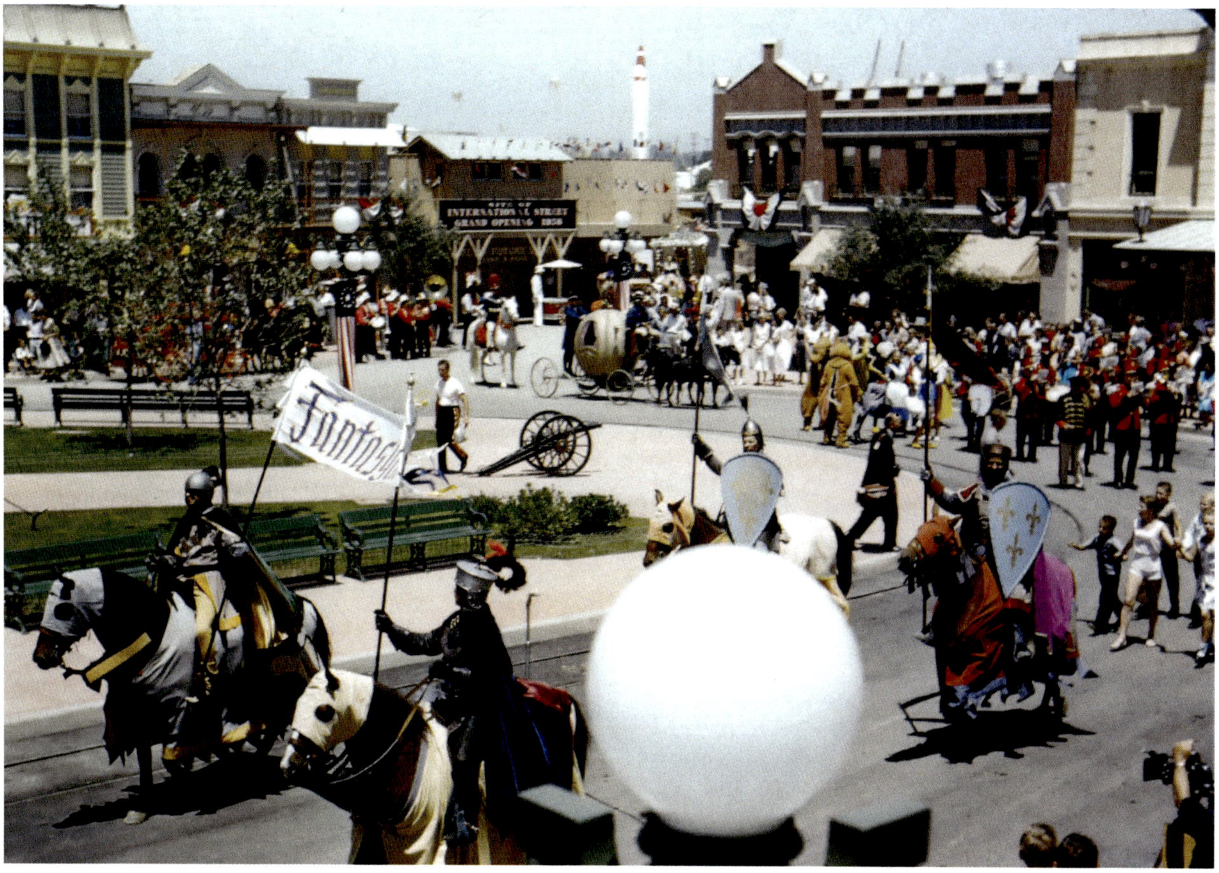

"A year ago, these 160 acres contained 11,000 orange trees. Today 22,000 invited guests swarmed through the gates and were dazzled by the wonders of yesterday and tomorrow, concocted by the imagination of Walt Disney and his fellow creators.

'It was nip and tuck but we made it,' sighed Disney. Dressed appropriately for the hot weather, he greeted arrivals in light blue slacks, white shirt with red polka dots and Tahitian straw hat.

He seemed satisfied as he surveyed his realm, even though it still needs a few finishing touches.

'We won't have some of the rides going until the public opening tomorrow,' the movie maker remarked.

'The Peter Pan Flight swayed too much so we can't use it yet. But we'll soon have everything in shape.'

Everywhere there were signs of the last-minute rush. A painter put finishing touches on the marquee of the Disneyland Opera House. Workers unloaded crates in the Turn-of-the-Century stores along Main Street and a crane hovered over the Mad Tea Party ride.

But most of the fantastic amusement park was finished enough to provide sheer joy for the children of the invited film stars, civic and business officials and press."

–***Associated Press***, July 18, 1955

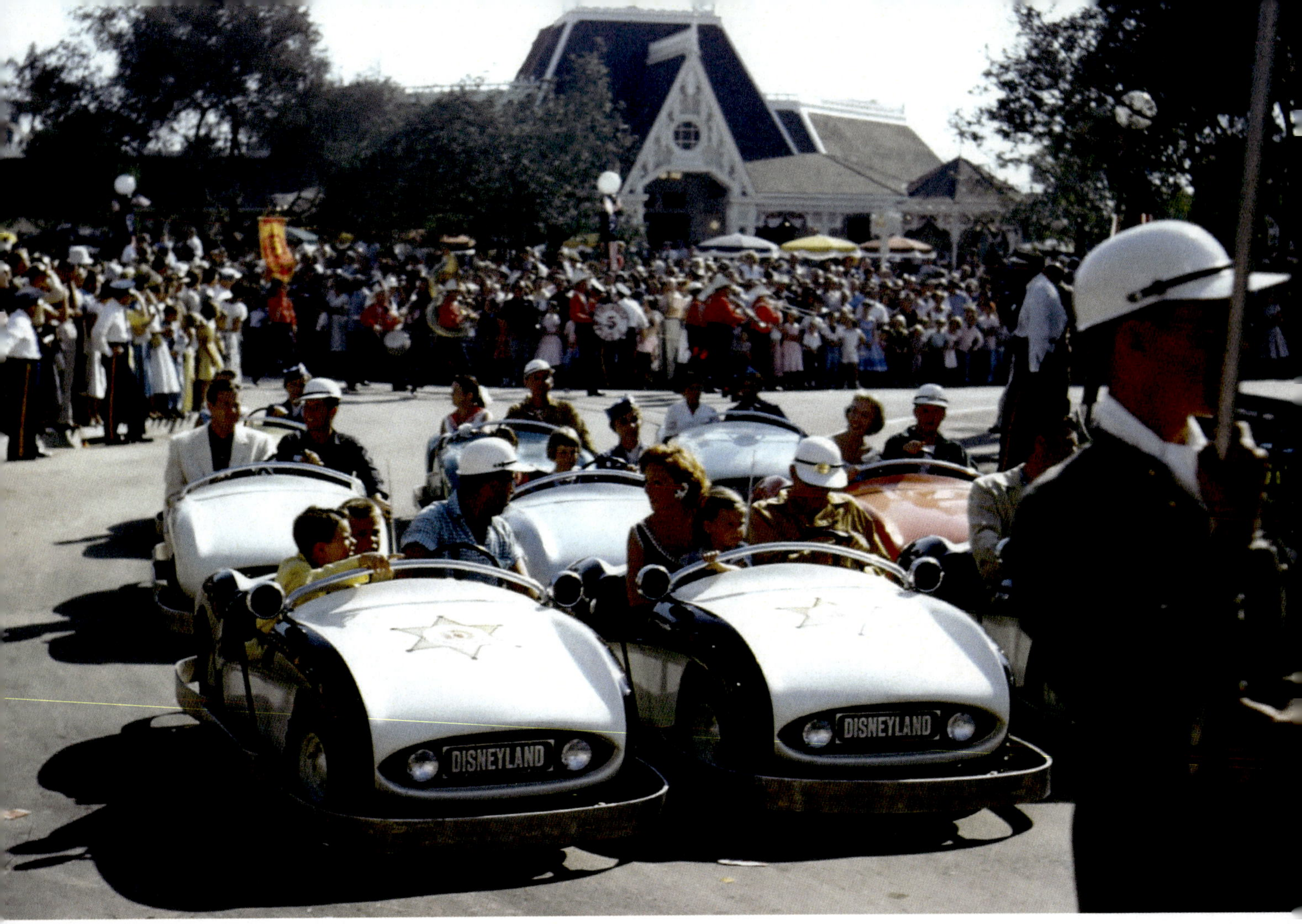

Actor Don DeFore, seated in the back left car, was best known as "Thorny" on ***The Adventures of Ozzie and Harriet*** and George Baxter on the television show ***Hazel***. DeFore was a friend of Walt Disney's and the proprietor of Don DeFore's Silver Banjo Barbecue restaurant in Frontierland from 1957 through 1962.

The woman in the car with the child on her lap is actress and singer Gale Storm. Bob Gurr is driving her two sons in the car next to her before they encountered Sammy Davis Jr.!

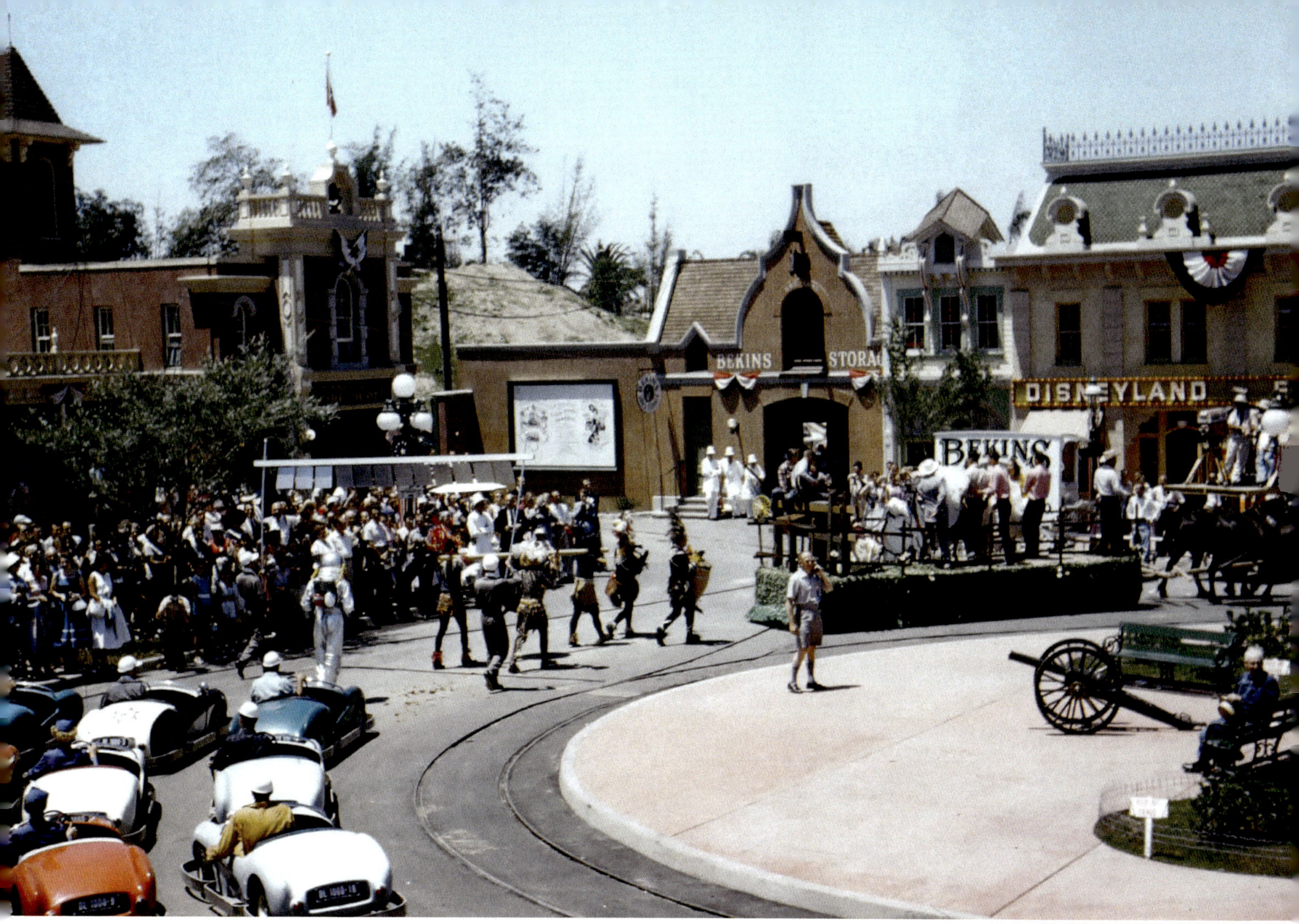

"The cross-country search inaugurated by Disneyland antique specialists for the Main Street and Frontierland areas of Walt Disney's fabulous wonderland in Anaheim would have delighted the heart of any antique collector.

This search covered the United States and parts of Canada, taking in everything from metropolitan collections to inconspicuous little junk shops in out-of-the-way villages. Even individuals were called upon to part with treasured objects to contribute to Disneyland's perfection.

One such case involved the magnetic electric fire alarm gong which is part of the Main Street fire house. The gong works on the same principle as the old telegraph key and was first used in Boston in 1851. The hunt for this was begun at the obvious place—the fire department. However, none were available at the local fire departments and Disneylanders were referred to an individual collector, who agreed to part with the gong only after hearing the story of Walt Disney's plan to reconstruct an entire Main Street of America's early days."

—*Long Beach Independent, July 15, 1955*

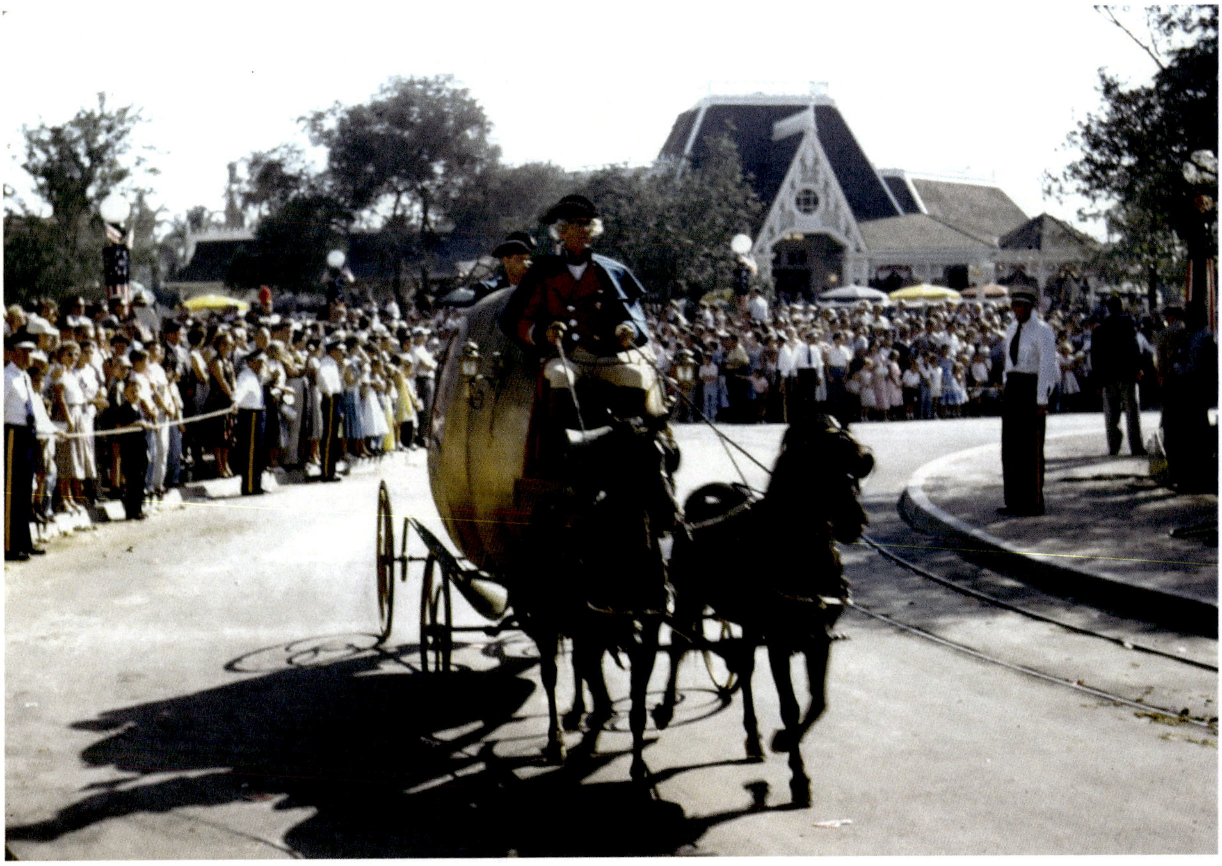

"Here is the world of imagination and dreams. In this timeless land of enchantment, the age of chivalry, magic and make believe are reborn—and fairy tales come true. Fantasyland is dedicated to the young and young-in-heart to those who believe that when you wish upon a star, your dreams come true."

—Fantasyland dedication plaque

"Only three weeks ago visitors to Disneyland exclaimed, 'It cannot possibly be ready for the July 18 opening!'

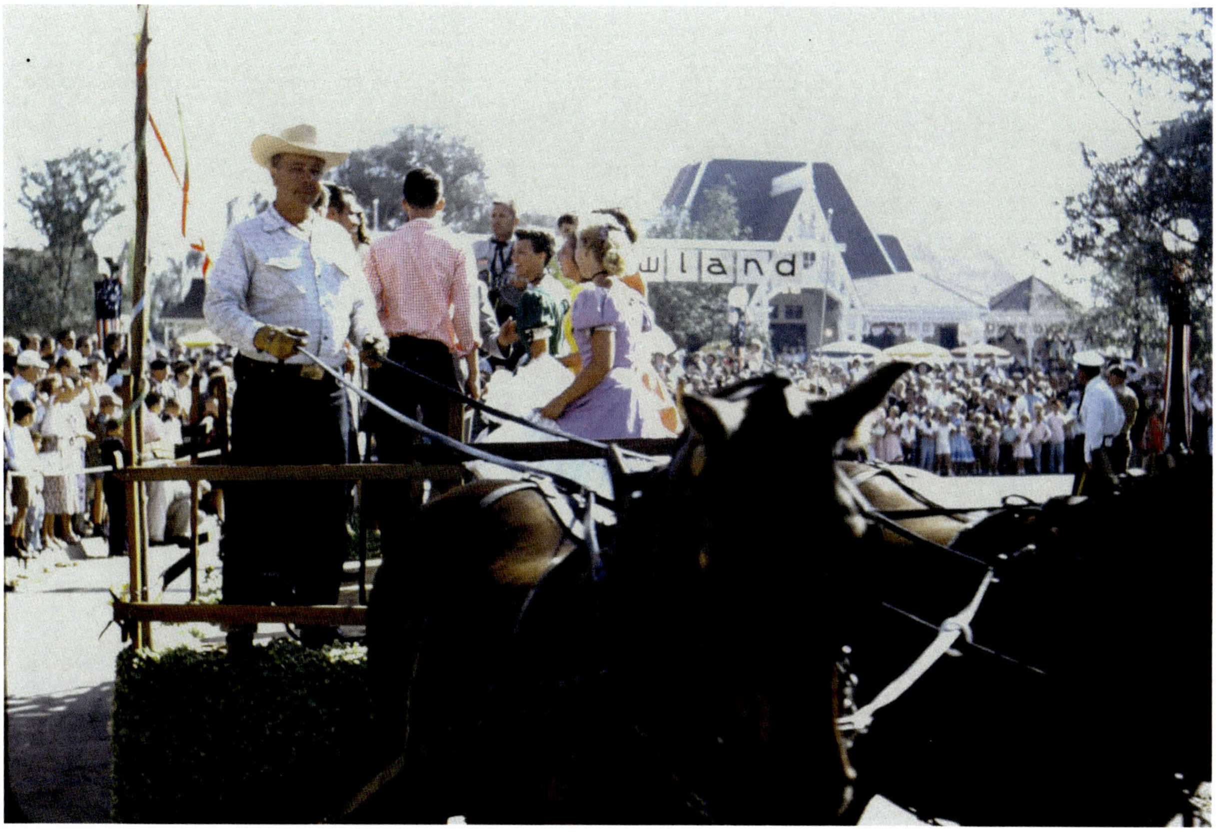

But they failed to reckon with the determination of Walt Disney and some 2,500 workmen on 10 hour shifts. For at 10 a.m. Monday, what Disney calls the 'magic kingdom of happiness and knowledge' will open to the first of an expected 5 million annual visitors, and all will be in order.

The will to complete the enormous job on time has been in evidence throughout the 160-acre park—workmen hurrying along with wheelbarrows of cement, hammering, sawing, painting, moving piles of dirt, paving roadways. Their pace has not been frantic—just determined.

And crudely-lettered signs have urged them on. One in the window of Main Street's Emporium reads: 'Sure we'll finish on time. We work.' Another in one of the woodworking shops states: 'Saturday's a work day—same as usual.'

Exactly one year and a day after ground was broken on the 160-acre orange grove in Anaheim, the multimillion dollar Disneyland will be complete."

– *Los Angeles Evening Citizen News*, July 16, 1955

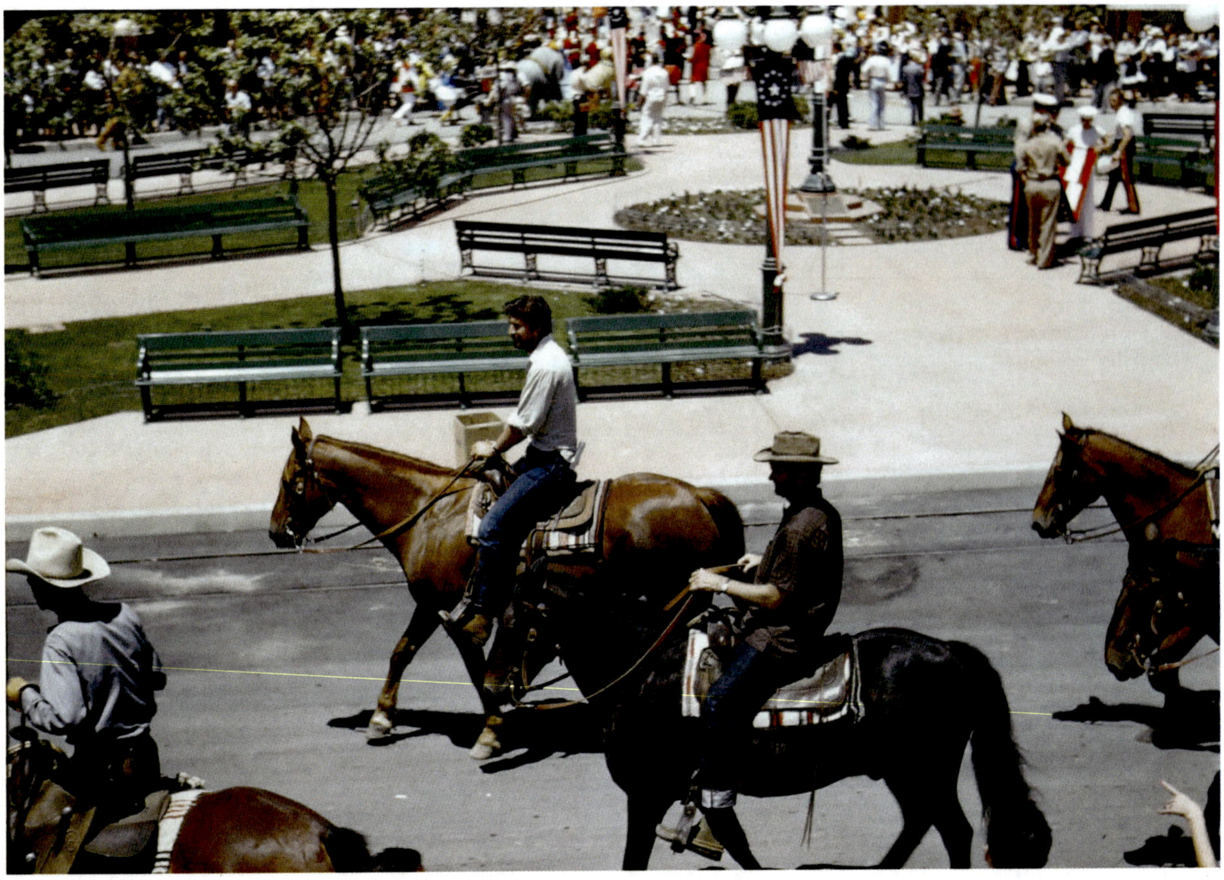

In order to make Walt's Disneyland dreams come true, he needed funding beyond what he and his brother Roy could financially come up with. This predicament led the Disney brothers to partner with the American Broadcasting Company (ABC). ABC was struggling for content at the time, so collaborating with Disney would provide the network with programming to broadcast. In return Disney would secure funding to bring Walt's Disneyland to life.

When Walt debuted his Disneyland television program, he promoted his upcoming park and brought original storylines to the airwaves, one of which was a serial about frontiersman Davy Crocket, starring Fess Parker.

"Son of a Texas ranch owner, 28-year-old Fess Parker, who is Davy Crockett on TV, was spotted by Disney in a small movie role. Disney decided Fess had the right smile to 'out grin a bear' and hired him to play Davy.

When Davy died on TV, so many protests poured in that Disney will launch Fess in a TV series, 'Legends of Davy Crockett.' Fess himself had to meet protests a few weeks ago when a teacher complained that kids did nothing but play Crockett games and needed to be calmed down."

—***Life***, April 25, 1955

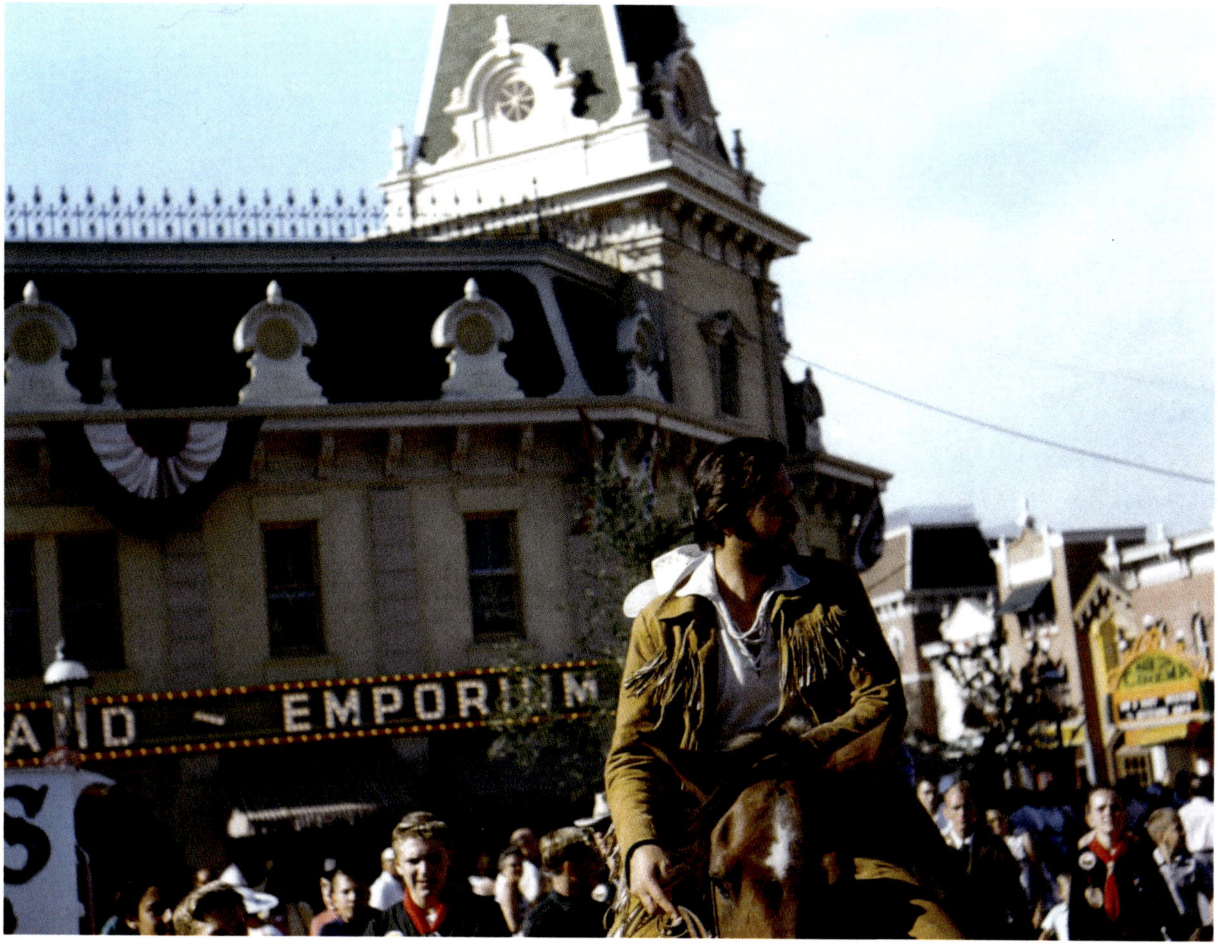

"The Crockett craze, unexpected even by the watchful Walt Disney, has produced a corresponding frenzy in commercial circles. Dozens of manufacturers are hustling to turnout more than 200 items, from baby shoes to wallets, which might conceivably be connected with Crockett's life. By June they will sell to the retail tune of $100 million—just about the largest merchandising feat of its kind.

Meanwhile, Walt Disney has made a full-length movie out of his TV film and booked it into 950 theatres for its opening month this June.

Sixteen versions of the Crockett ballad which was introduced on the TV show, have been recorded, not counting the Davy Crockett Mambo."

–***Life***, April 25, 1955

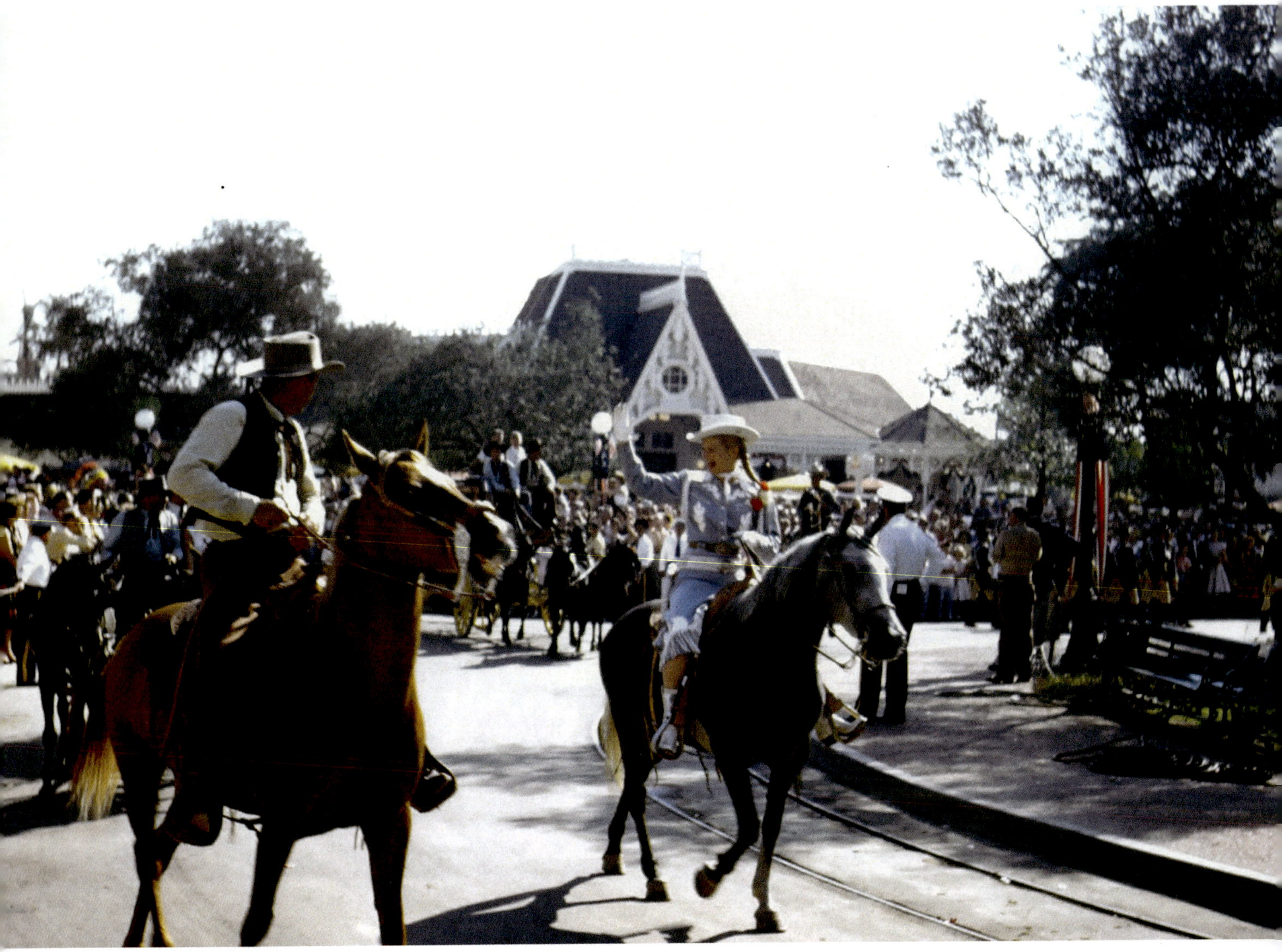

Gail Davis played Annie Oakley in the ***Annie Oakley*** television series, which ran for eighty-one episodes.

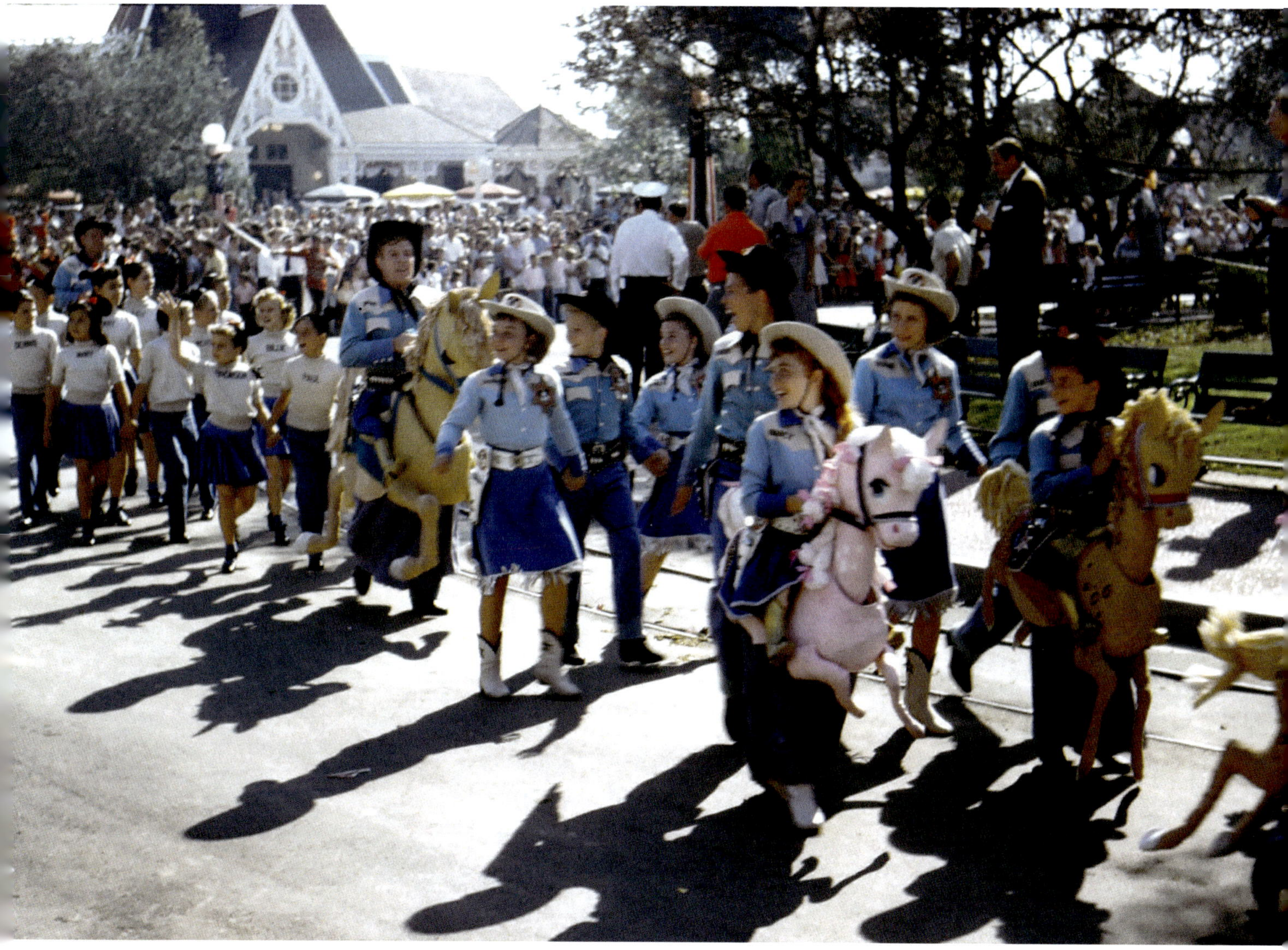

July 17, 1955 featured two Disney debuts: the Disneyland park being one, obviously, but it was also the first time the country was introduced to the youngsters who were starring in Walt's second television series, *The Mickey Mouse Club*, which came to TVs across the country in October of 1955.

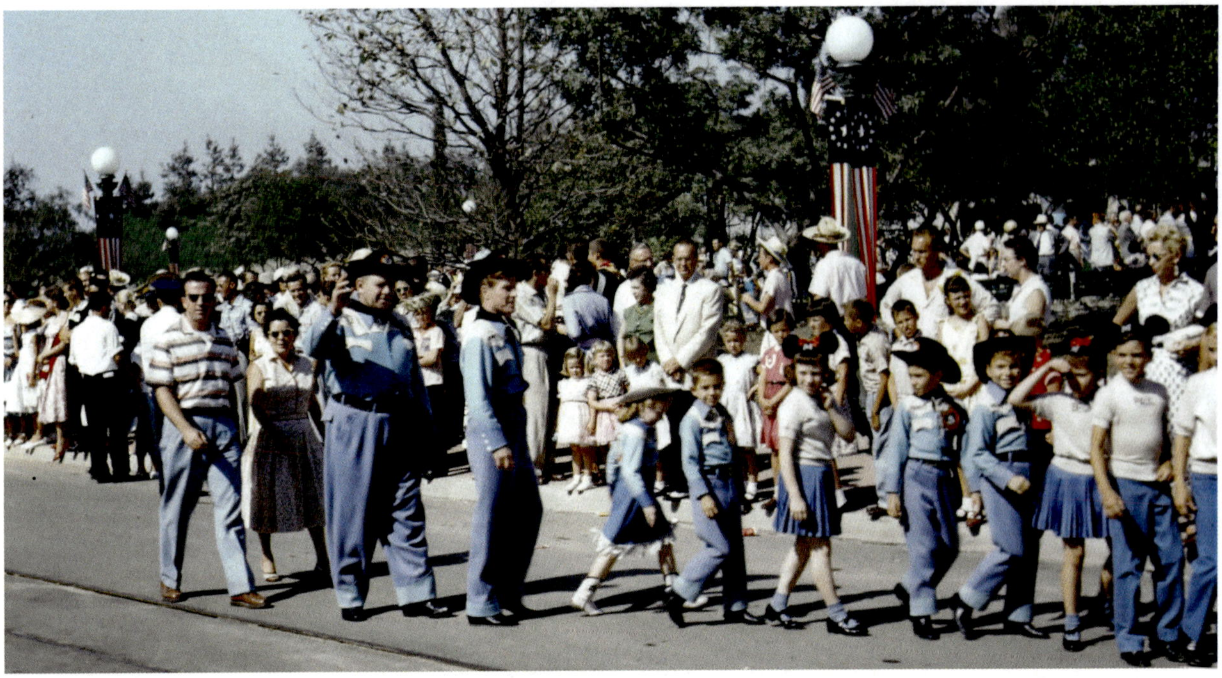

See the big fella in the back raising his hand? That's Roy Williams. Roy made his debut at Disneyland as "Big Roy," the mouseketeer on Walt Disney's upcoming television series, *The Mickey Mouse Club*. And by the way, not only was Roy an outstanding artist and story man for the studio, and a beloved adult mouseketeer, but he was also the inventor of the Mickey Mouse ear caps seen in Disney theme parks around the globe—Williams was inspired by the 1929 Mickey Mouse short "The Karnival Kid," in which Mickey tipped his ears to Minnie.

"Williams, who looks more like an ex-football blocking guard than an artist—or anybody except football guards, for that matter, usually do—has worked with Walt Disney all his adult life, even while he was going to art school, with Disney paying for his training. Six feet in height, weighing 300 pounds, he got his first job with Disney 23 years ago. A high school cartoonist at the time, he took a bunch of his drawings around to the Disney studio, then in a one-room garage, and asked to see Walt.

While waiting he talked drawing to the office boy. After a half hour or so he began to gather up his drawings.

'Mr. Disney isn't going to show up, I guess,' he said, 'I'll come back tomorrow.'

'I'm Walt Disney,' said the 'office boy' and 'you're hired!'

Williams was the 15th man hired. Now the organization has 1500 employees and the plant covers 35 acres in Burbank, with a main building that cost $4,000,000."

—***Brooklyn Daily Eagle***, January 18, 1953

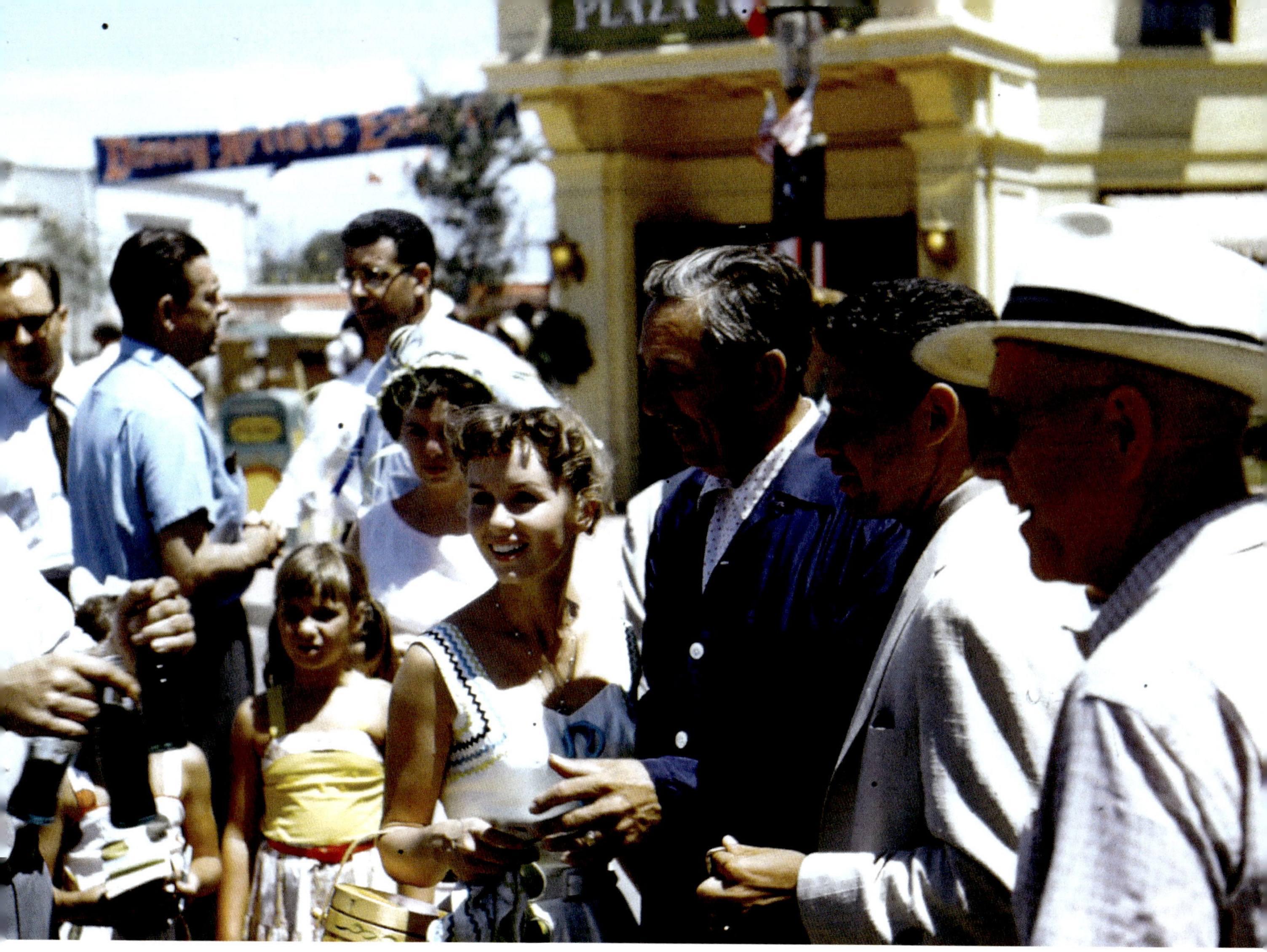

Debbie Reynolds, Walt Disney, and Eddie Fisher wait for a few sodas. Contrary to Disney legend and lure, the day was not as hot and humid as everyone remembered.

Note, in the background, the gentleman on the left side of the photo wearing sunglasses is Cornelius Vanderbilt ("C. V.") Wood—more on him on pages 128–130.

The gentleman opposite Wood, with dark hair and glasses, is Card Walker. E. Cardon Walker ("Card") was hired by the Disney studio in 1938 as a traffic boy. By 1971 he was named president of the company, and in 1976, he added the duty of chief executive officer. He was elected chairman of the board in 1980.

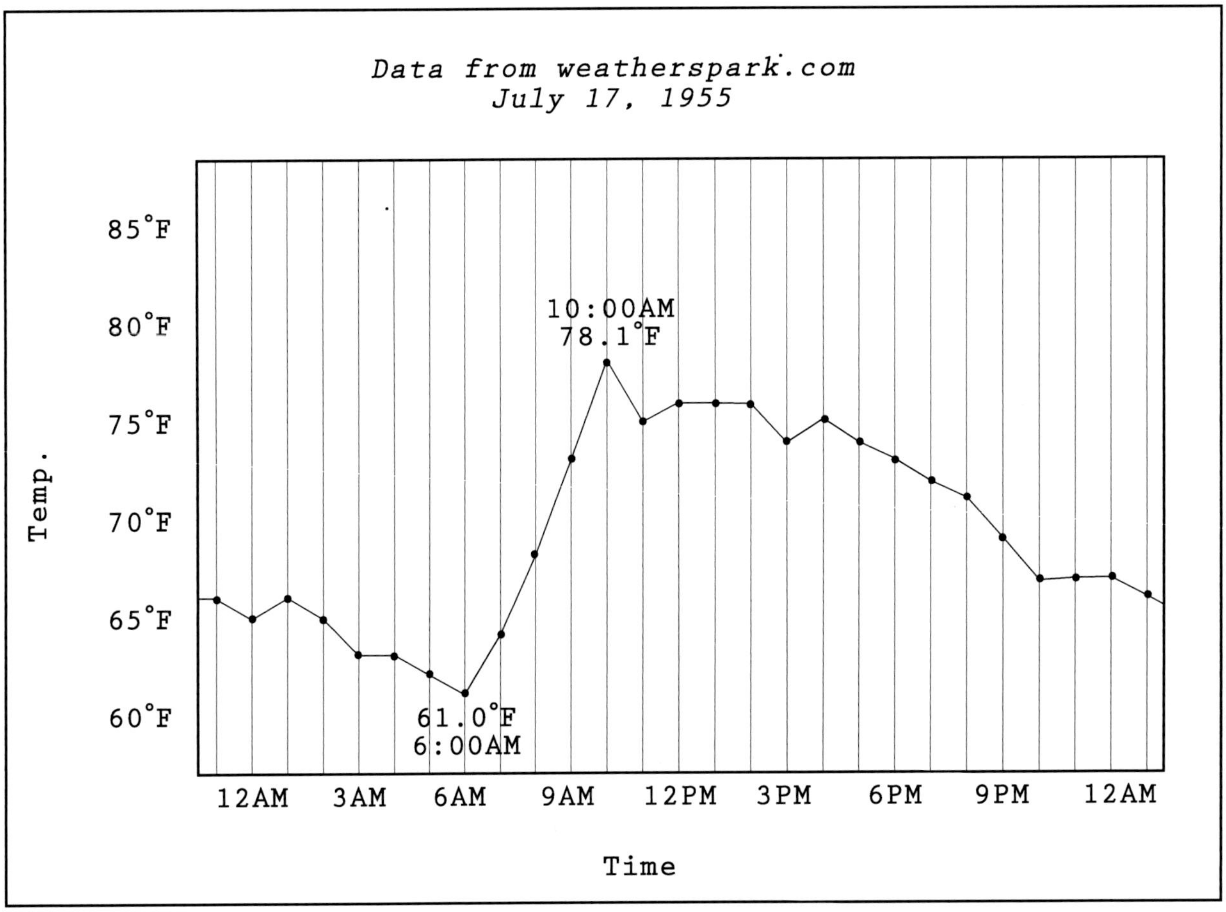
Data from weatherspark.com
July 17, 1955
85°F
80°F
75°F
70°F
65°F
60°F
Temp.
10:00AM
78.1°F
61.0°F
6:00AM
12AM
3AM
6AM
9AM
12PM
3PM
6PM
9PM
12AM
Time

LOCAL TEMPERATURES - Sunday's maximum and minimum temperatures at Southern California points, as reported to the Los Angeles office of the U.S. Weather Bureau, were as follows:

Station-	Max.	Min.
Los Angeles	87	63
Beaumont	99	55
Bishop	104	55
Blythe	104	85
Burbank	91	62
Campo	97	55
Culver City	73	58
Daggett	108	70
El Centro	101	82
Long Beach	84	59
L. A. Airport	78	61
Montebello	87	58
Mt. Wilson	85	70
Needles	108	88
Newport Beach	71	60
Palmdale	103	59
*Pasadena	88	59
Paso Robles	94	49
Riverside	98	65
Sandberg	92	64
San Bernadino	100	62
San Diego	73	64
San Gabriel	93	58
San Pedro	76	61
Santa Ana	82	58
Santa Barbara	79	54
Santa Monica	77	61
Thermal	103	80
Torrance	81	58

* Unofficial reading

From The Los Angeles Times
July 18, 1955 Edition

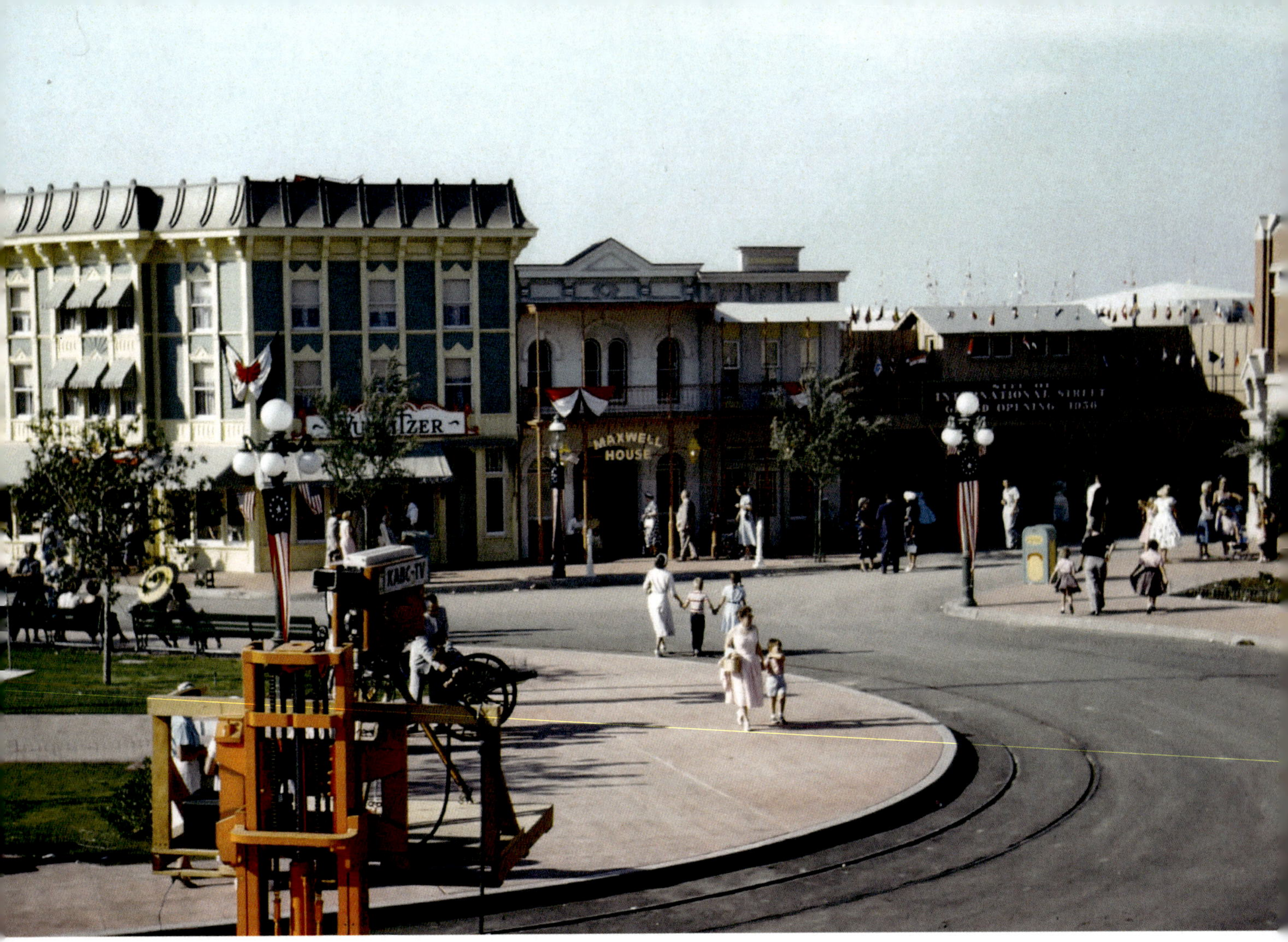

On the far-right side of the photo you can spot a sign for International Street. As early as December 1954, the street was mentioned in stories about Disneyland's construction. When the park finally opened, signage was posted stating International Street would debut in 1956. If you look closely, you can even see guests looking through holes that were intentionally created in the wall, offering a sneak peek of what was to come.

As late as January 1957, the press was still reporting on the park's upcoming premiere of International Street. However, by 1958 plans for Liberty Street overtook International Street. Unfortunately, neither of these concepts came to fruition.[8]

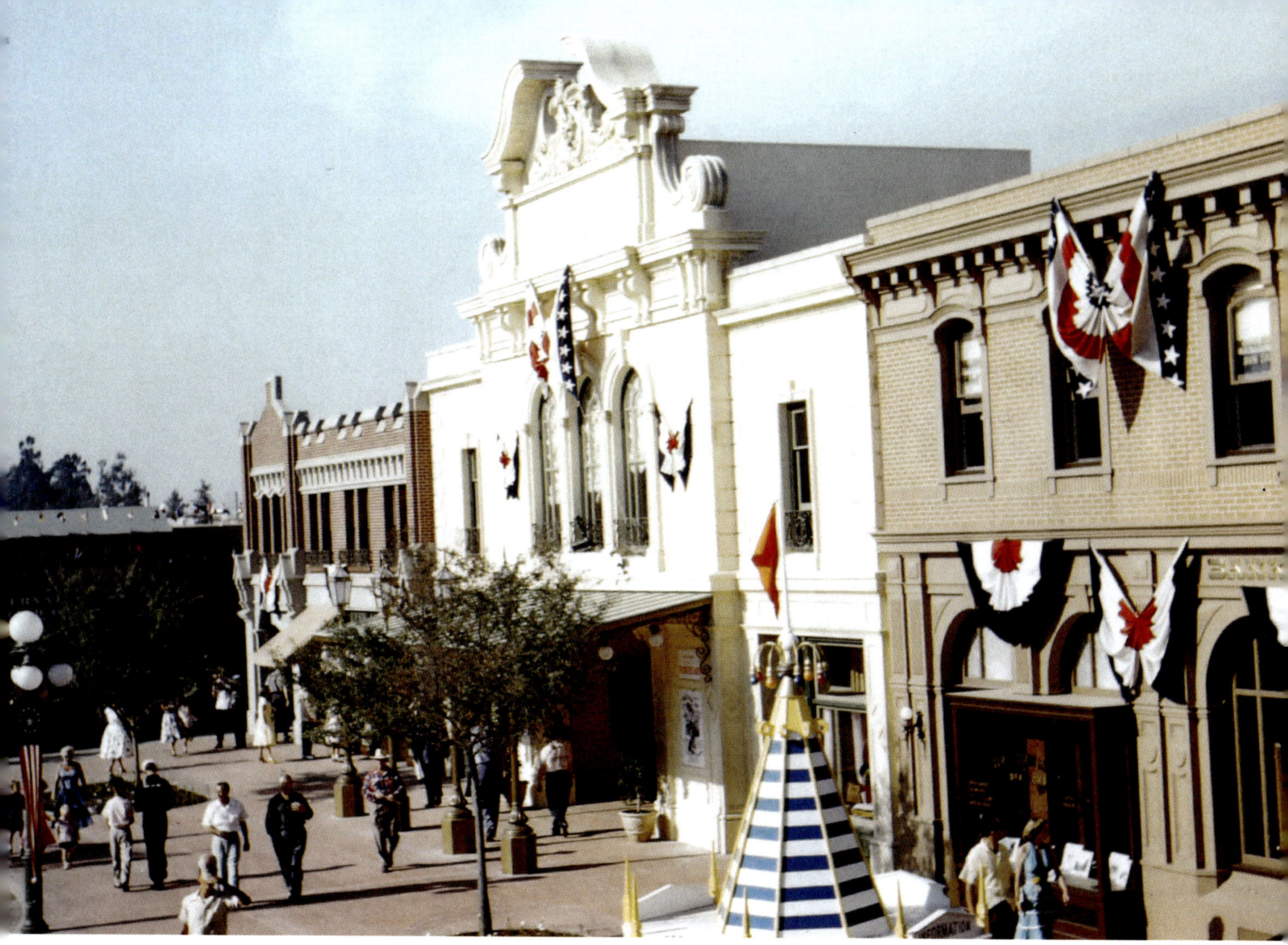

The Disney brothers had a long history with Bank of America. As Mickey Mouse was out conquering the world, the studio's coffers were becoming depleted. Starting in 1931, funding to support the studio was often obtained from Bank of America.

Over the decades since Mickey became a sensation, the Disneys would chattel mortgage many of their previous cartoon shorts for future projects. When production for *Snow White and the Seven Dwarfs* was coming to a close and the studio needed funds to complete the project, Bank of America executive Joseph Steinberg showed confidence in their first full-length animated feature and approved the loan to wrap up production.

It seemed only fitting when Walt wanted an actual bank operating on Main Street at Disneyland, Bank of America would be his choice.

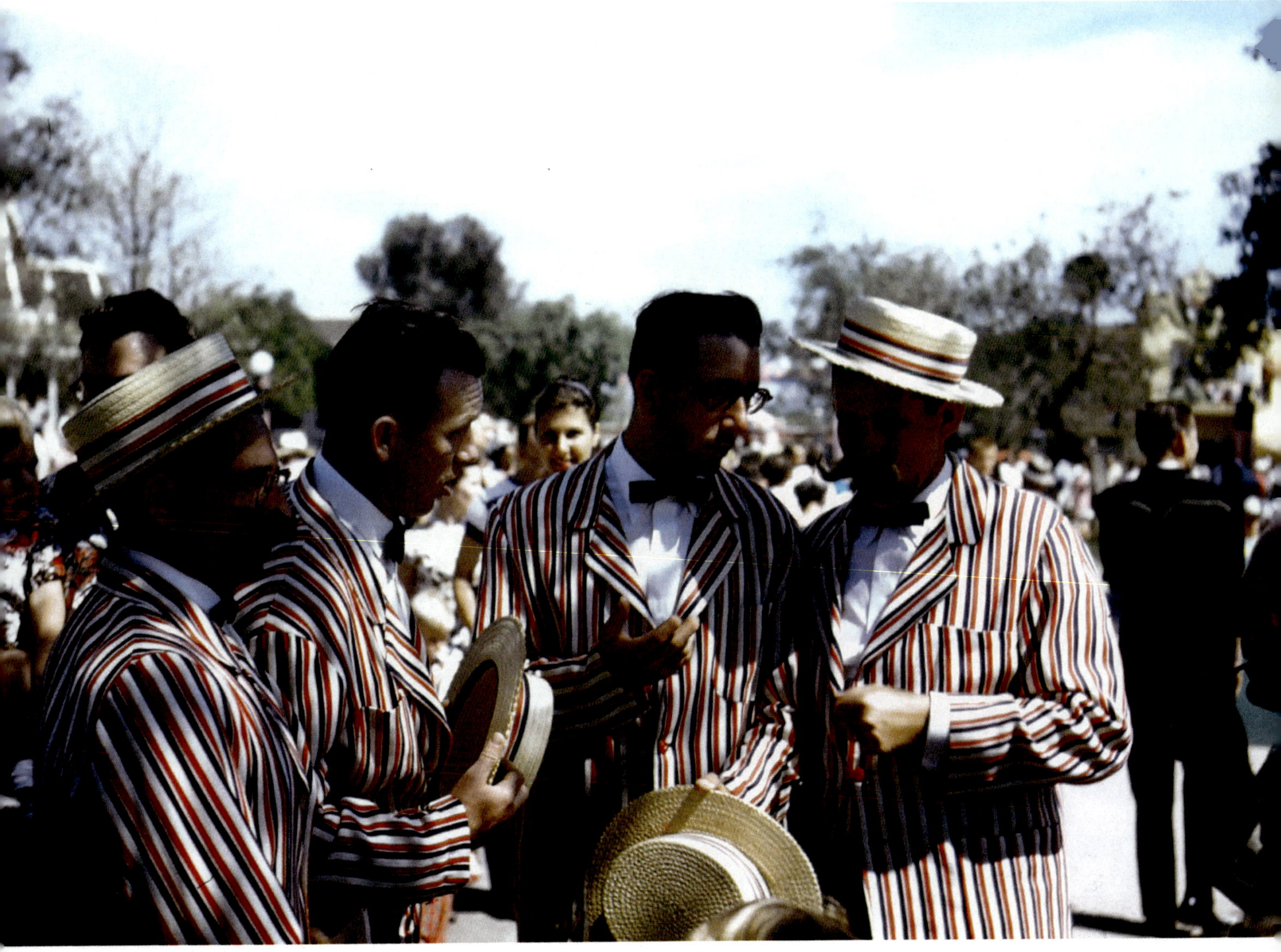

"Hundreds of schoolteachers, nurses and other Orange County residents will have weekend employment at Disneyland. Hal Hensley is holding classes to train the estimated 1200 employees in how to meet Disneyland's public. 'Disneyland must be a way of life,' he cautions. 'You've got to get a "new world" feeling about this place.'"

—*Los Angeles Mirror,* June 10, 1955

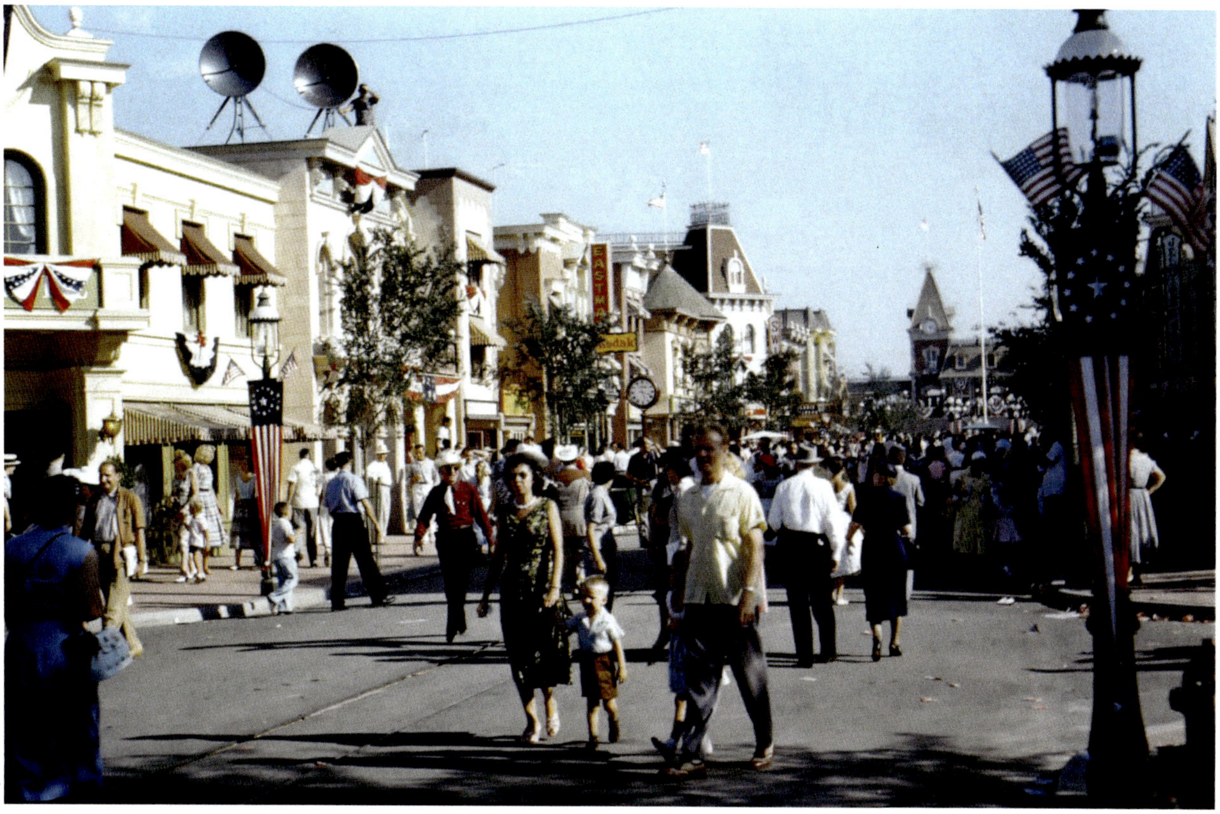

Art Linkletter, host for Disneyland's television debut, was a good friend of Walt Disney's and a pretty astute businessman. When Walt asked if Art would like to invest in Disneyland, Art turned him down (but he did invest in the Hula-Hoop). Art did, however, get a pretty sweet deal with another endeavor he collaborated on with Walt.

Around Disneyland's thirty-fifth anniversary, Linkletter described how money was so tight for Walt when he was opening Disneyland that Linkletter was only paid union scale to be the host for telecast. He persuaded Disney to throw in an extra that handsomely repaid him: the film and camera concession. "It was the highest-priced performance of any performer, I'm sure, ever got, considering the worth of that—a couple million dollars."[9]

While Linkletter cashed in on his film deal, Eastman Kodak had a presence on Main Street, alongside the other shops representing the turn of the twentieth century's Anytown, USA.

"The professional photographer's studio will be an exact replica of the Nineties with a photographer and model posed with her head in the metal headrest typical of that period. All the cameras and equipment will be exact replicas of that used during that period.

The displays historical exhibit will include a study of stereophotography through the years, an exhibit of old time 'detective' cameras and an old time Kinetoscope, forerunner of the movies."

—***Evansville Press***, Sept 8, 1955,

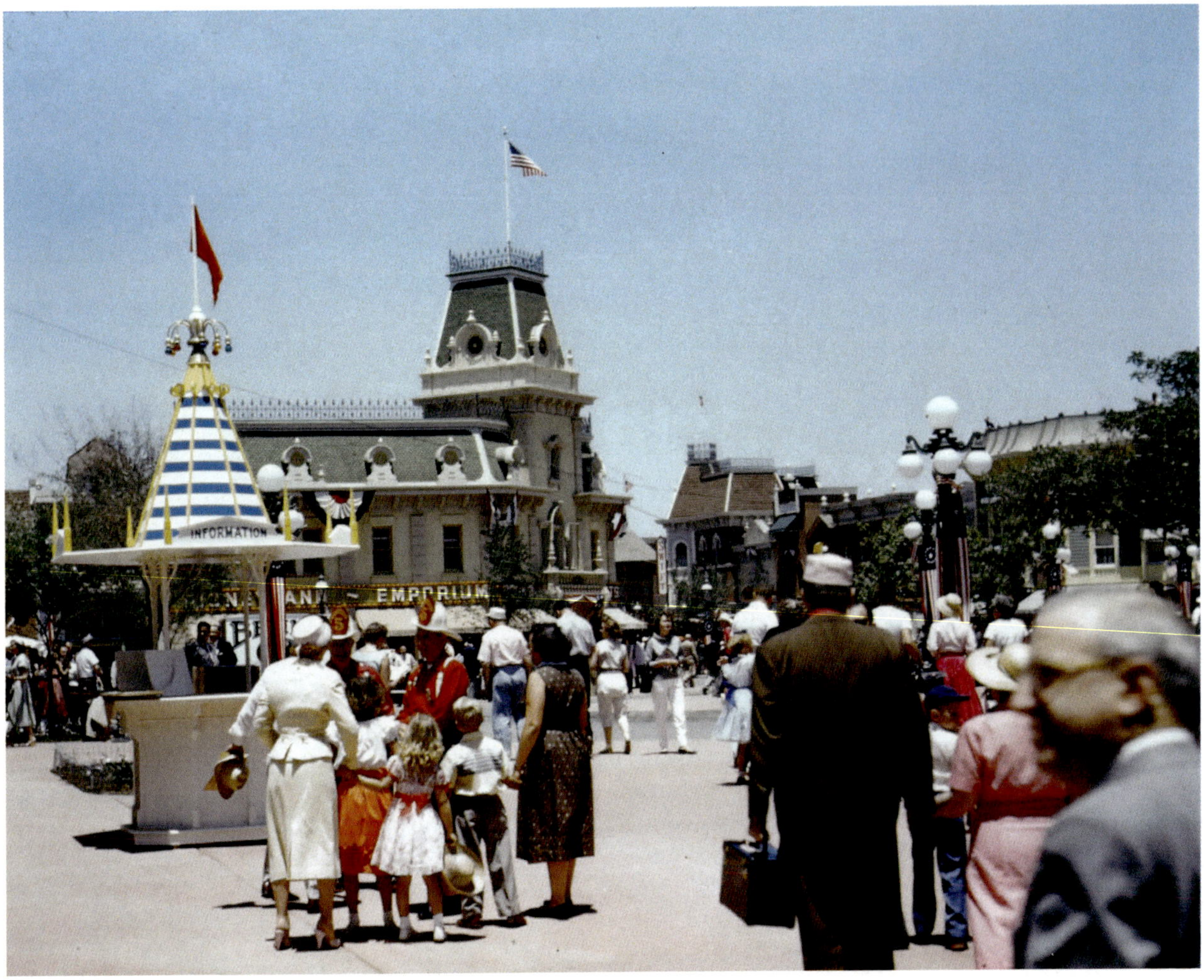

Walt Disney loved his country; he also loved flags. A quick trip down Main Street, even today, showed Walt's appreciation for flags on full display.

"We'll have flags all over the place. At the entrance we'll have a big one with 48 stars. In Frontierland, the flags will have as many stars as there were in that time. And in Tomorrowland, the flags will have 50 stars—for Hawaii and Alaska."

—***Oakland Tribune***, May 8, 1955

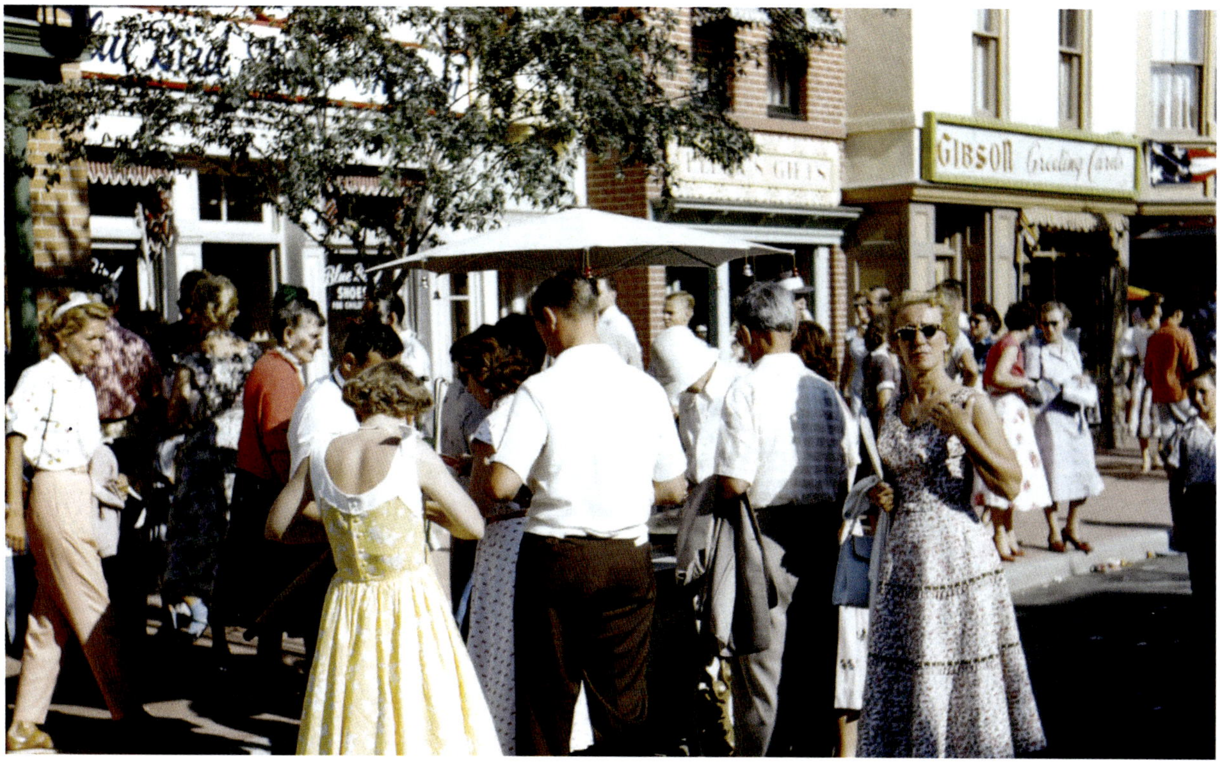

On opening day, and for quite some time after Disneyland opened, the majority of the shops along Main Street were just that: shops for the public to patronize and purchase everyday items, not exclusively Disney merchandise.

Visitors could browse for greeting cards, hats, fine china, glassware, shoes, and even ladies' undergarments. You can see the obstructed sign behind the tree for Blue Bird Shoes, which was Kirby's Shoe Store's nationally advertised children's brand and the exclusive children's shoe store in Disneyland.

"The Wonderful Wizard of Bras, famed of the Hollywood-Maxwell Brassiere Company and major domo of the novel, eye-popping exhibit prepared by Disneyland by this manufacturer of intimate apparel is one of the major magicians in the nation's greatest magic land.

The Wonderful Wizard highlights the Hollywood-Maxwell display which is one of fifty 'famous names in American businesses selected by Disneyland officials to populate Main Street U.S.A., an exact replica of an American town of the 1890-1910 period.

The Hollywood-Maxwell exhibit features the Wonderful Wizard of Bras on a revolving stage, on one side of which is a complete re-creation of the fashions and intimate wear of the 1890s and on the other side a showing of the fashions of today—inner and outer wear.

On stage acting as master of ceremonies, via a tape recorder, is the Wonderful Wizard who, with presto-change charm, explains the basic theme of the show.'"

—***Long Beach Independent,*** July 15, 1955

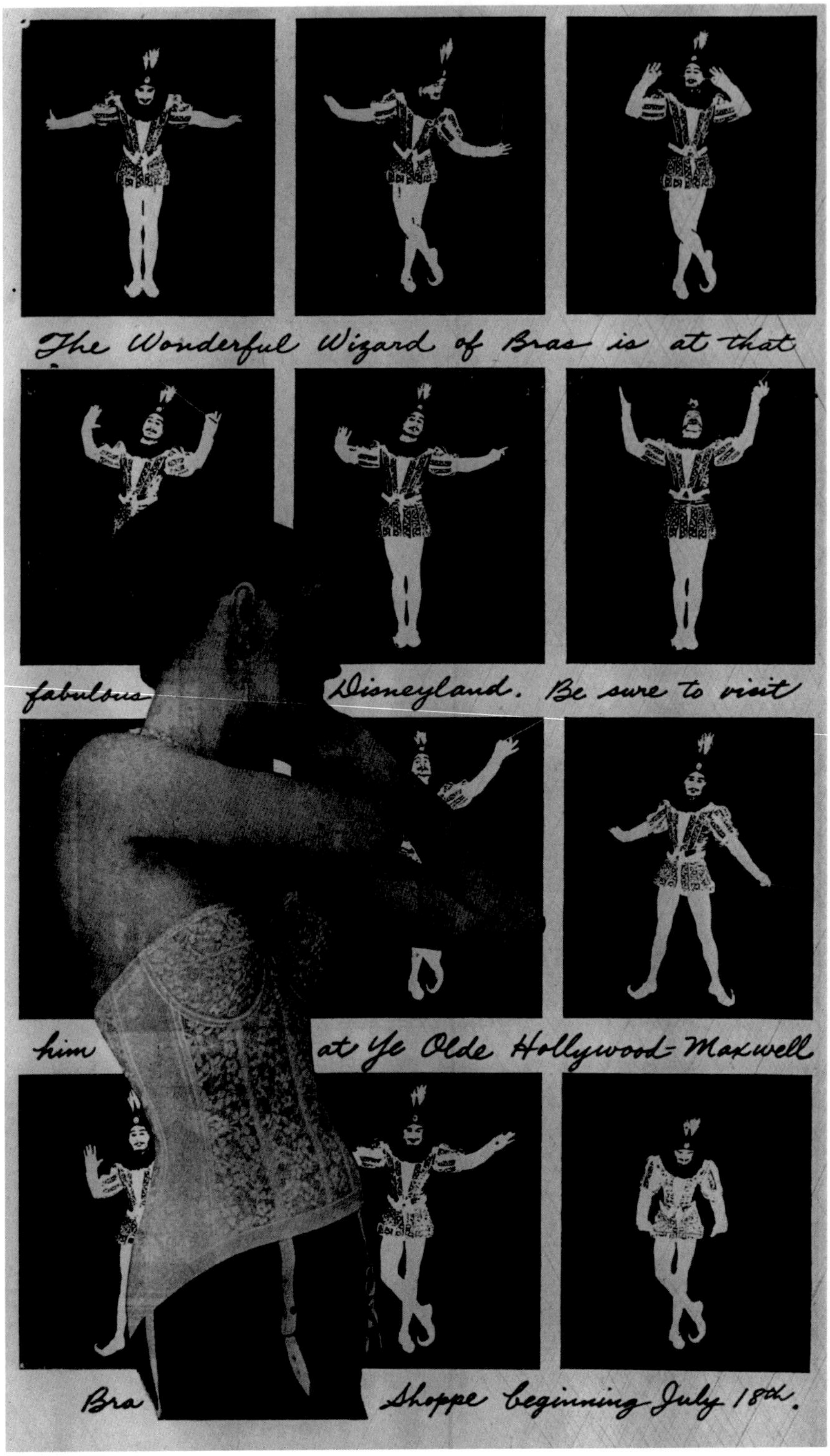

"The Wonderful Wizard of Bras is at that fabulous Disneyland. Be sure to visit him at Ye Olde Hollywood-Maxwell Bra Shoppe beginning July 18th."

—***Long Beach Independent***, July 15, 1955

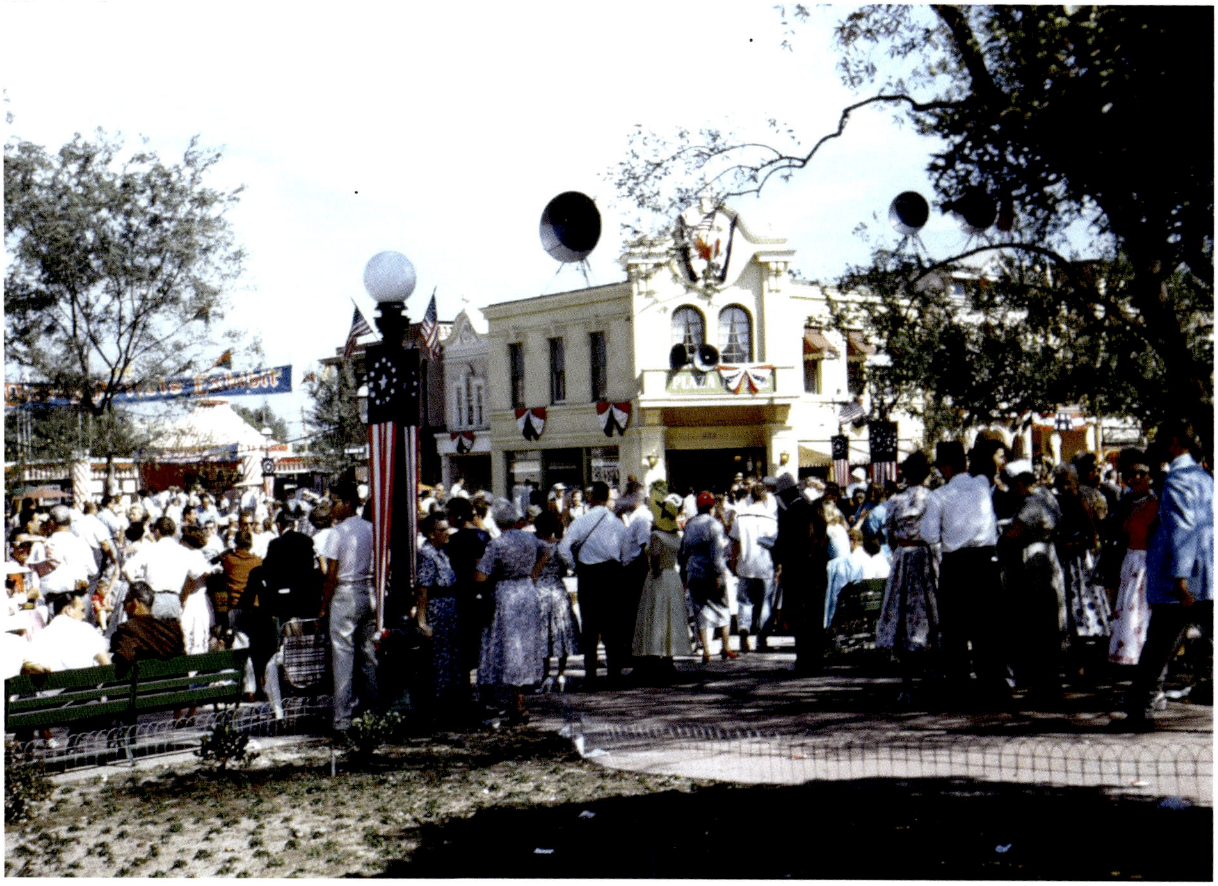

"When they come here, they're coming because of an integrity that we've established over the years. And they drive hundreds of miles. I feel a responsibility to the public."

— Walt Disney speaking about Disneyland from the Walt Disney Productions Tenncenial Press Clippings

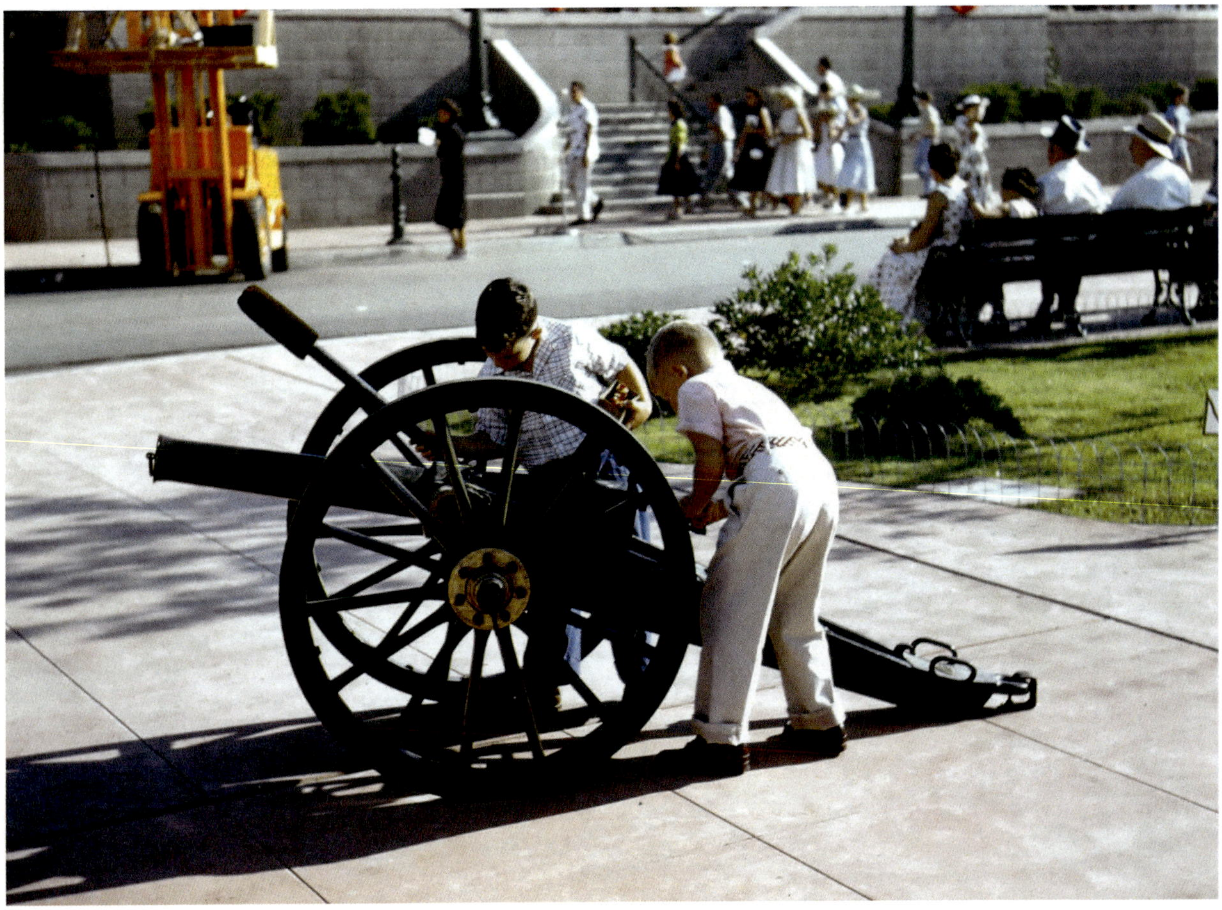

"You can't live on things made for children—or for critics. I've never made films for either of them, Disneyland is not just for children. I don't play down."

— Walt Disney speaking about Disneyland from Walt Disney Productions Tencennial Press Clippings

"I love nostalgia myself. I hope we never lose some of the things of the past."

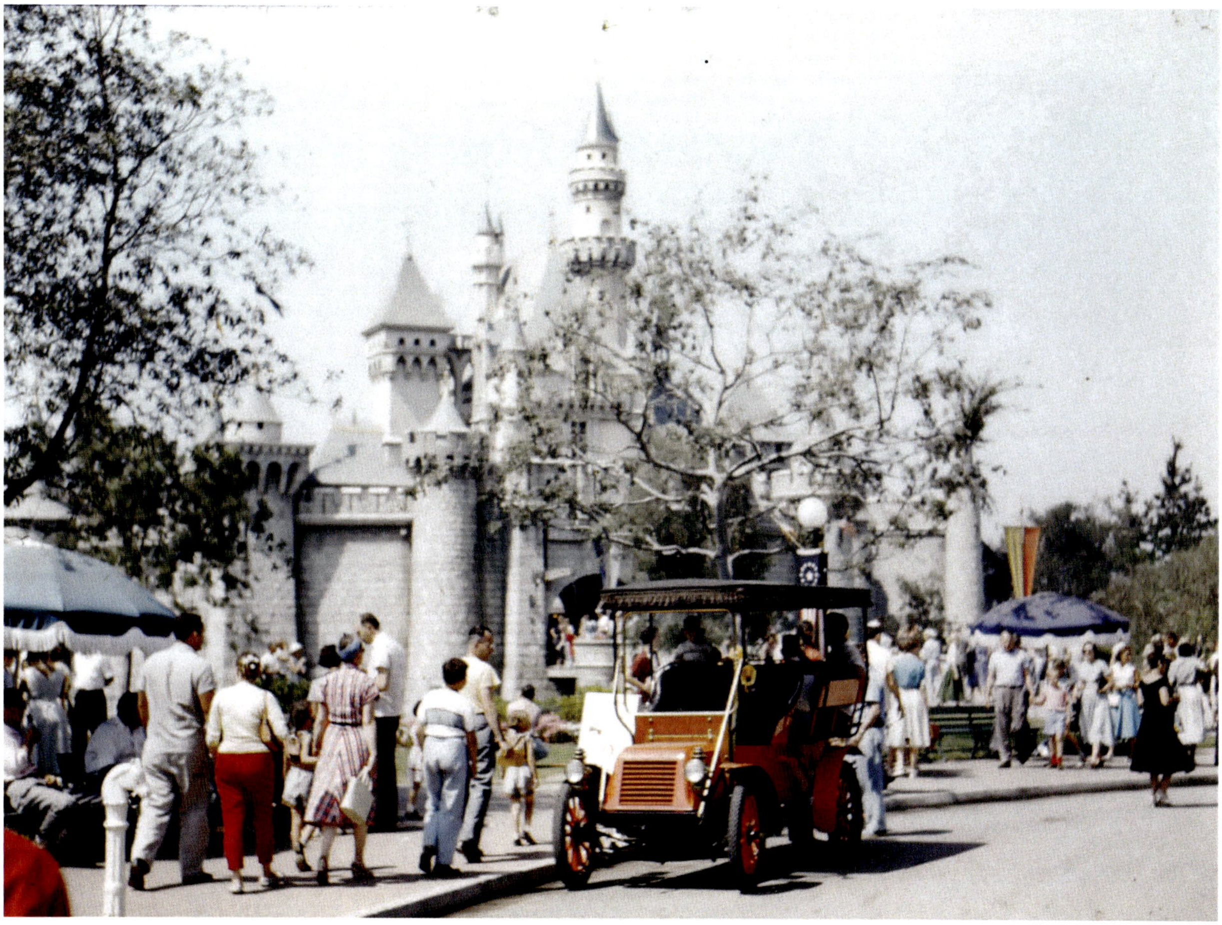

—Walt Disney speaking about Disneyland from Walt Disney Productions Tencennial Press Clippings

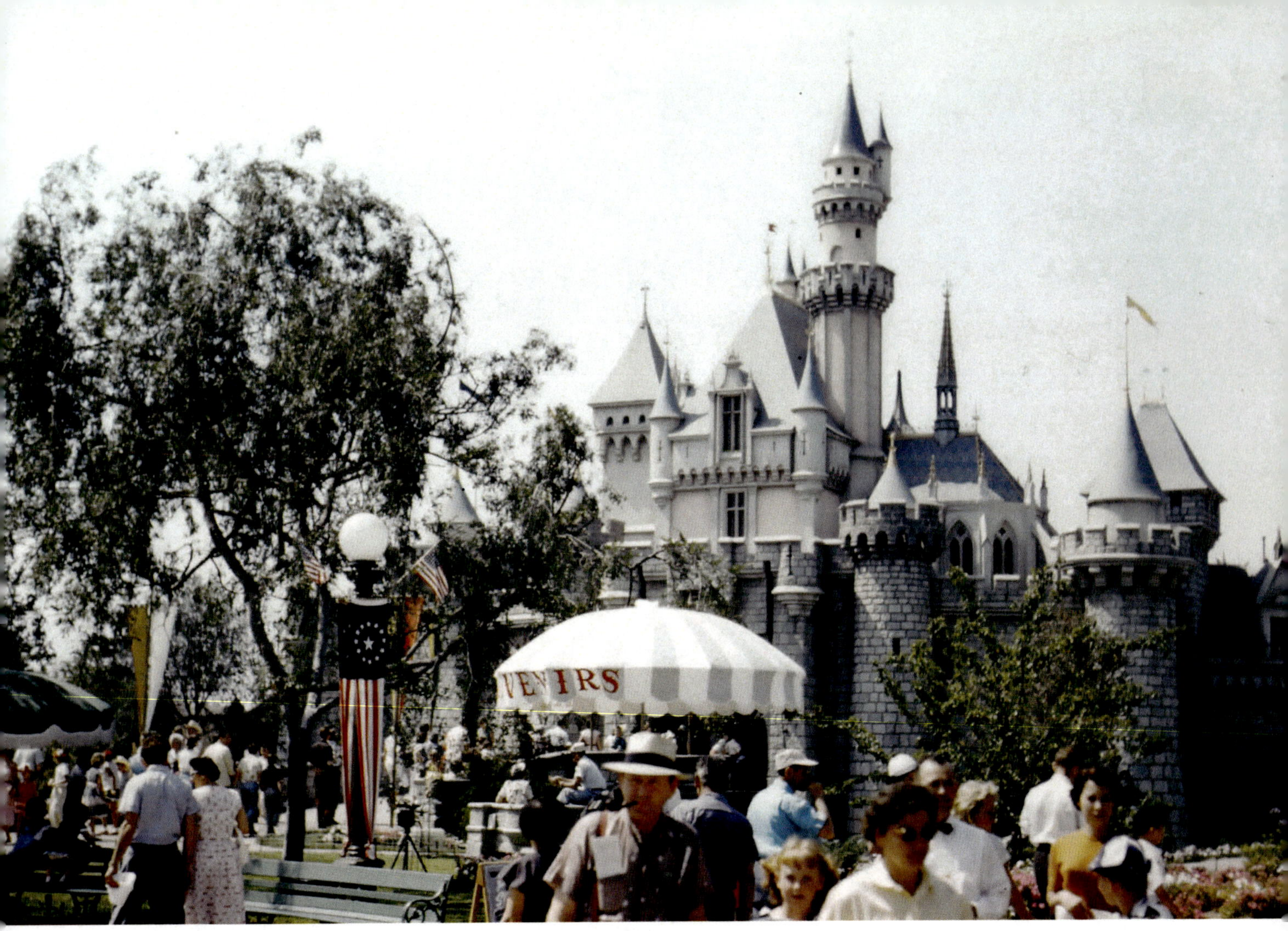

"To keep an operation like Disneyland going you have to pour it in there. It's what I call 'Keeping the show on the road.' You have to keep throwing it in; you can't sit back and let it ride. Not just new attractions but keeping it staffed properly . . . you know, never letting your personnel get sloppy . . . never let them be unfriendly. That's been our policy all our lives. My brother and I have done that and that is what has built our organization."

— Walt Disney speaking about Disneyland from Walt Disney Productions Tencennial Press Clippings

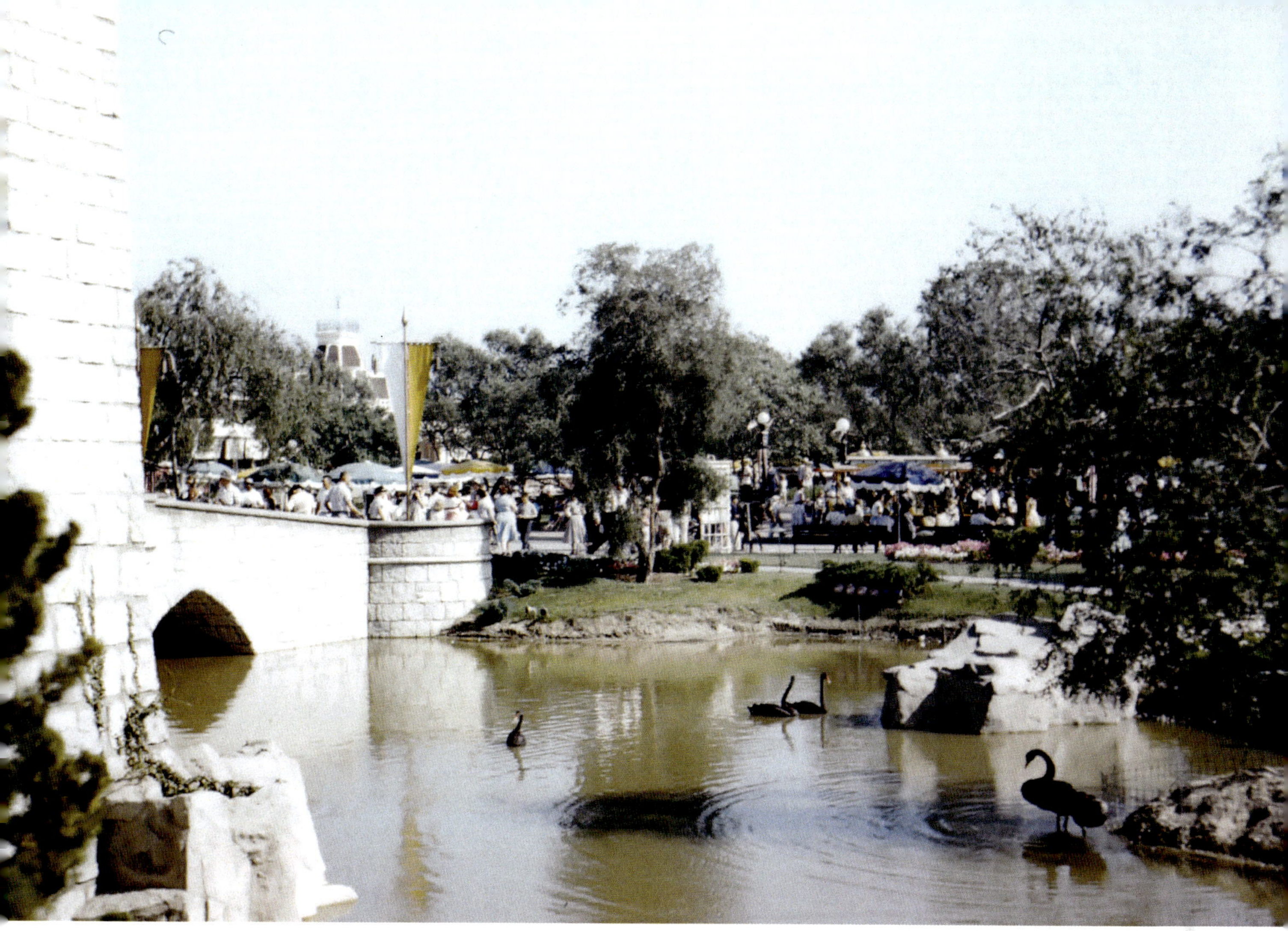

"The way I see it, Disneyland will never be finished. It's something we can keep developing and adding to. A motion picture is different. Once it's wrapped up and sent out for processing, we're through with it. If there are things that could be improved, we can't do anything about them anymore. I've always wanted to work on something alive, something that keeps growing. We've got that in Disneyland."

— Walt Disney speaking about Disneyland from Walt Disney Productions Tencennial Press Clippings

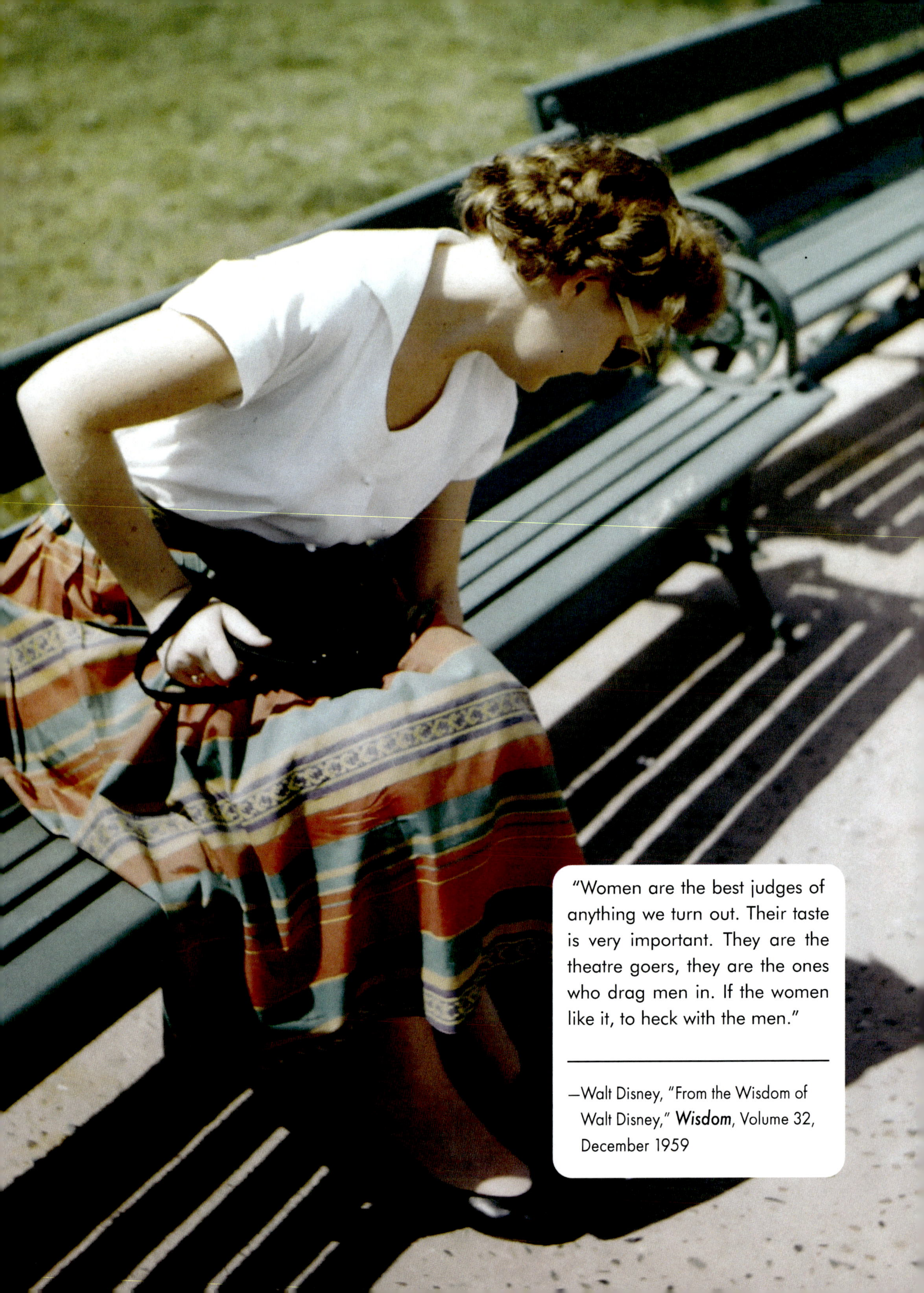

"Women are the best judges of anything we turn out. Their taste is very important. They are the theatre goers, they are the ones who drag men in. If the women like it, to heck with the men."

—Walt Disney, "From the Wisdom of Walt Disney," ***Wisdom***, Volume 32, December 1959

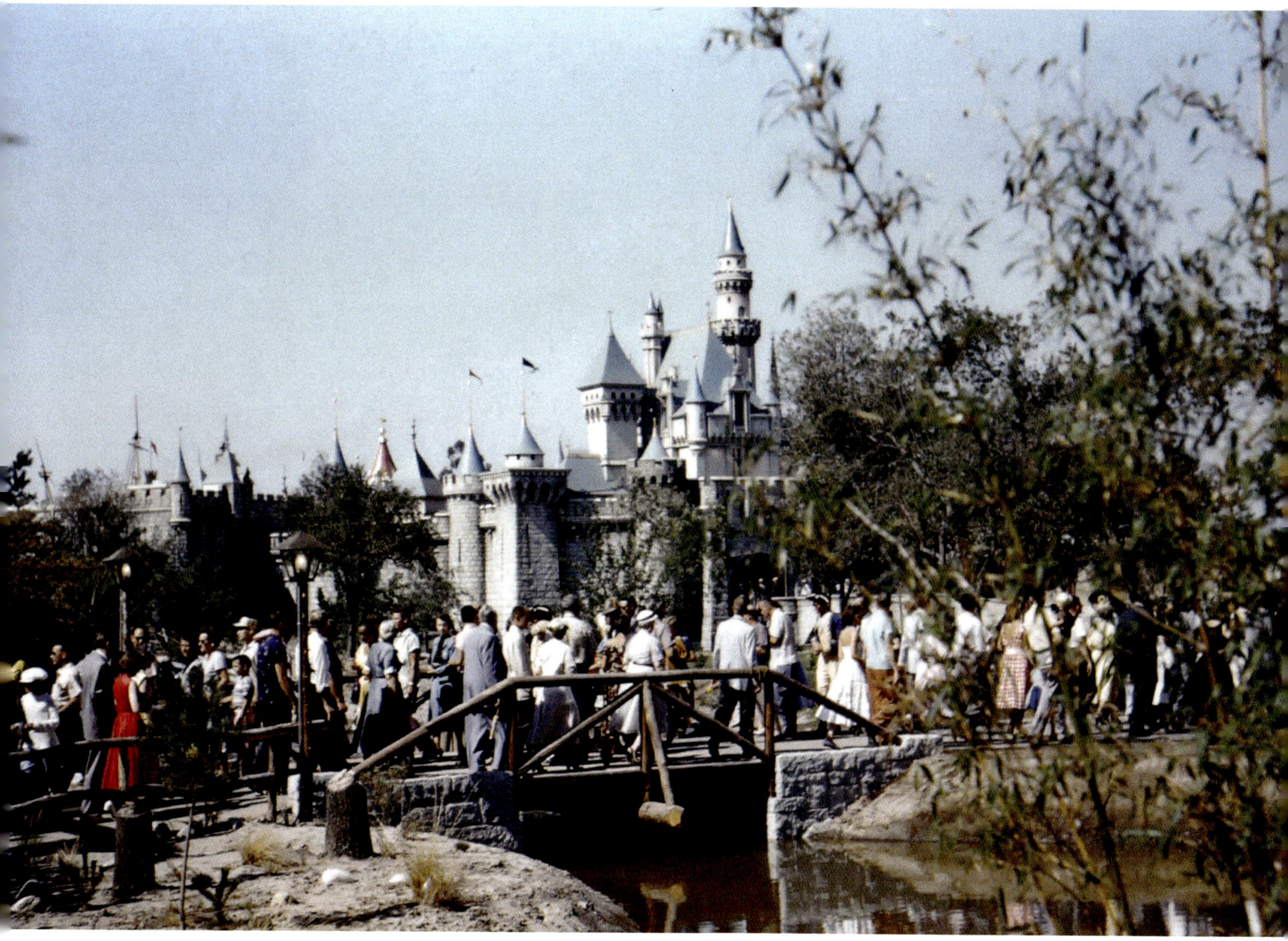

"I could have got most of my costs back with a beer concessions alone, a lot of adults will come here but Disneyland is primarily for children, and I don't think kids and liquor mix."

—Walt Disney, ***Orlando Sentinel***, August 14, 1955

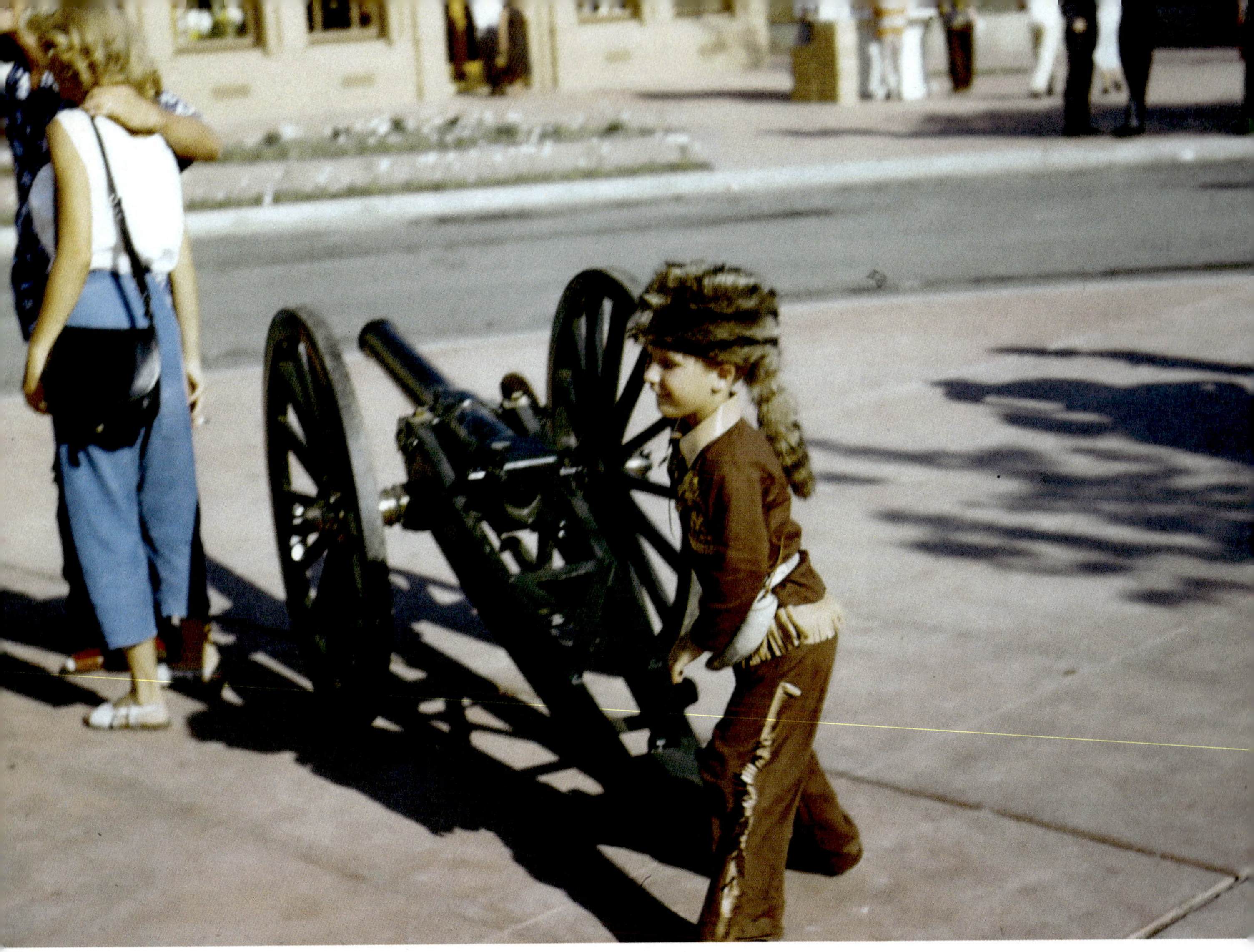

"The most acute Crockett crisis has hit the coonskin market. Raccoon tails used to sell for 2 cents a piece, but with shrill demand for coonskin hats, the market soared to 8 cents, and has now become an open question which will be exhausted first: the supply of raccoons or the parents who have to buy the caps."

—***Life***, April 1955

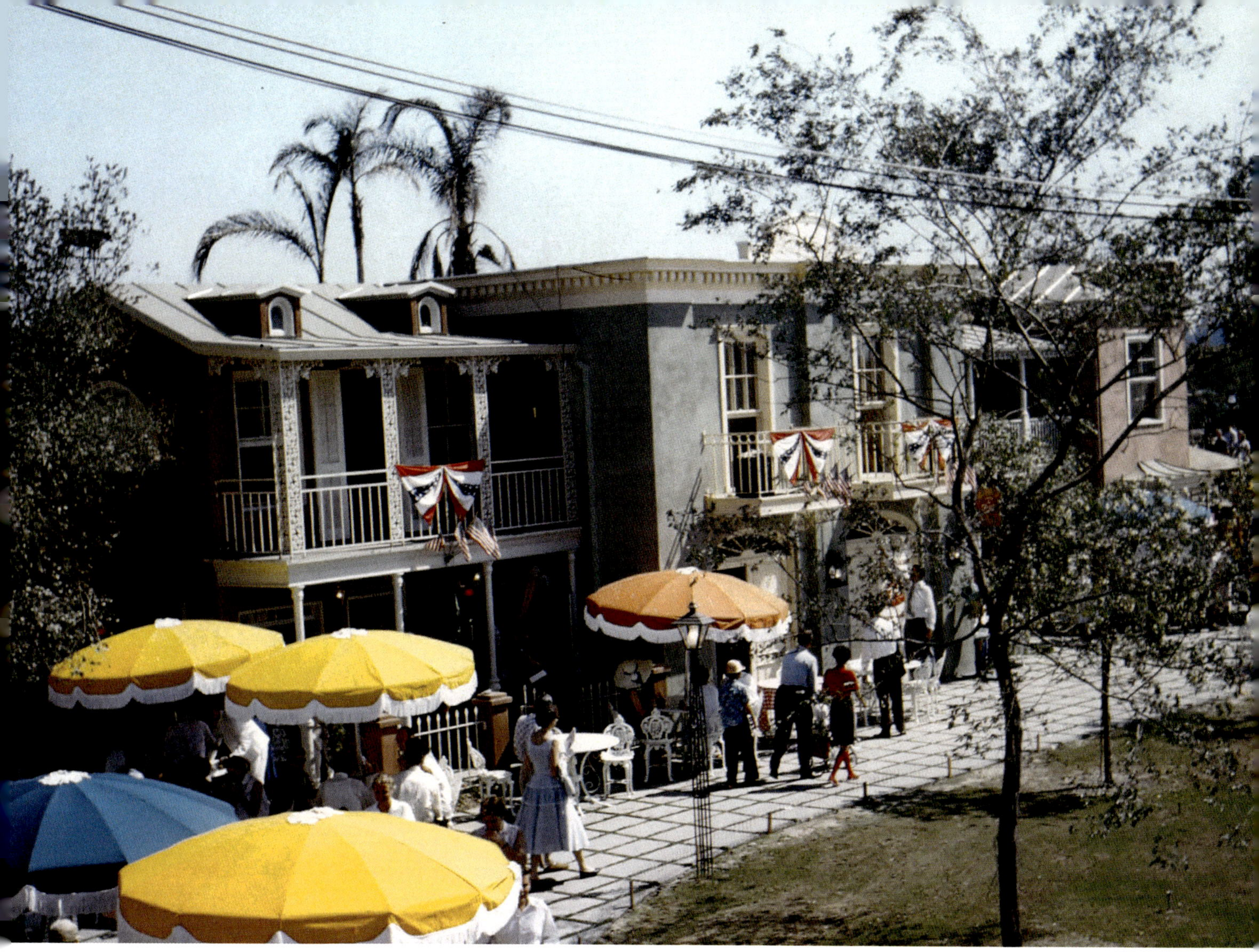

"What has been your biggest problem? 'Trees. We need lots of big ones, but it's hard to find and transplant them, except for palms.'"

—*Oakland Tribune*, May 8, 1955

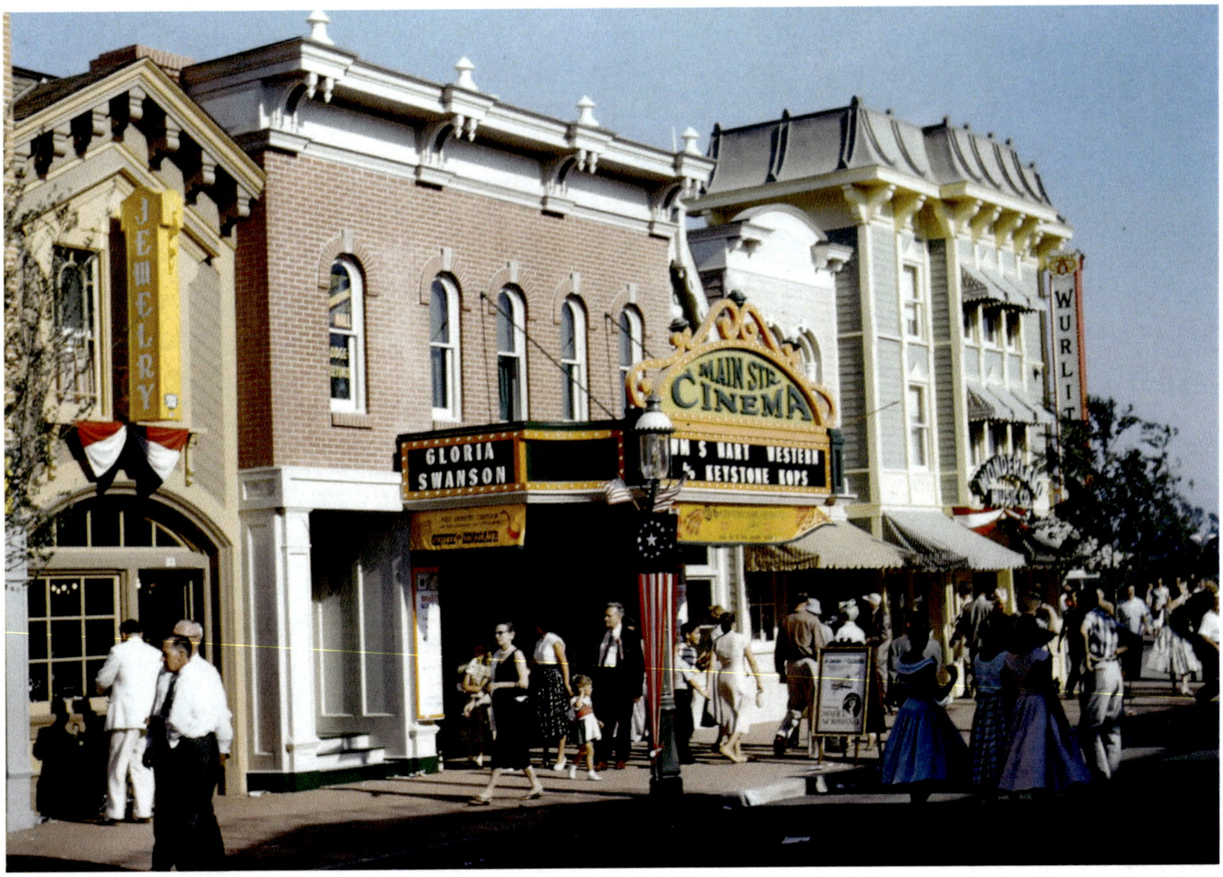

"The Rudolph Wurlitzer Co, whose Cincinnati store has been a landmark in the Queen City for more than 50 years, has been selected by Walt Disney as official representative of the musical-instrument industry at Disneyland, Anaheim, California. R. C. Rolfing, president of the Wurlitzer company, announced the selection yesterday.

The Wurlitzer store at Disneyland, which will be opened to the public next Monday, is reproduced on the corner of 'Main Street, U.S.A.' at the playground. Architecture of the store reflects the Victorian era. In the windows will be old-style pianos, phonographs, pianinos, organs and other musical instruments. Inside the store, contemporary Wurlitzer products will be displayed."

—***Cincinnati Enquirer***, July 12, 1955

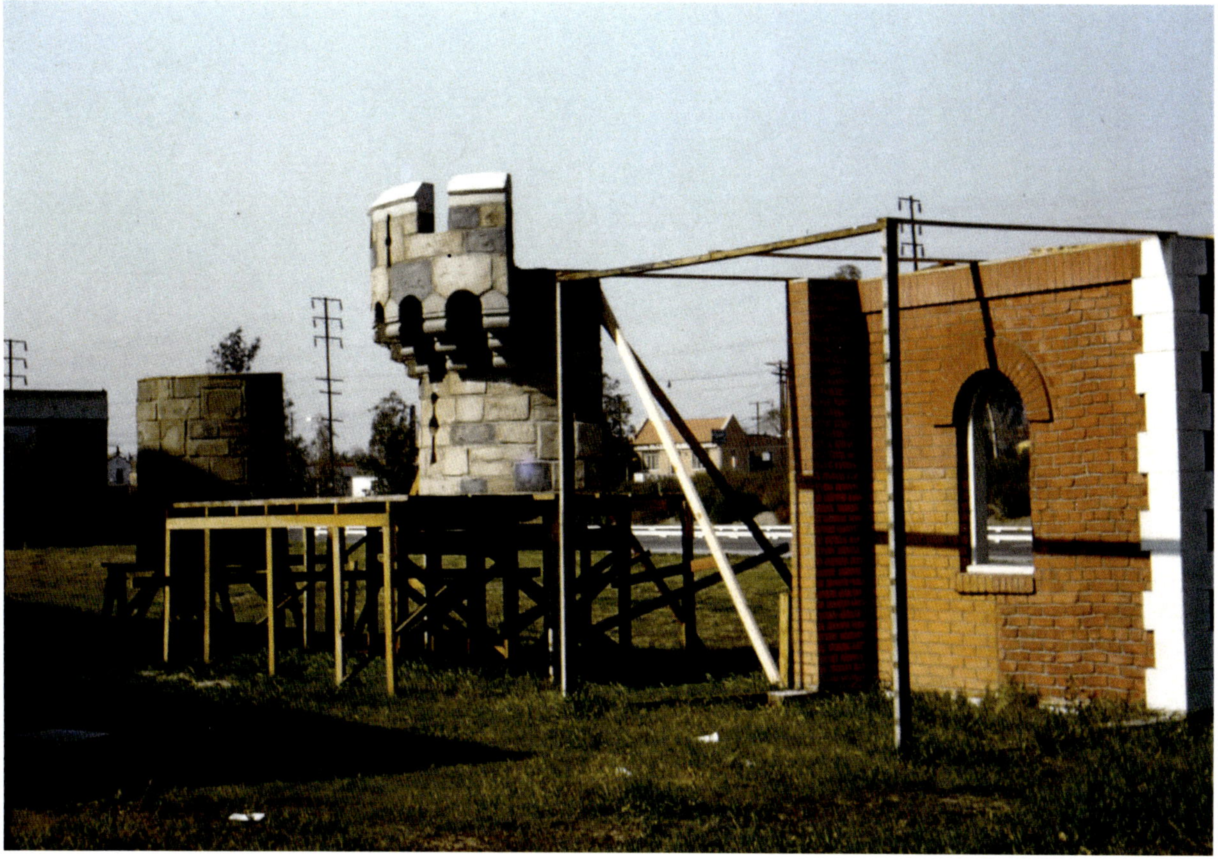

Well, here it is! An exceptional photograph of the legendary—or maybe I should say infamous—"test wall," which can currently be found off of Main Street down Center Street. Is it actually a "test wall" illustrating how the different types of brickwork look? Or was it meant to be a transitional wall to the never built International Street? Does this photo add to the legend and lore, or perhaps it takes away from it?

Upon seeing the photo, Tom Morris—a preeminent Disney historian and a former creative development executive at Walt Disney Imagineering—explained to me that the parking lot in the background is the Alameda Street parking lot. Today, at the Disney studio in Burbank, the Frank Wells building stands where the lot once was. The closest building on the left side of the photo is Ub Iwerks's optical lab.

The aerial view of the studio from 1954 on the next page aligns with what is in the background of the "test wall" photo—an empty field and the Alameda Street parking lot.

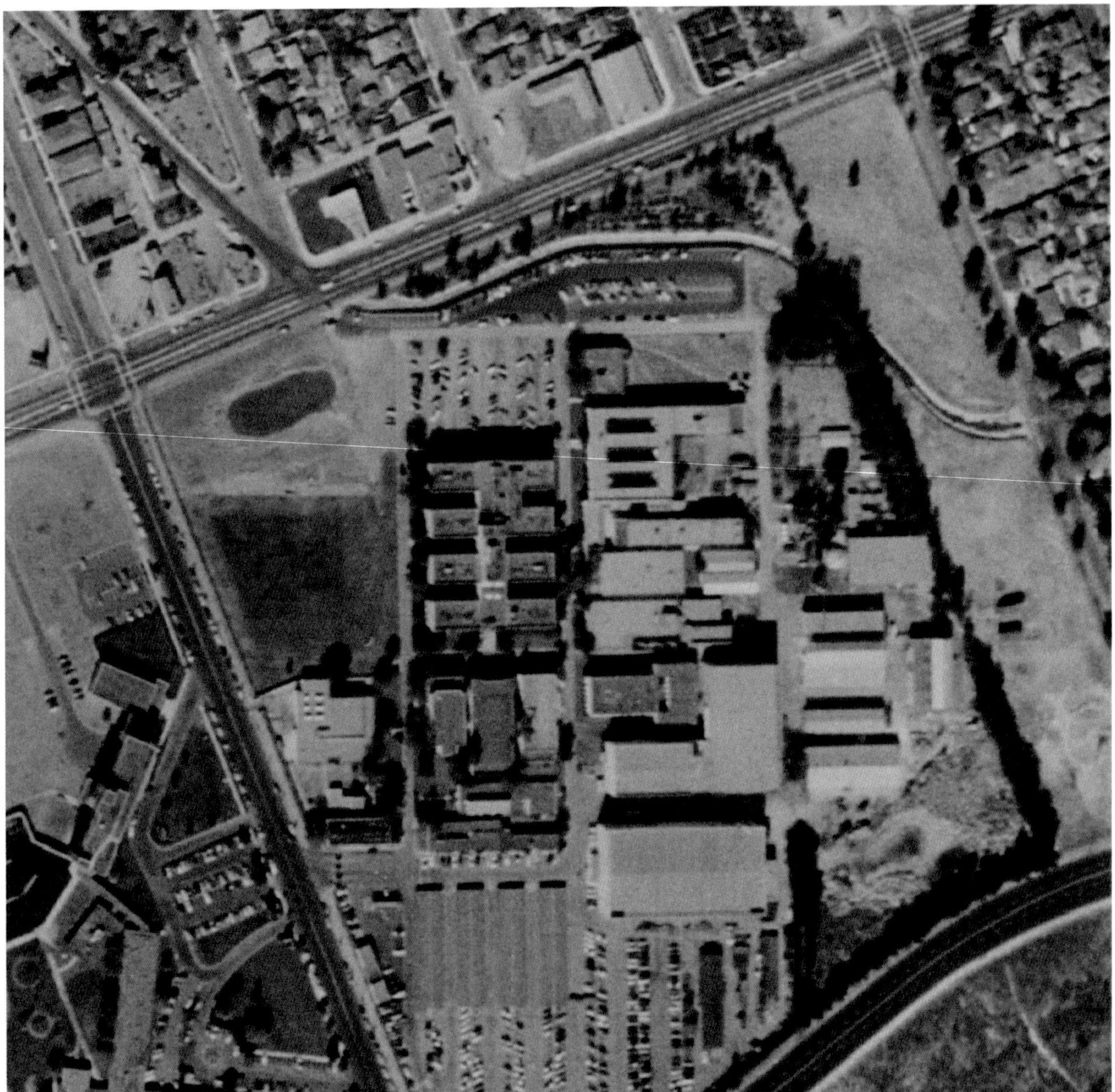

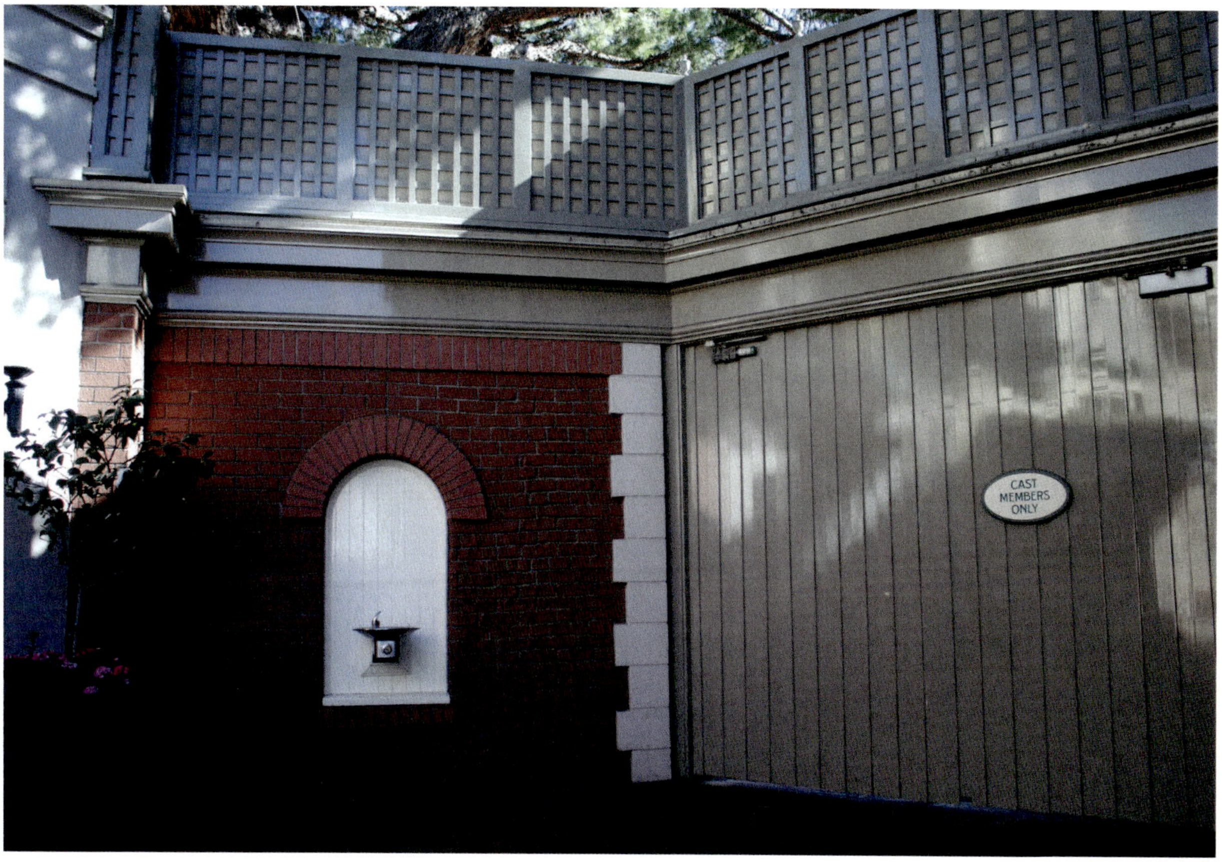

January 2023, Photo Credit Paulina De Artola

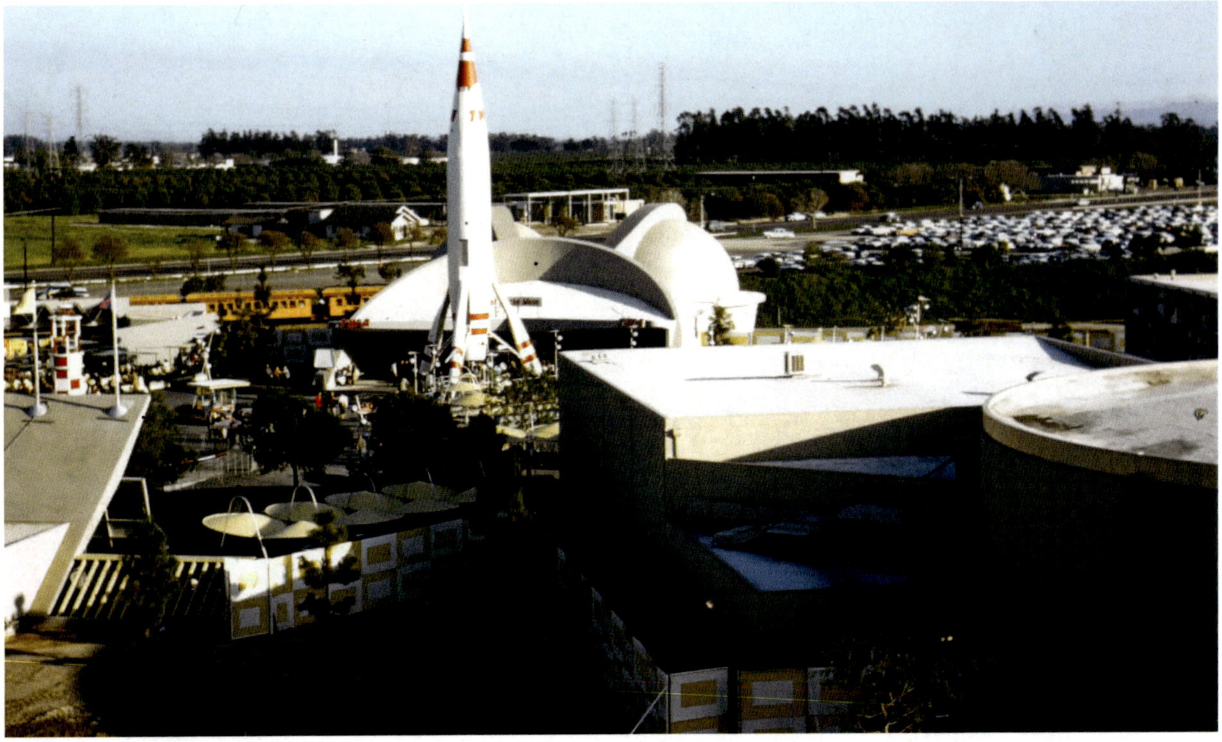

"Long recognized as one of the West's outstanding builders, McNeil Construction Co., was called upon for the construction of Disneyland. And in less than a year the Los Angeles firm converted the orange and nut groves into the fabulous Disneyland.

Much of the construction was unique for the firm for it meant going well back into yesterday in building the Main St., U.S.A. area. Castles of old and such structures were new to the workers but they took them in stride. But building of Tomorrowland was nothing unique for the McNeil firm. Throughout their long career in the Southland they have been building for tomorrow. The firm did much in converting Los Angeles from a mere country town into one of the great cities many years ago.

Moving equipment onto the Disneyland site in mid-July 1954, McNeil crewmen first had to remove 12,500 orange trees, 700 eucalyptus trees and 500 walnut trees. Immediately after the trees were removed, work was started on site development and installation of underground utilities.

Nearly 2 million board feet of lumber went into the buildings constructed: 5,000 cubic yards of concrete went into construction; 350,000 cubic yards of earth were moved; 4,000 linear feet of sewer line installed; 2,000 lineal feet of storm drain piping; 4000 feet of gas line and 7,000 feet of waterline installed.

Over 1,000,000 square feet of asphalt paving was done in the parking area and streets inside the park. All of the millwork, wrought iron work and staff work was done right on the jobsite by McNeil forces. Over 60 subcontractors were employed on the project and materials were purchased from several hundred sources in Southern California or elsewhere as the need arose."

—***Long Beach Telegram***, July 15, 1955

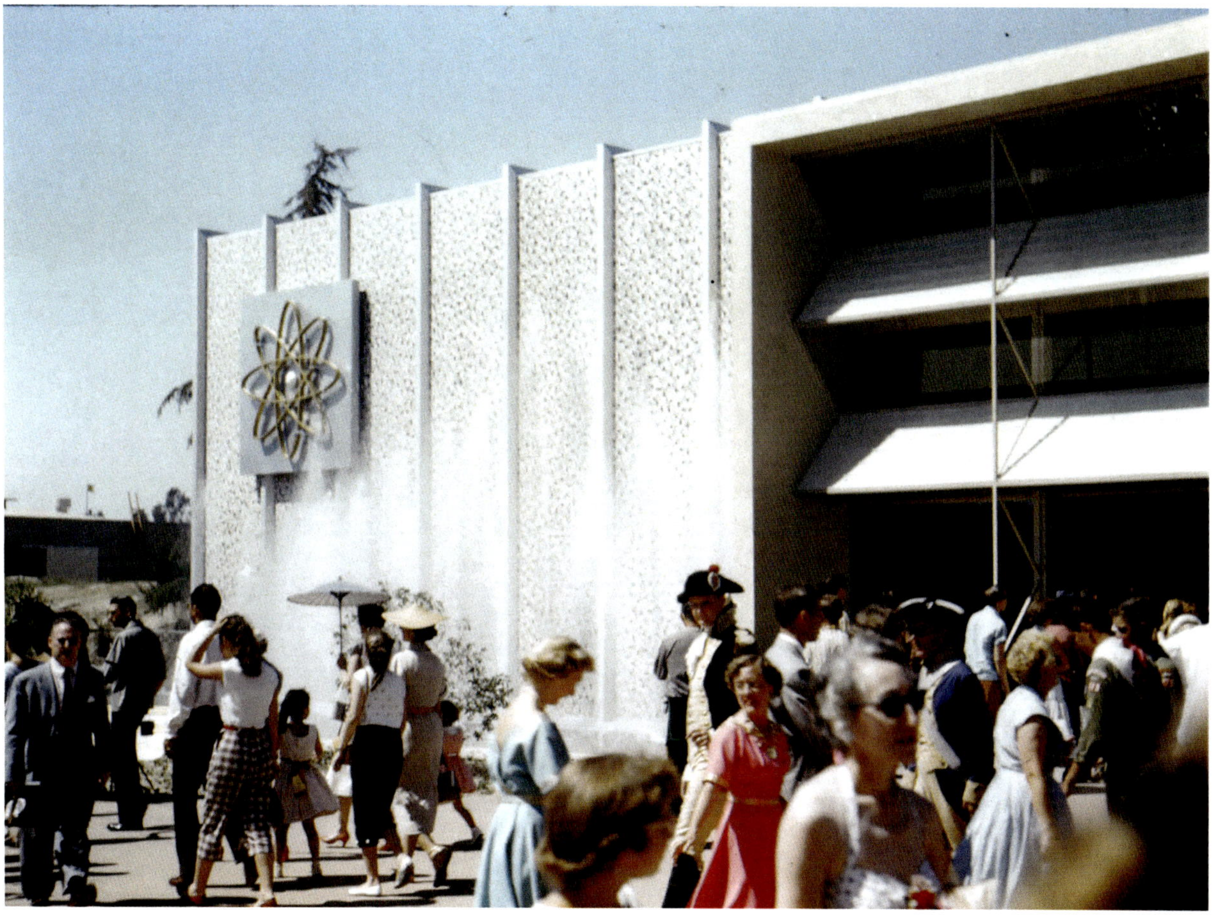

"Here's the place! Don't miss it!—Monsanto's Hall of Chemistry is the first attraction you will see in the first building to your right as you enter 'Tomorrowland.' No visit will be complete without seeing the contributions of chemistry in Tomorrowland.

Upon entering Monsanto's Hall of Chemistry, you will see CHEMATRON . . . huge shining test tubes of the eight basic materials found in nature, from which countless chemicals and plastics can be made."

—*Los Angeles Times Supplement,* July 15, 1955

(Side note: judging by their costumes, it looks like a few guys are out of place in Tomorrowland!)

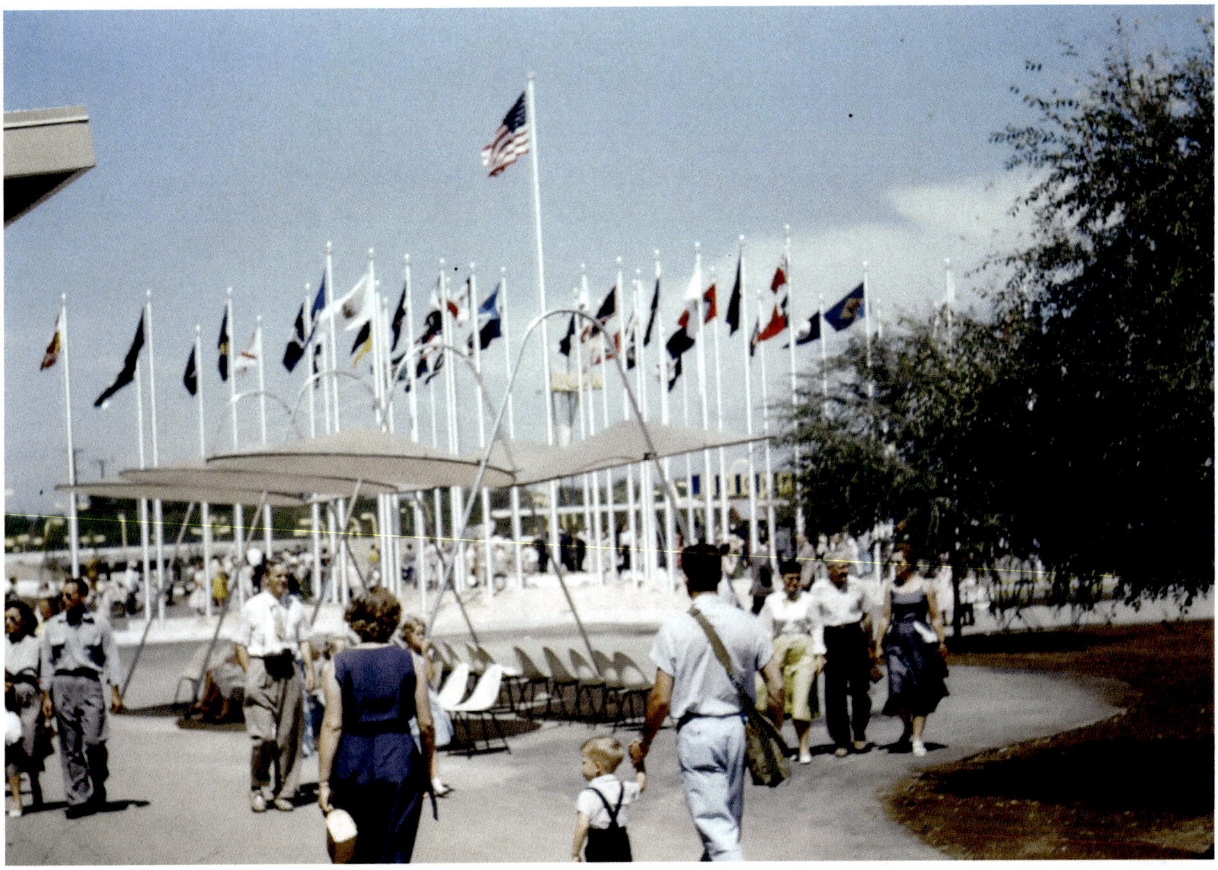

"Beyond the clock is the Court of Honor. The Court is an eight-pointed star, 80 feet in diameter, with six flags radiating out from the center toward each point. The flags atop the 30-foot poles, represent each state of the Union, while the American flag waving from a 45-foot pole, stands in the center."

—***Long Beach Independent***, July 15, 1955

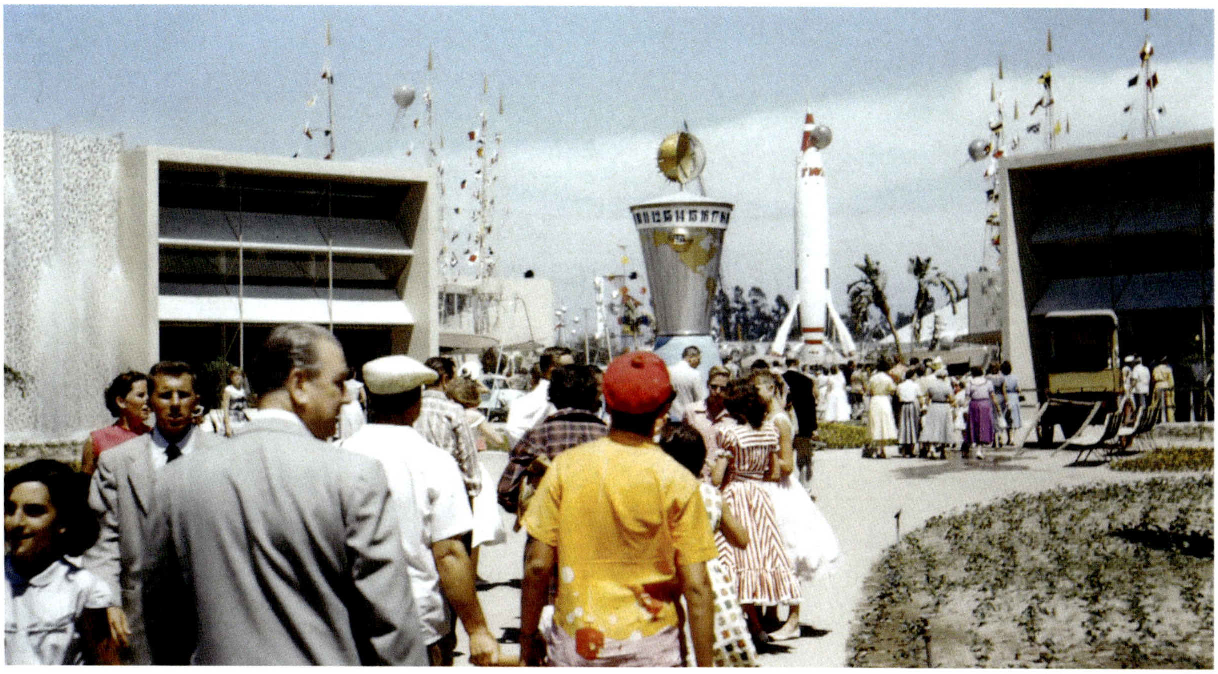

"The Clock of the World at Tomorrowland's entrance where a rotating motif represents the sun and the moon. The sun's warm rays will come from a gold aluminum half-sphere, which is lit form the inside. At night, the moon reflects the sun's light complying with the pattern of the universe. The clock itself is stylized hour glass shape. Its background is of silver aluminum and applied on that are countries of the world in gold aluminum. Roof and base of the clock are imported Italian glass mosaics and the entire structure sits on a brilliant floral pattern indicating the cardinal points of the compass."

—***Long Beach Independent,*** July 15, 1955

"What the incredible Disney calls Tomorrowland, here is where TWA has installed a rocket ship, Diana, flying regular round trip schedules to the moon. Do not be alarmed at the thrust of the jet takeoff, the stewardess said, and there we were, going straight up. Above we could see the moon approaching; below we watched the earth receding."

—***Abilene Reporter-News***, August 15, 1955

The Moonliner, which was the centerpiece for the Rocket to the Moon attraction sponsored by TWA, was a science-factual round trip to the moon. The trip was simulated by seat vibrations and circular screens and scanners showing take off and approach of both the planet and of Earth's moon. The seat vibrations were operated by air compressors synchronized with the viewing screens. The viewing screens and scanners were located on the floor of the spaceship. Sixteen millimeter film was projected onto the scanners and synchronized with the seat vibrations and the sounds of the launch and "mission" recorded on tape.

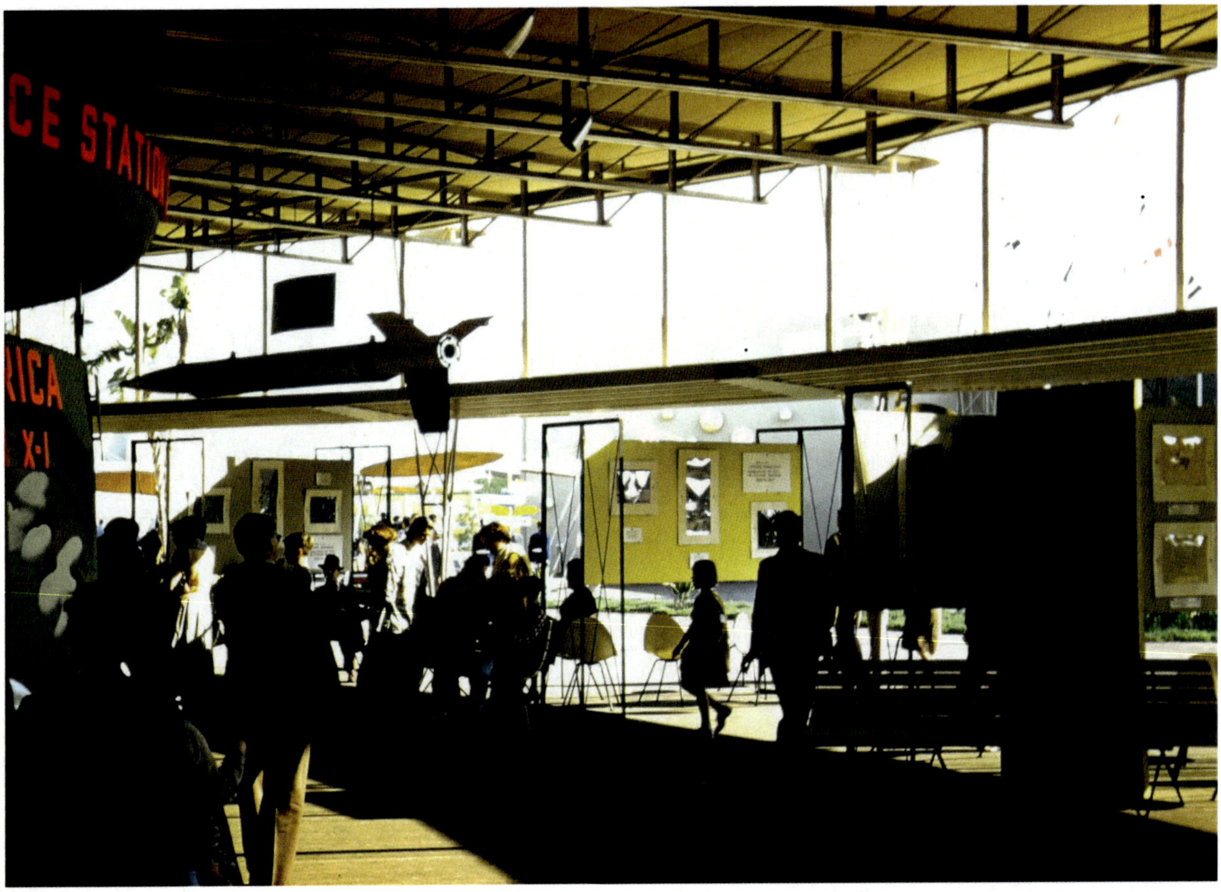

"The subject is Space Station X-1 at Disneyland. It measures 100 feet across and 300 feet around. It was produced under the supervision of Walt Disney, with Peter Ellenshaw directing. All the facilities of Disney's vast Burbank studios were placed at Ellenshaw's disposal.

Six months were required to finish it, working from a smaller model, and another six weeks were required to assemble and interlock the parks. Jim McCann, under the direction of Ellenshaw, was in charge of Disney's scenic artists—scores of them working on the project.

The raised effect is an optical illusion. Imagine you are traveling in a space ship 500 or more miles above the United States. Well, that's it. Below is the United States in all its vast detail, and you see it from a platform that moves slowly from East to West. Florida, New York, the Great Lakes, the Illinois and Iowa corn country, the great marching ridges that are the Rockies, the prairies, the High Sierras and the Pacific States. It is stunning, revealing, really gigantic. The illusion is perfect, with its night and day effects."

—***Valley Times***, November 26, 1955

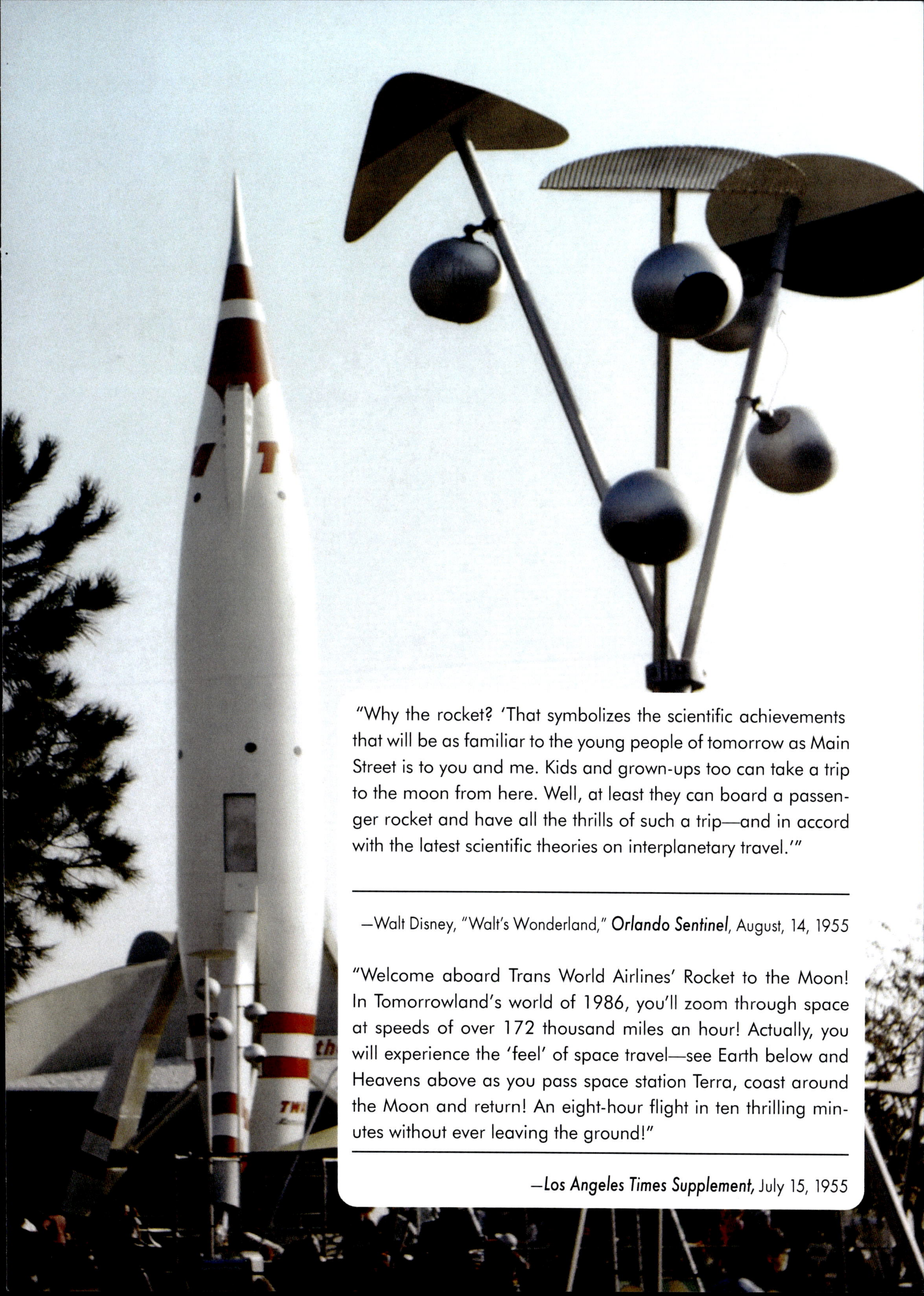

"Why the rocket? 'That symbolizes the scientific achievements that will be as familiar to the young people of tomorrow as Main Street is to you and me. Kids and grown-ups too can take a trip to the moon from here. Well, at least they can board a passenger rocket and have all the thrills of such a trip—and in accord with the latest scientific theories on interplanetary travel.'"

—Walt Disney, "Walt's Wonderland," ***Orlando Sentinel***, August, 14, 1955

"Welcome aboard Trans World Airlines' Rocket to the Moon! In Tomorrowland's world of 1986, you'll zoom through space at speeds of over 172 thousand miles an hour! Actually, you will experience the 'feel' of space travel—see Earth below and Heavens above as you pass space station Terra, coast around the Moon and return! An eight-hour flight in ten thrilling minutes without ever leaving the ground!"

—***Los Angeles Times Supplement,*** July 15, 1955

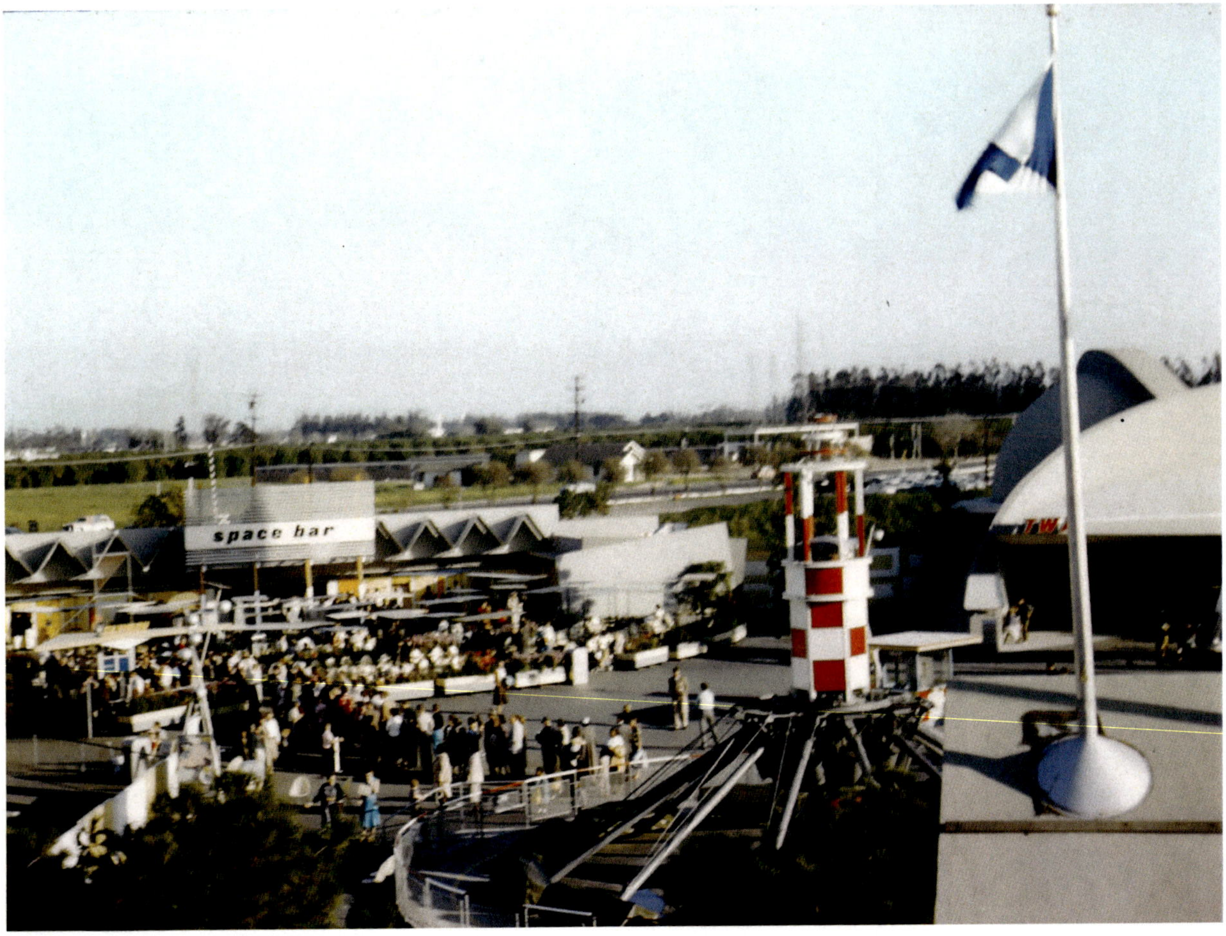

"Dinnertime 1986 . . .You will enjoy a delicious dinner of the future delivered to you from an immaculate, fully automatic food service. Just push a button of your selection—seconds later you will have a complete piping hot meal. Then you eat in the midst of all the splendor of Walt Disney's 'Tomorrowland' at family-sized tables in a shaded resting place overlooking freeways of tomorrow."

—***Long Beach Independent***, July 15, 1955

A bit of artistic license was certainly used when describing Space Bar in Tomorrowland. Visitors to the Space Bar dined on burgers and hot dogs—your typical quick service-type fare from a run of the mill restaurant—and vending machines fulfilled the push button aspect mentioned in the description.

In the "Welcome to Disneyland" newspaper supplement from the ***Los Angeles Examiner*** on July 15, 1955, Space Bar was actually called "Stratosnack"and had a bit of a different façade on the building—this name was the name given to the restaurant in the initial planning of the restaurant concept.

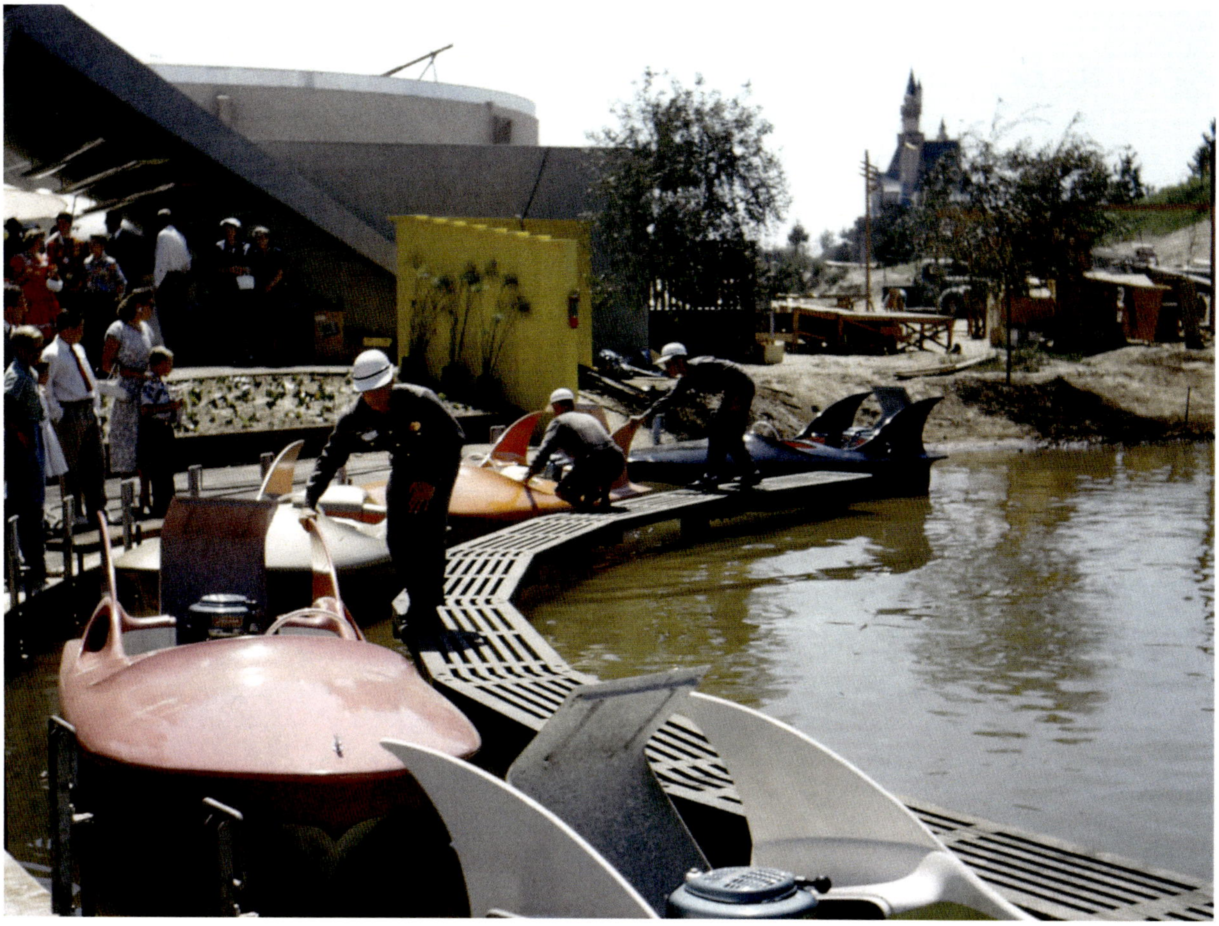

Disneyland's opening year featured many attractions with watercraft. Here you see one of the more dubious boat rides, the short-lived Tomorrowland Boats. About a month later they were renamed "Phantom Boats." Opening day advertising touted fourteen boats for guests to commandeer around Tomorrowland Lake.

According to Disney Legend Randy Bright, "Each boat that left the dock seemed to have only a 50-50 chance of making it back without having to be towed." The Phantom Boats were a short-lived attraction, only sticking around for roughly two years. They looked cooler than they were physically—their motors would often overheat.[10]

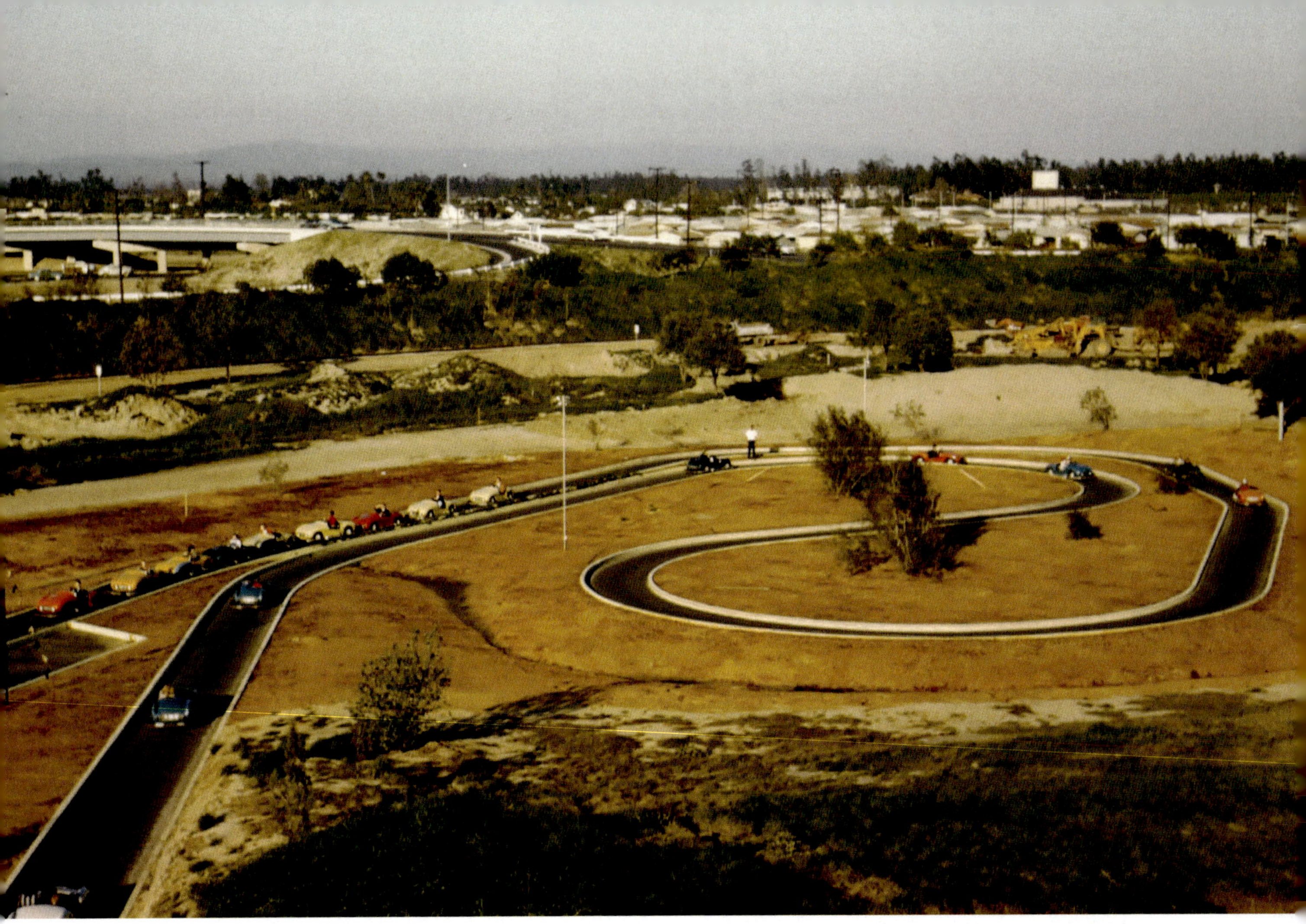

"Whether you're 6 or 60, the Richfield Autotopia is one of the very special things you won't want to miss when you visit Walt Disney's magic kingdom—Disneyland. The Autopia is a real model freeway, and the cars are gas-engine automobiles powered with New Richfield Ethyl. It's absolutely safe, yet a real thrill to get behind the wheel of one of the brightly colored cars. Be sure to visit the Richfield Autopia in Tomorrowland when you visit Disneyland."

—***Long Beach Independent,*** July 15, 1955

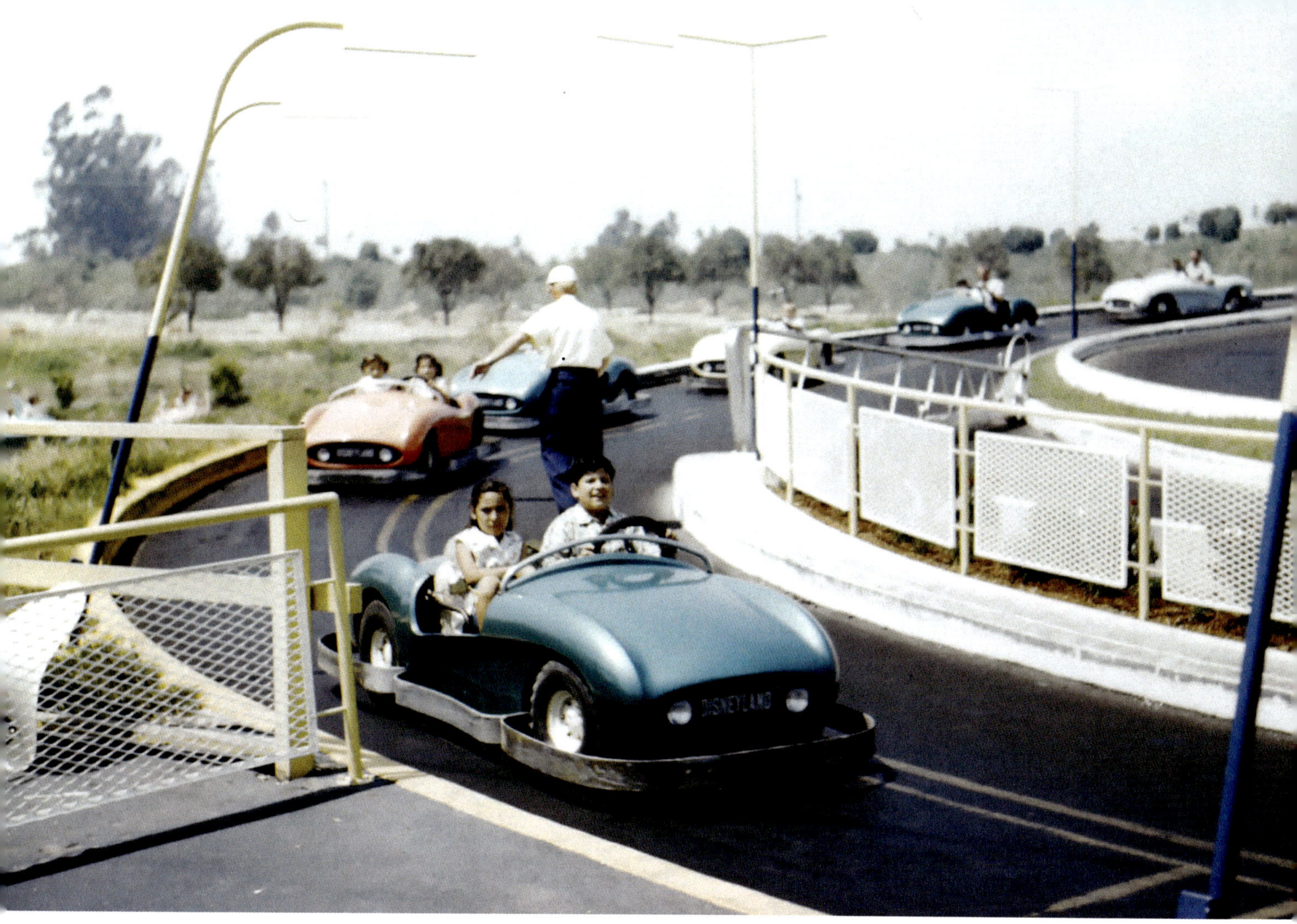

"These little cars designed for everyone from 7 years old and up, are so completely safe that any child might push or pull any control without endangering himself or the automobile. Brake and throttle controls are all spring loaded and the brake is operated from the outside. A governor on the carburetor allows the speedsters a fast clip of 11 miles per hour. Based on square tubular frame with seven and one-half horsepower Gladden engines, the cars are equipped with centrifugal clutch and surrounded by aluminum bumpers designed with control springs on the inside of the frame.

The rear portion of the body, which is made of fiberglass, swings upward to facilitate servicing of all mechanical parts. Demountable wheels are finished with aluminum hubs and the steering wheel is of special aluminum casting. Steering gear is of the rack and pinion type.

Just as the word 'autopia' stresses safety and good driving, Disney's craftsmen designed the Disneyland Autopia and the Autopia Freeway as the ultimate in automobile safety."

—***Long Beach Independent***, July 15, 1955

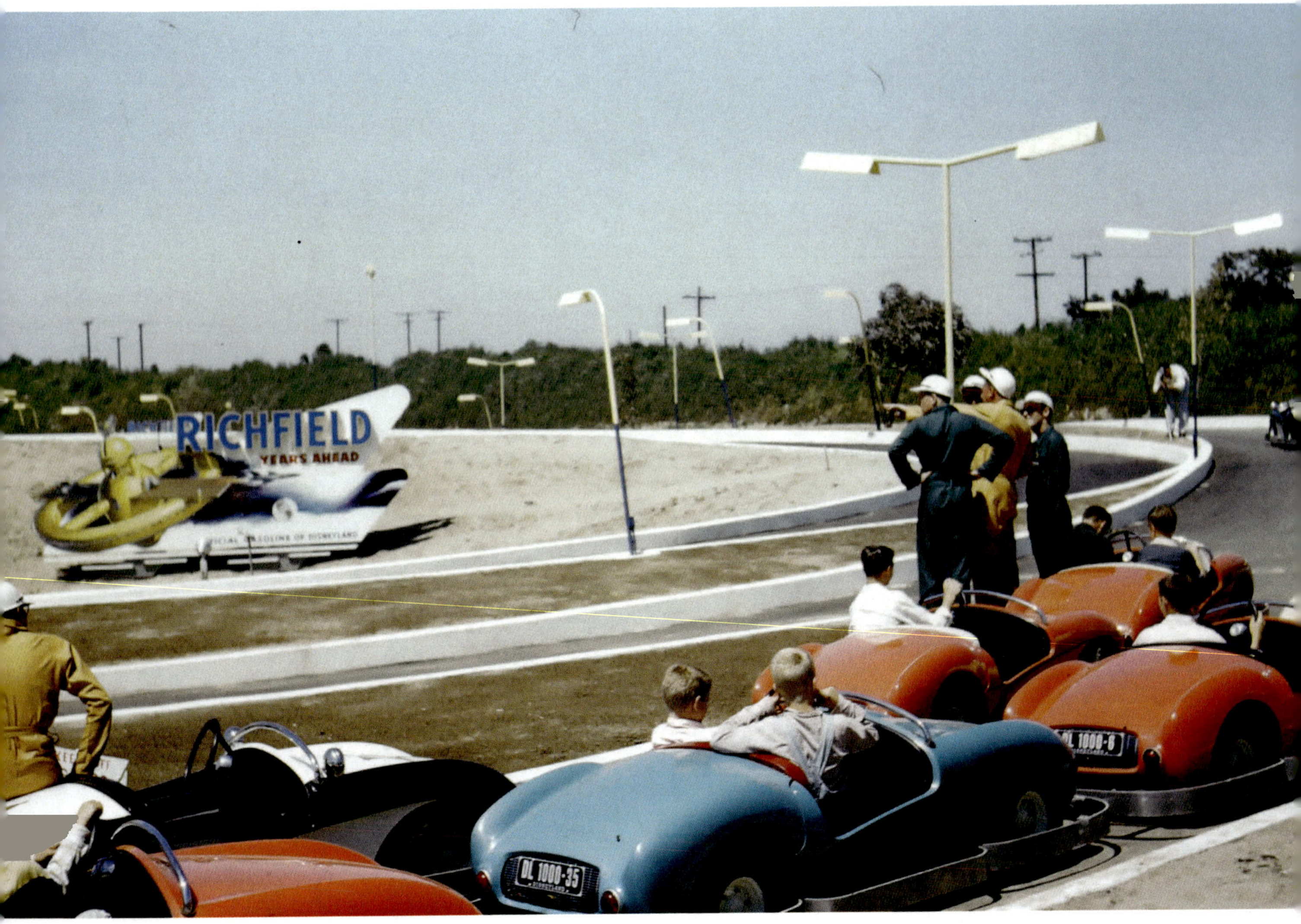

"Disneyland is one of the most widely advertised ventures in history. Since the inception it has been given wide publicity in newspapers, magazines and on the air. Then Richfield Oil Corp. incorporated the Disneyland motif in its 1955 sales campaign.

Within a week's time, dealers gave away 500,000 Disneyland comic books and a second edition of 750,000 is being distributed. The comic book story tells the adventures of an imaginary family from outer space visiting Disneyland."

—***Long Beach Independent***, July 15, 1955

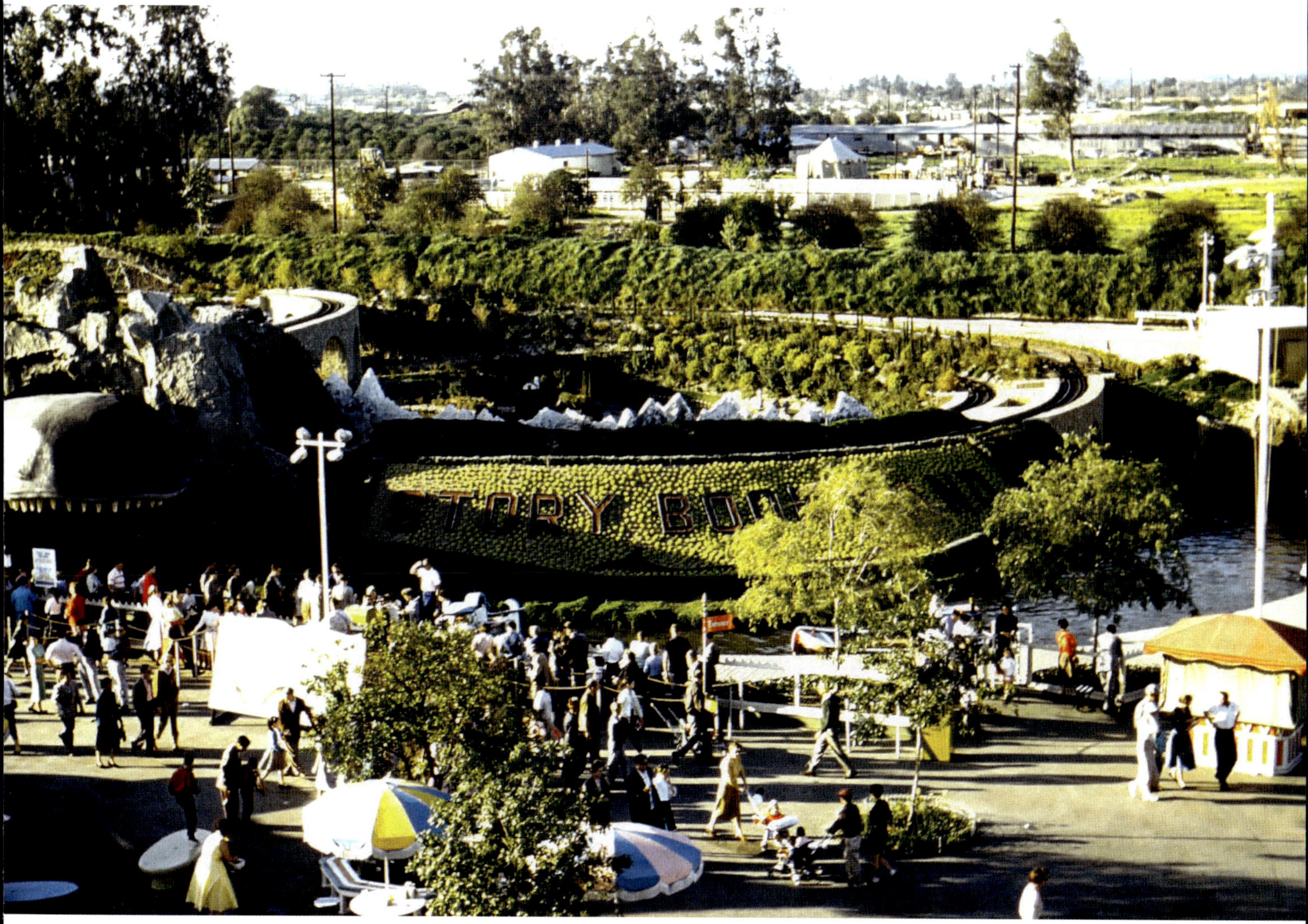

"Fantasy, if it is really convincing, can't become dated, for the simple reason that it represents a flight into a dimension that lies beyond the reach of time."

— Walt Disney, "From the Wisdom of Walt Disney," ***Wisdom***, Volume 32, December 1959

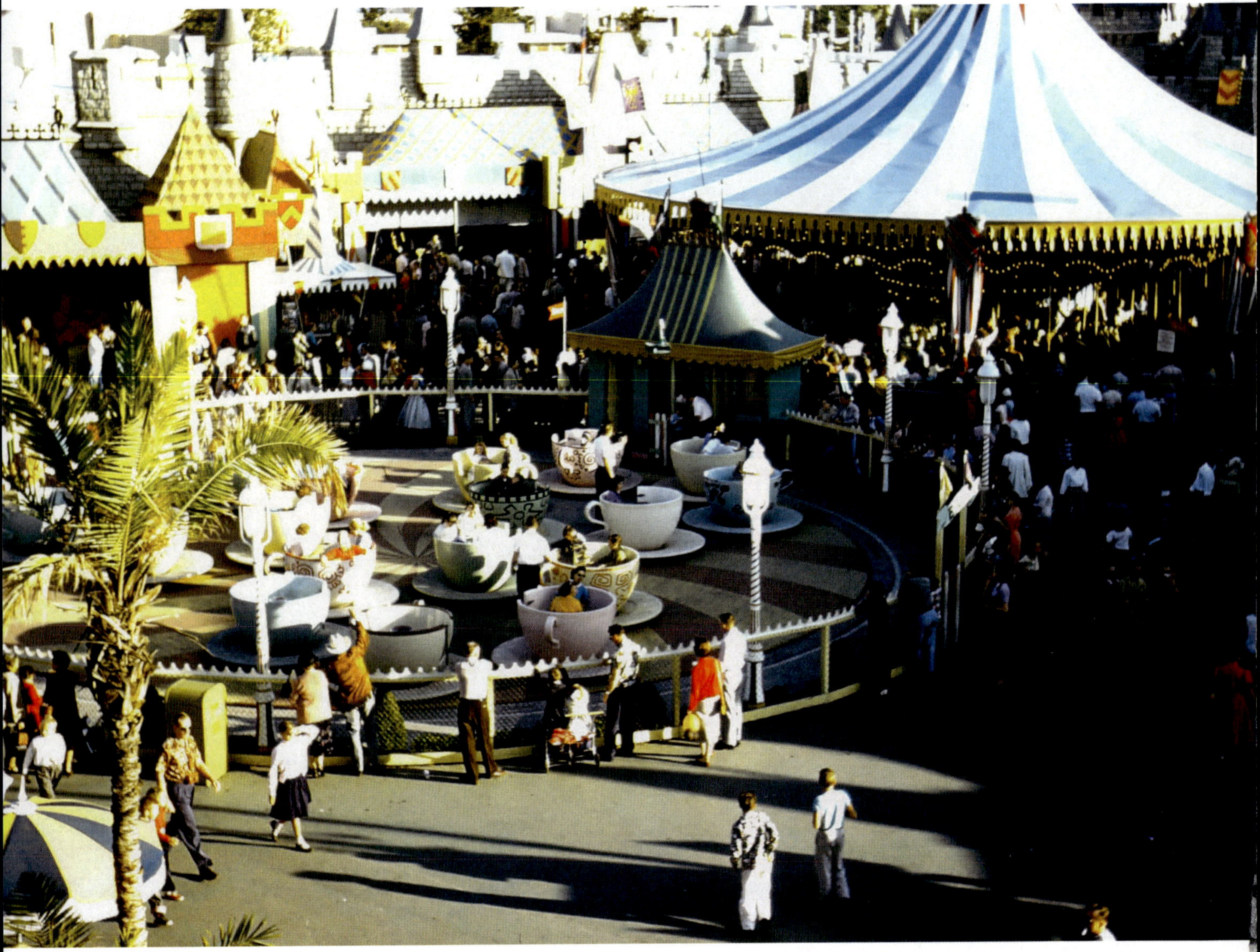

"Beyond the carrousel is the Mad Hatter's Tea Party where guests go for a merry and unusual spin in a cup and saucer, and the Mad Hatter and the March Hare debate furiously atop a sugar bowl."

—***Long Beach Independent***, July 15, 1955

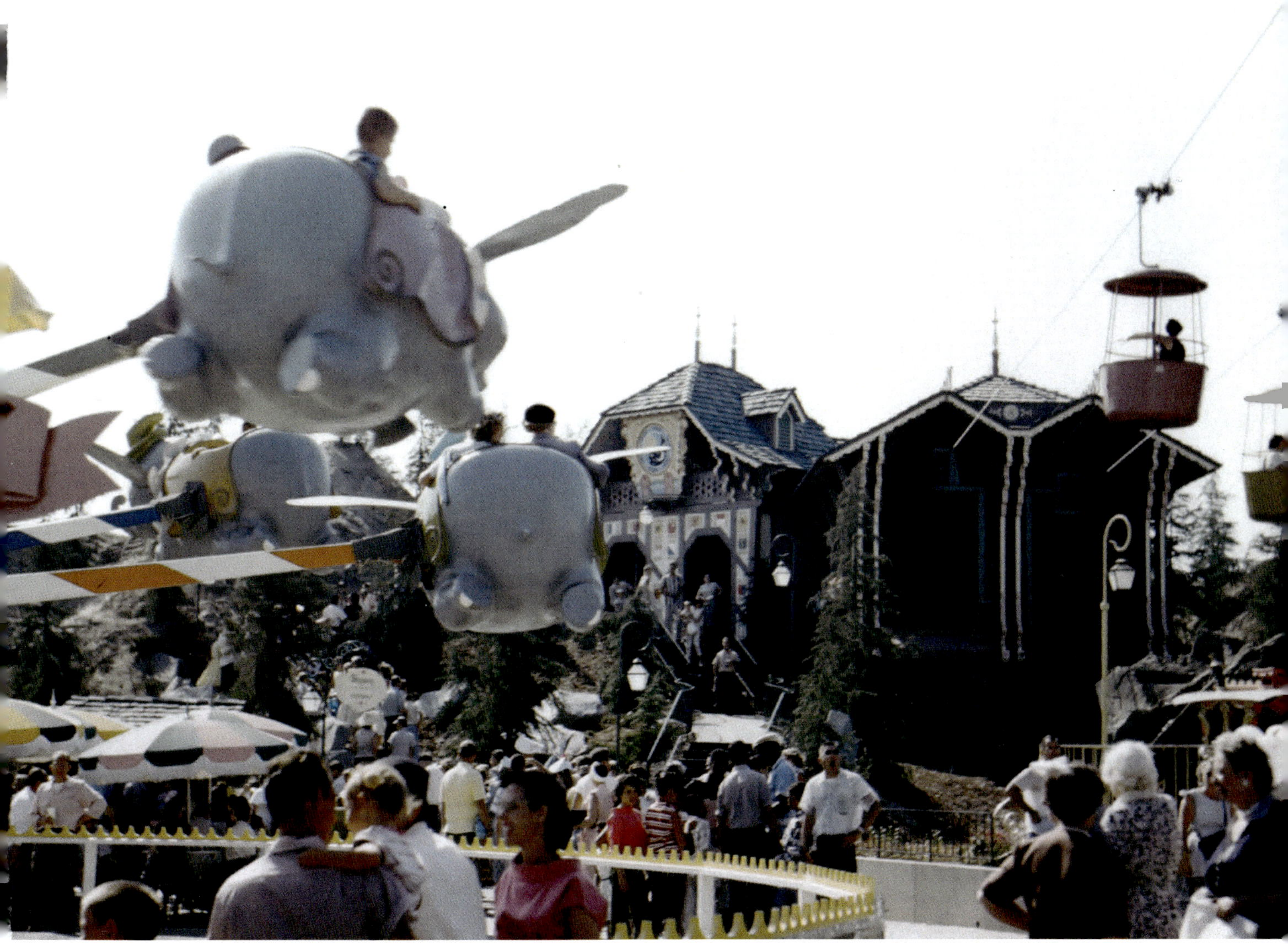

When the film *Dumbo* was in released in 1941, it was such a sensation through '41 and into 1942 that *Time* magazine was going to make Dumbo the magazine's "Mammal of the Year" (along the lines of their Person of the Year!).

The Disney studio even created a cover for the magazine honoring everyone's favorite pachyderm. Unfortunately, the country wouldn't get to see it as Pearl Harbor was attacked on December 7, 1941. The news changed the world, and General Douglas MacArthur graced the cover of *Time* that had been slotted for Dumbo.

(Photo not from opening day)

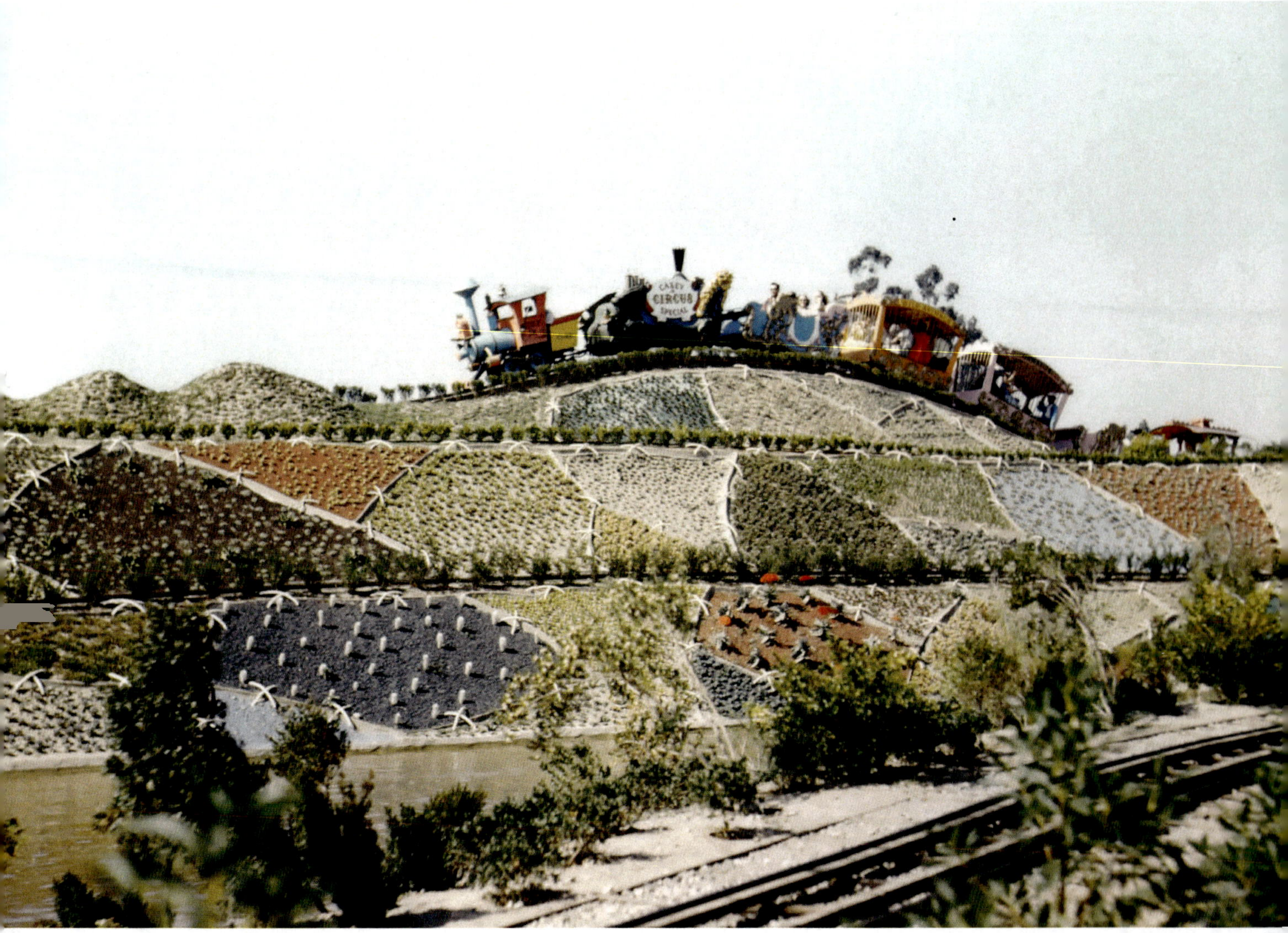

"The Casey Jr. Train—as nearly human as a train can get—almost laughs out loud as it pulls six circus cars of merry riders up hill and down dale and over the Canals of the World. Casey Jr. carries its own music in the Calliope Car and boasts two animal cars, two chariots and a caboose."

— ***Long Beach Independent***, July 15, 1955
(Photo not from opening day)

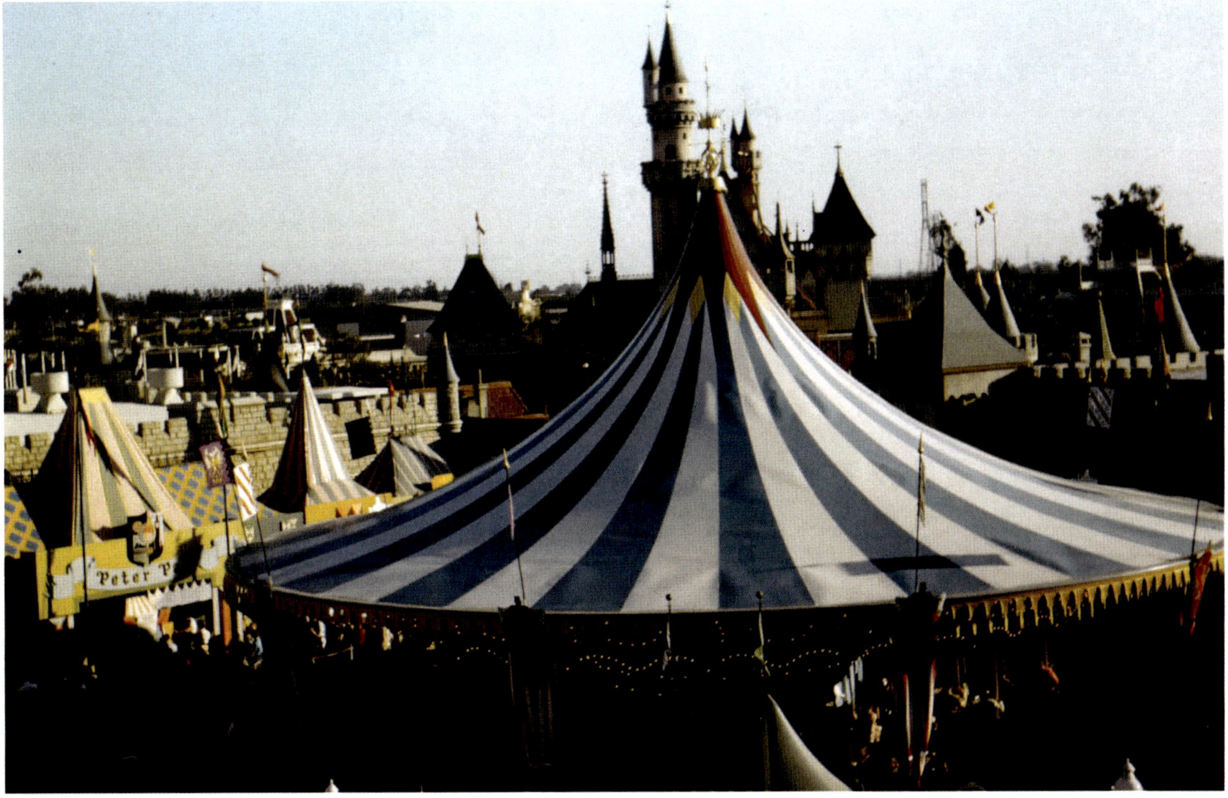

"Dear Sirs:

I think it goes without saying that I am as critical as you people are of many facets of American life. Lord knows I've raised my voice often enough. But when someone like Julian Halevy equates Disneyland and Las Vegas (The Nation, June 7), I begin to doubt his or my sanity.

Not that I haven't met his type before. The world is full of people who, for intellectual reasons, steadfastly refuse to let go and enjoy themselves. Mr. Halevy damns himself immediately when he states he is glad he didn't take a child with him to Disneyland. I did better than take a child; my first visit, I accompanied one of the great theatrical and creative minds of our time, Charles Laughton. I've never had such a day full of zest and good humor. Mr. Laughton is no easy mark; he has a gimlet eye and a searching mind. Yet he saw, and I found, vast reserves of imagination before untapped in our country. I admit I approached Disneyland with many intellectual reservations, myself, but these have been banished in my seven visits. Disney makes mistakes; what artist doesn't? But when he flies, he really flies. I shall be indebted to him for a lifetime for his ability to let me fly over midnight London looking down on that fabulous city, in his Peter Pan ride. The Jungle Boat ride, too, is an experience of true delight and wonder. I could go on, but why bother?

I have a sneaking suspicion, after all is said and done, that Mr. Halevy truly loved Disneyland but is not man enough, or child enough, to admit it. I feel sorry for him. He will never travel in space, he will never touch the stars."

—Ray Bradbury

"Letters to the Editor," ***The Nation***, June 28, 1958

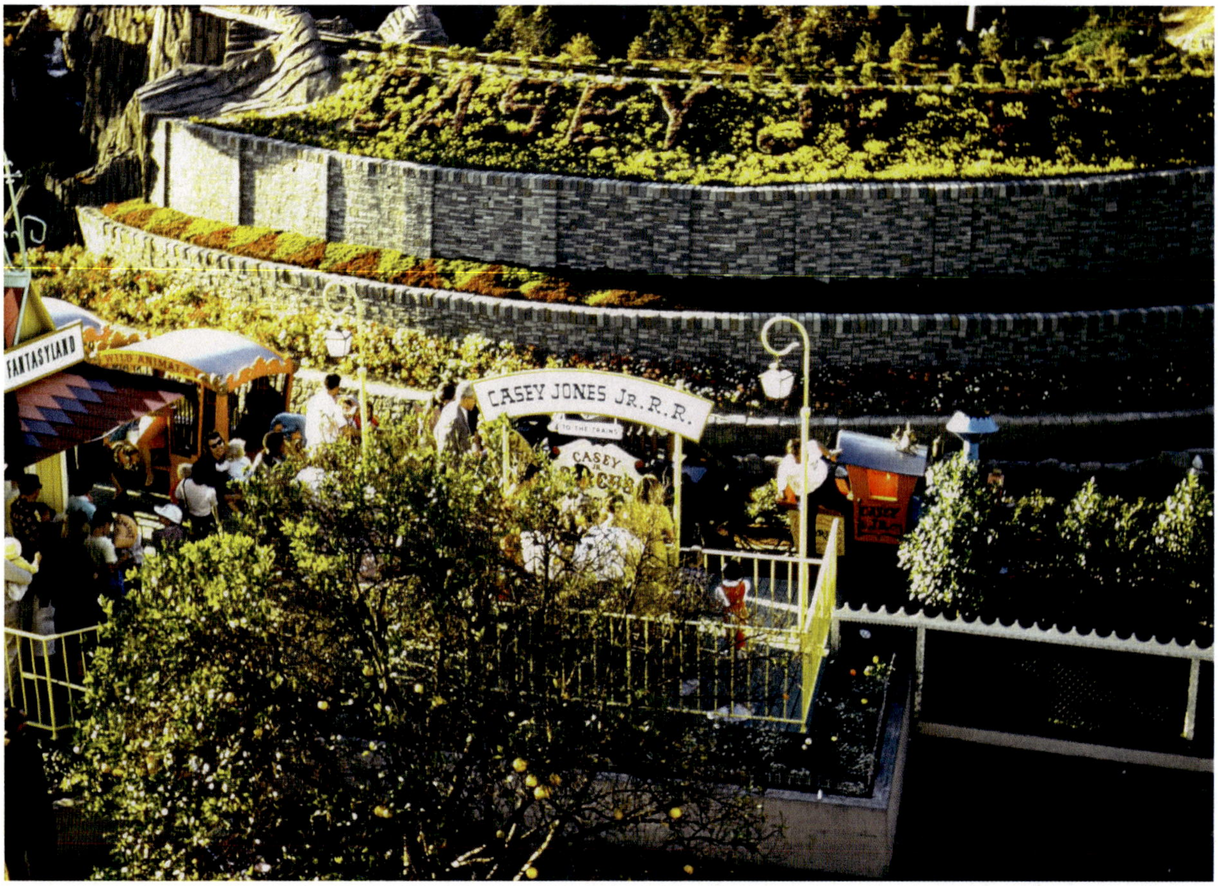

While doing press for the park's opening, Walt was asked which land at Disneyland was his favorite. He responded, "Fantasyland, that's why I use the castle for the symbol on the TV show. I think fantasy captures more of the imagination than anything else."[11]

(Photo not from opening day)

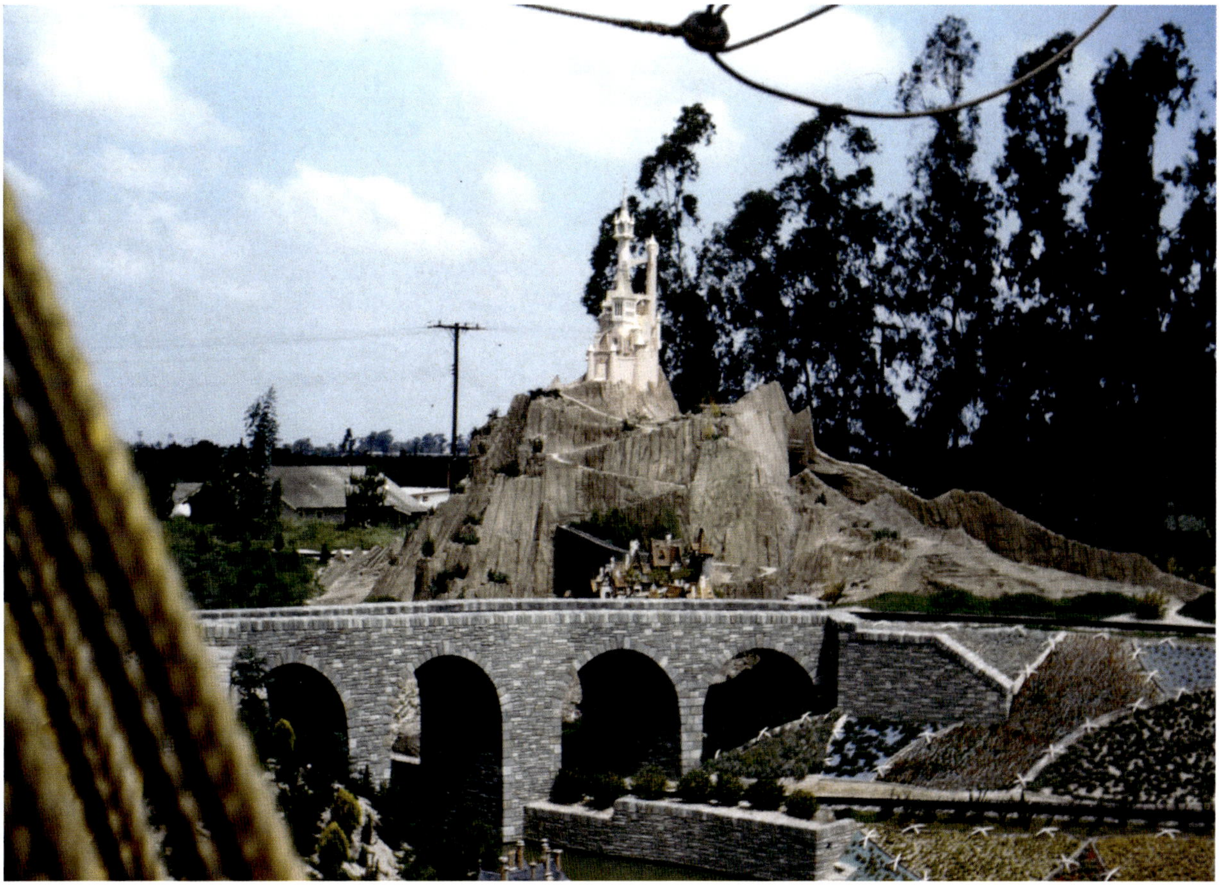

"Of all the fascinating realms in Disneyland, none are better known to Pasadena area children than Fantasyland.

For this is the home of the fairytale folk that Walt Disney has immortalized in film, book, and television—Peter Pan, the Seven Dwarfs, Sleeping Beauty, Mr. Toad ('From Wind in the Willows') and many more. By crossing the moat and passing through the archway of Sleeping Beauty Castle, you may ride or stroll with these folk through worlds of color and art that are almost beyond imagination.

And through it all—in the background—you will hear the soft music created by Walt Disney for each of these stories that are told . . ."

—***Pasadena Independent***, December 18, 1955

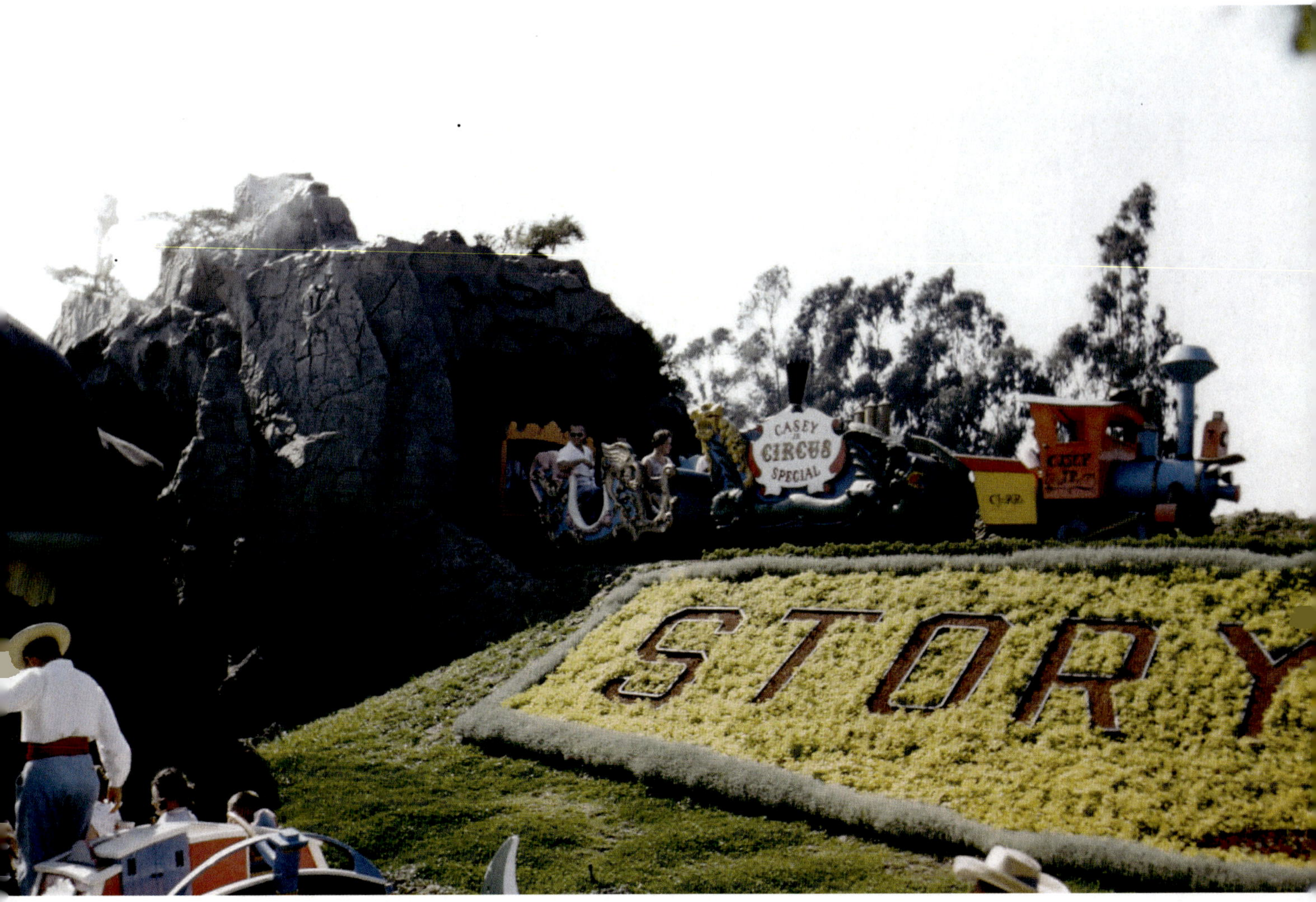

"Everybody thinks that park [Disneyland] is a gold mine—but we have had our problems. You've got to work it and know how to handle it. Even trying to keep that park clean is a tremendous expense. And those sharp pencil guys will tell you, 'Walt, if we cut down on maintenance, we'd save a lot of money.' But I don't believe in that—it's like any other show on the road; it must be clean and fresh."

— Walt Disney speaking about Disneyland from Walt Disney Productions Tencennial Press Clippings

(Photo not from opening day)

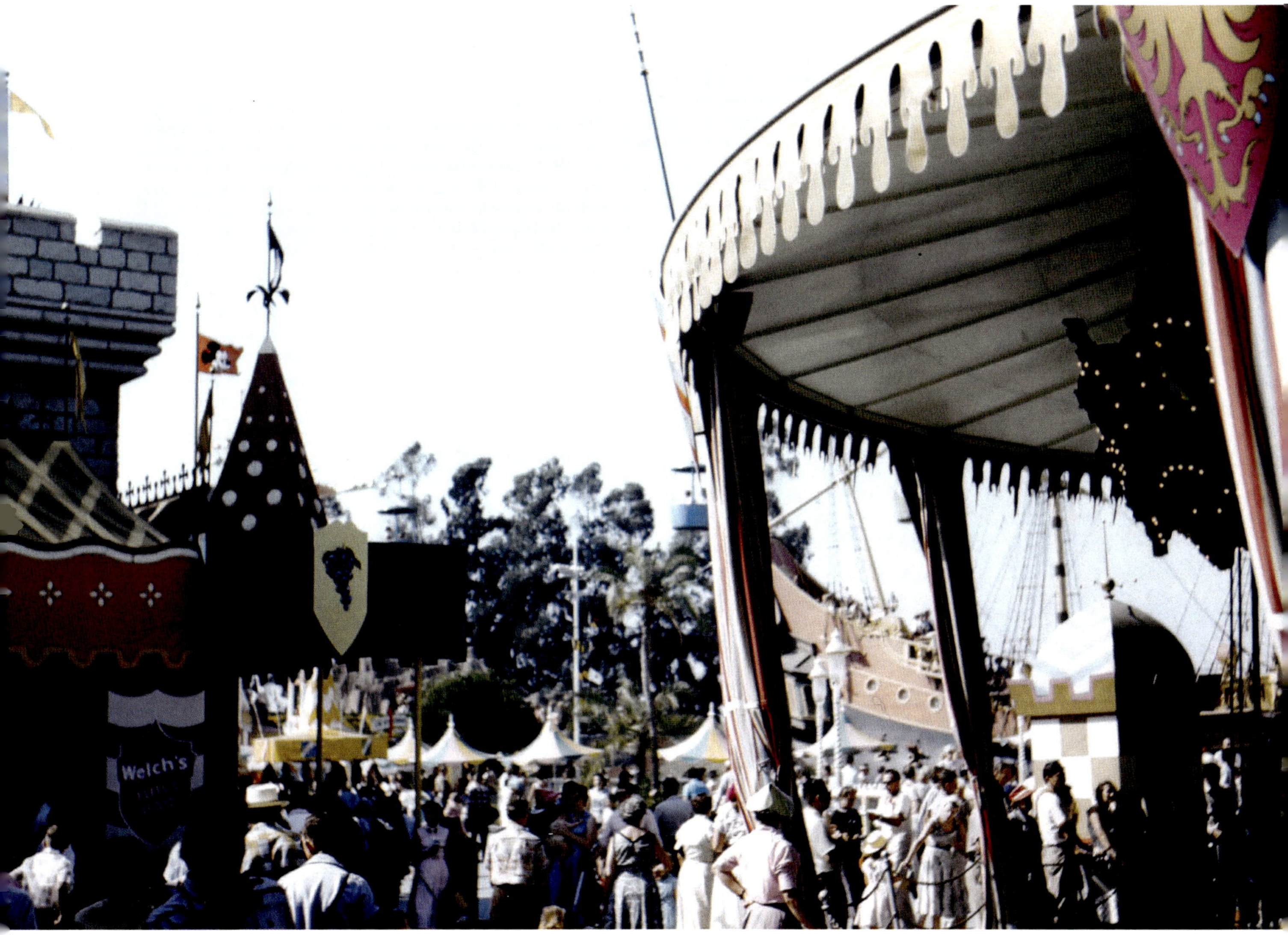

"You'll meet lots of old and good friends in Fantasyland. One of the best, especially when you're thirsty—is cool, delicious Welch's Grape Juice. Look for the gay and colorful Welch Grape Juice Bar right at the Mickey Mouse Theatre. Make it your headquarters for healthful refreshment."

— ***Los Angeles Times Supplement***, July 15, 1955

(Photo not from opening day)

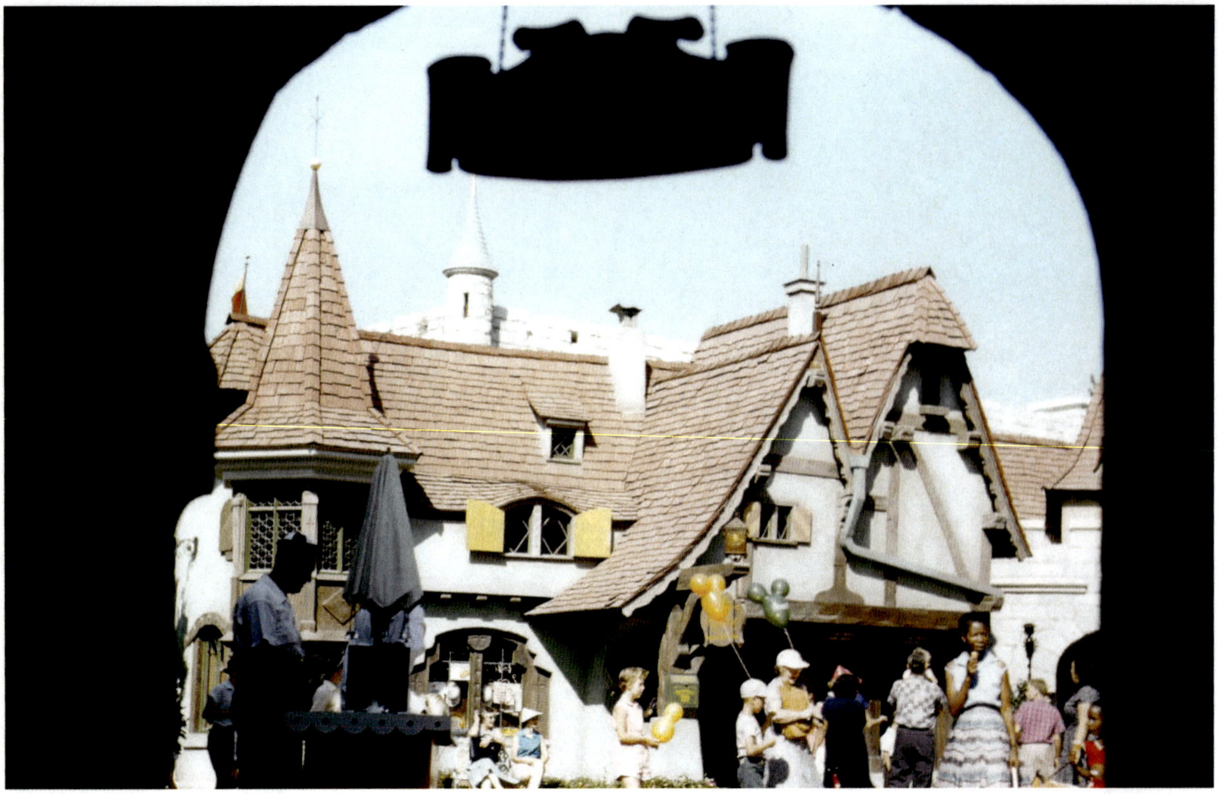

"Disneyland, since July 17, 1955, has been a powerful magnet in drawing thousands of visitors daily to view and ride the colorful and amazing attractions.

Besides paying for admission and the offerings, thirsty and hungry patrons shower coins for soft drinks and food in addition to souvenirs ranging from Japanese trinkets to Mickey Mouse balloons. These extra services are operated by concessionaires (or lessees as the management terms them).

Contributing a dime for a refreshment or 25 cents for a balloon doesn't seem like much. But they add up. Total gross from all concessions for the week ended July 28 came to $170,722 vs. $117,020 in the same period last year.

Of the 3,000 people currently working at Disneyland, 1,000 are employed by concessionaires. Remainder are Disneyland workers. After peak season these figures dip a bit.

Where it can be measured, concessionaires pay a rental fee on a square foot basis. All have five-year leases. Before being accepted, potential concessionaires must supply an affirmative answer to these questions: Will it be something people want? Is it a service? Will it be interesting? (No Coney Island-type tenants are considered.) Final acceptance comes from the operations committee and a policy committee at Disneyland Productions.

Students find summer work for concessionaires an excellent way to earn money. Typical is Richard Mauerhan, 15-year-old balloon seller from Anaheim. In an eight-hour especially good day yesterday, he boasts, he sold 500 balloons at 25 cents each. His take: 10%."

–*Los Angeles Mirror*, August 15, 1957

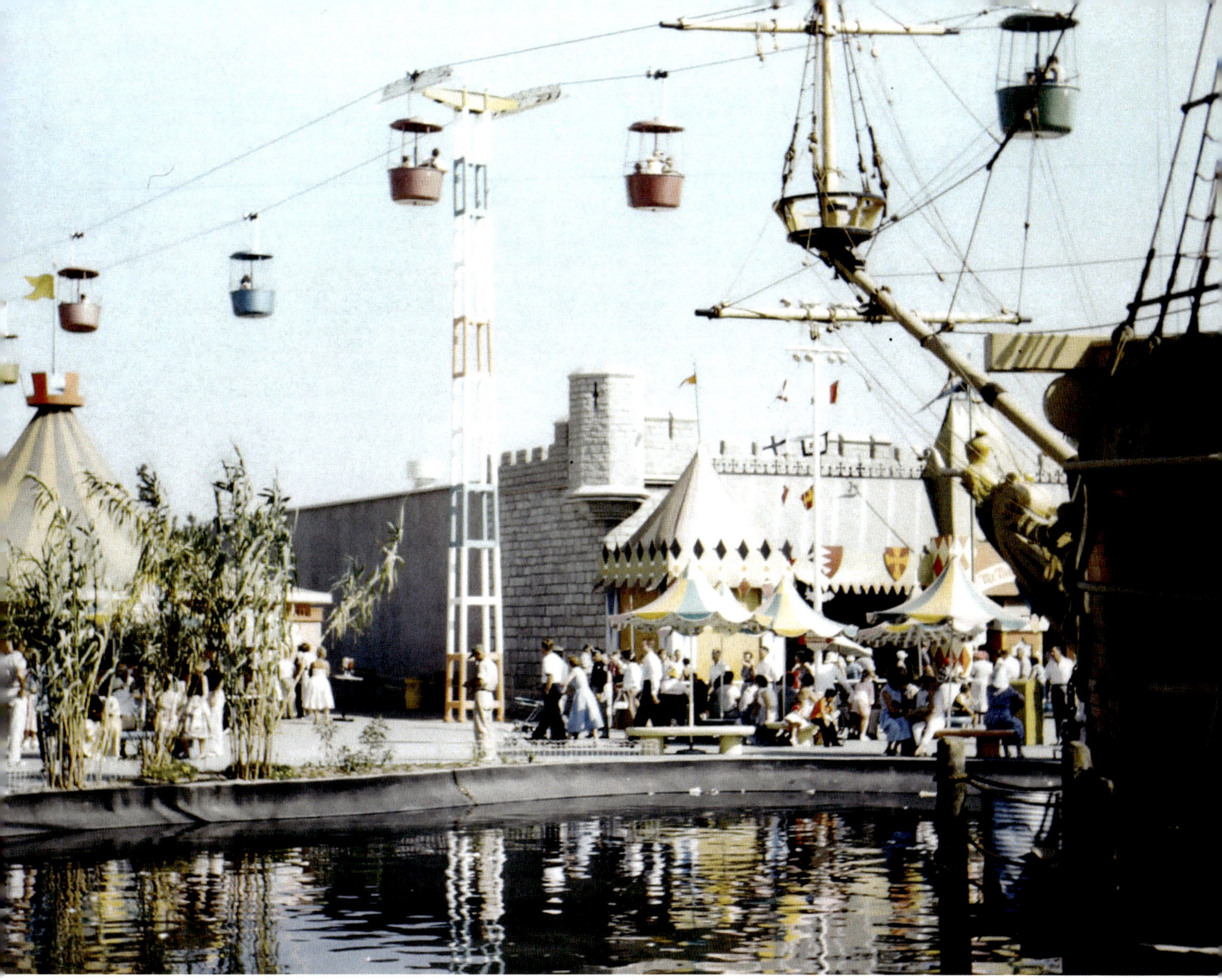

The Skyway to Fantasyland wasn't an opening day attraction. This photo is from the summer of 1956, when the Skyway debuted. The attraction was very similar in principle to a ski lift. The forty-nine buckets that carried passengers were designed at WED Enterprises (later known as Disney's Imagineering division) and assembled at Disneyland. The rest of the mechanical apparatus came from Switzerland.

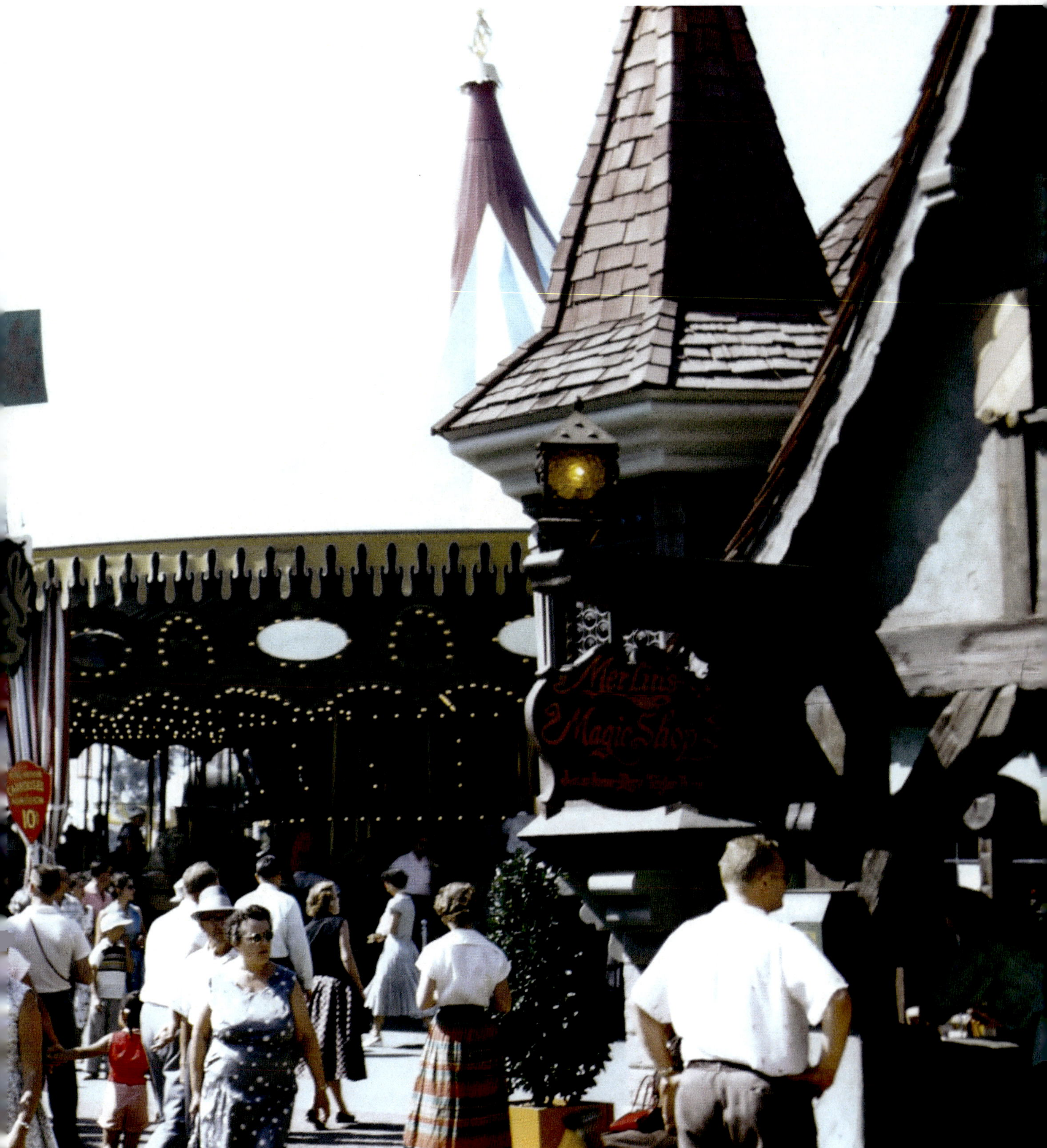
Merlin's
Magic Shop
10

Merlin's Magic Shop was owned and operated by Taylor and Hume Inc. Merv Taylor and James Hume made up this magical partnership. Taylor was an art and sheet metal teacher at Freemont High School in Los Angeles for fifteen years. With the country at war and metal becoming scarce, Taylor grew frustrated with his occupation as a metal shop teacher and launched a second career.

"During the war years, he got so disgusted with trying to teach metal work with no metal and training would-be war workers completely unfit for work that his health broke, forcing his retirement at 42. By entering the magic trick business, he said to himself, he could be his own boss and at the end of the day have fun by demonstrating his products whenever he could corral an audience. It worked out so well he completely regained his health, not a little of which he attributes to the fact that he set up his plant in the valley."

—*Valley Times, February 19, 1947.*

Well, there you go: another life saved by magic. By the late 1940s, Taylor was one of the largest creators, distributors, and suppliers of magical equipment and accessories in the country. As the story goes, Walt Disney approached Merv to open up a magic shop in Fantasyland—Merv already had a retail shop in North Hollywood.

Long before he became a Grammy, Emmy, and Academy Award winner, entertainer Steve Martin was an employee of Merlin's Magic Shop.

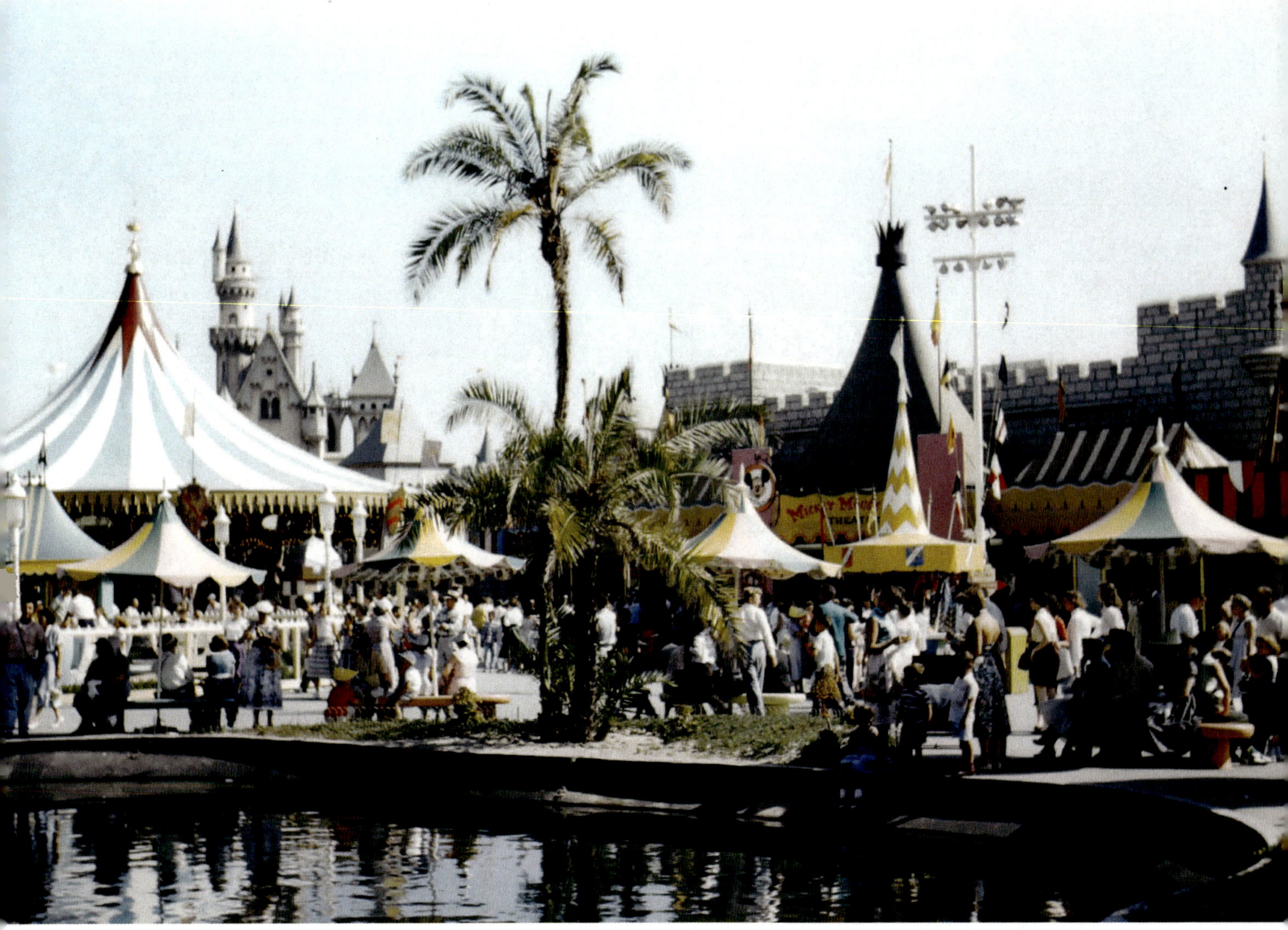

"Would you say that you're a success now? 'I must be,' he said with a laugh. 'I owe the banks $8 million.'"

— "Walt's Wonderland," ***Orlando Sentinel***, August 14, 1955

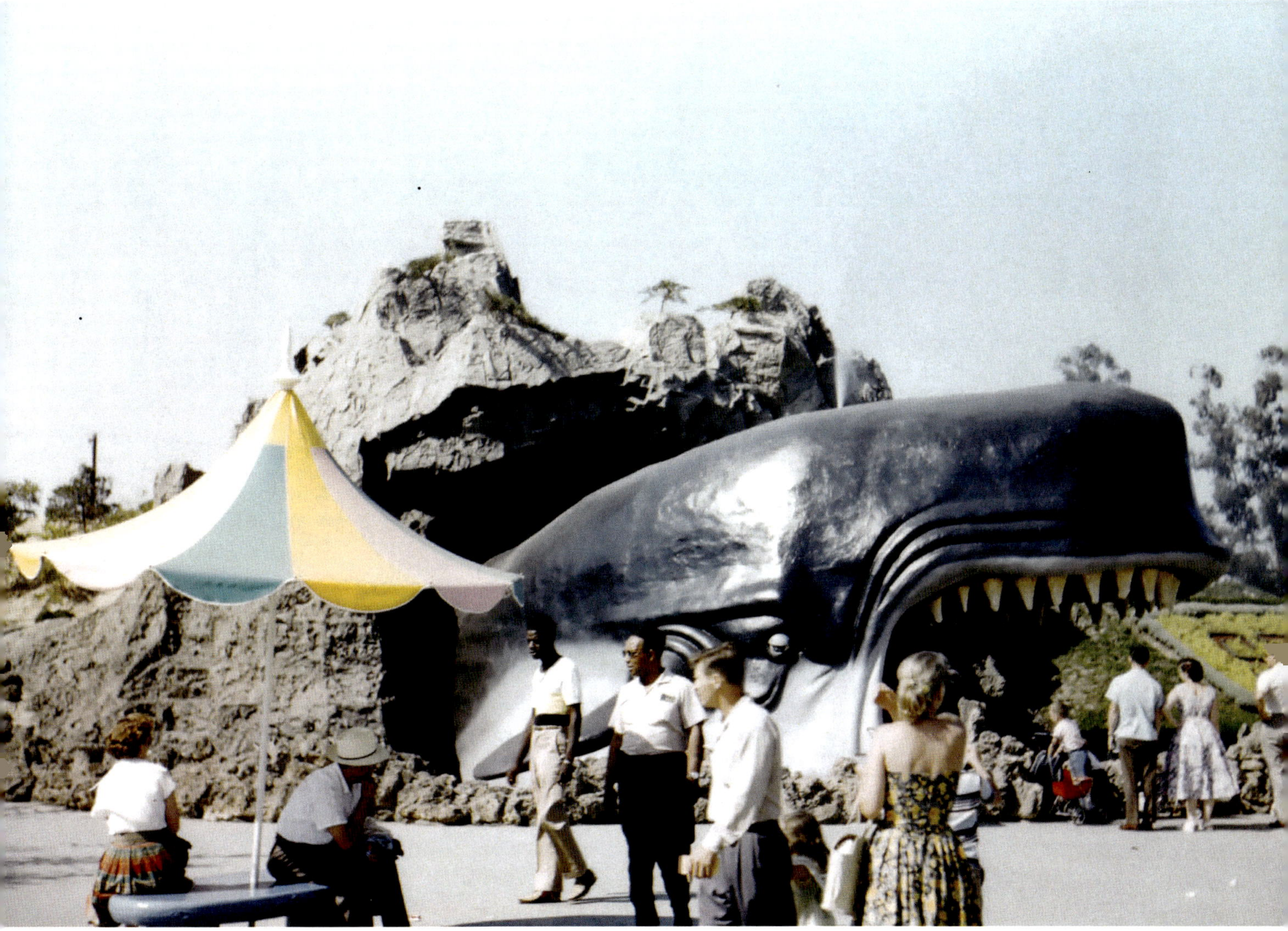

Opening day at Disneyland featured the short-lived Canal Boats of the World. By the summer of 1956, this attraction morphed into the Storybook Land Canal Boats, its entrance—the mouth of Monstro from ***Pinocchio***—seen here.

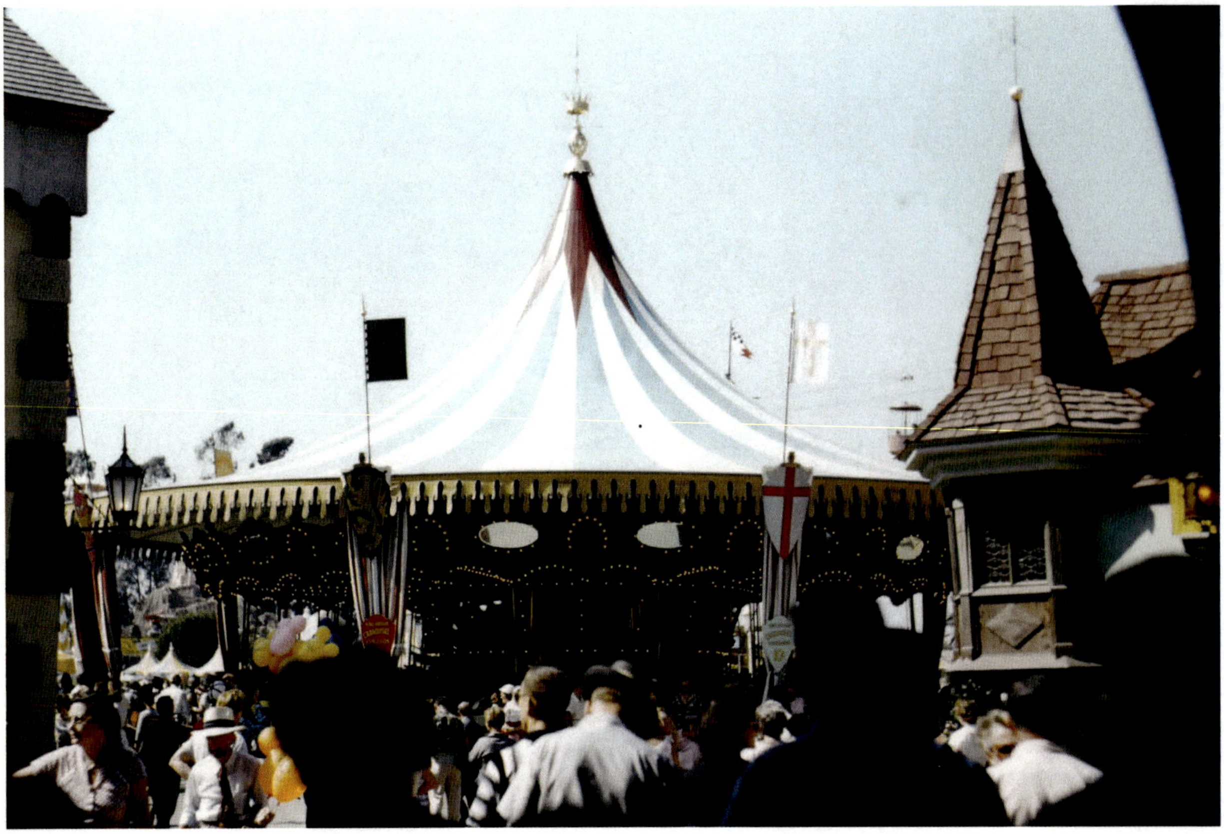

"When Walt Disney first planned his multi-million dollar project, a carrousel of a size and vintage appropriate to the courtyard of Sleeping Beauty's Castle was considered imperative. A continent-wide search ensued.

Eventually the ideal model was found—in Toronto Canada, where it had been uprooted to make way for an advancing freeway. The model is known as a Dentzel—lineal descendent of America's first merry-go-round. Its decorative woodwork is in the priceless hand-carved style of the time. But changes were necessary. In its original state, the carrousel carried lions, elephants, tigers and other wild and semi-wild animals—as well as horses.

Yet, the Canadian carrousel was for the entertainment of visitors to the medieval castle. And King Arthur never mounted anything but a horse. The animals obviously would have to be limited to horses.

Here again, the Disneyland struggle for perfection was illustrated. If any horses were found merely standing, their legs were broken and horses reformed into jumpers."

— ***The Pomona Progress Bulletin,*** October 27, 1955.

(Photo not from opening day)

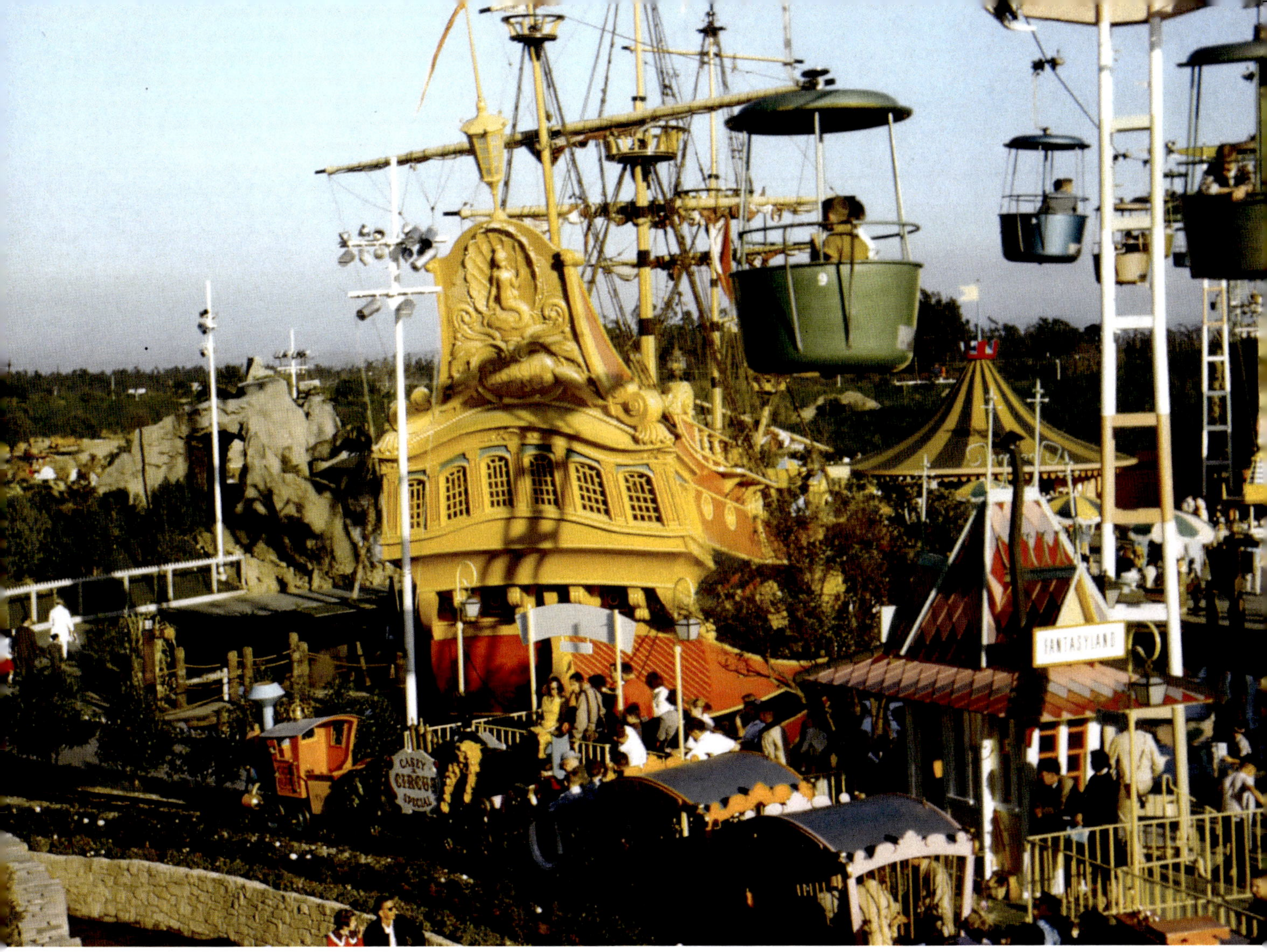

"All the pirates you've ever heard of would feel right at home topside this galleon, but they'll get a big surprise below deck. Here is one of the most unique restaurants you'll ever find, serving, tuna, oyster, shrimp and other seafood the likes of which no pirate captain ever found in all his travels on the seven seas. "

— *Long Beach Independent,* July 15, 1955

(Photo not from opening day)

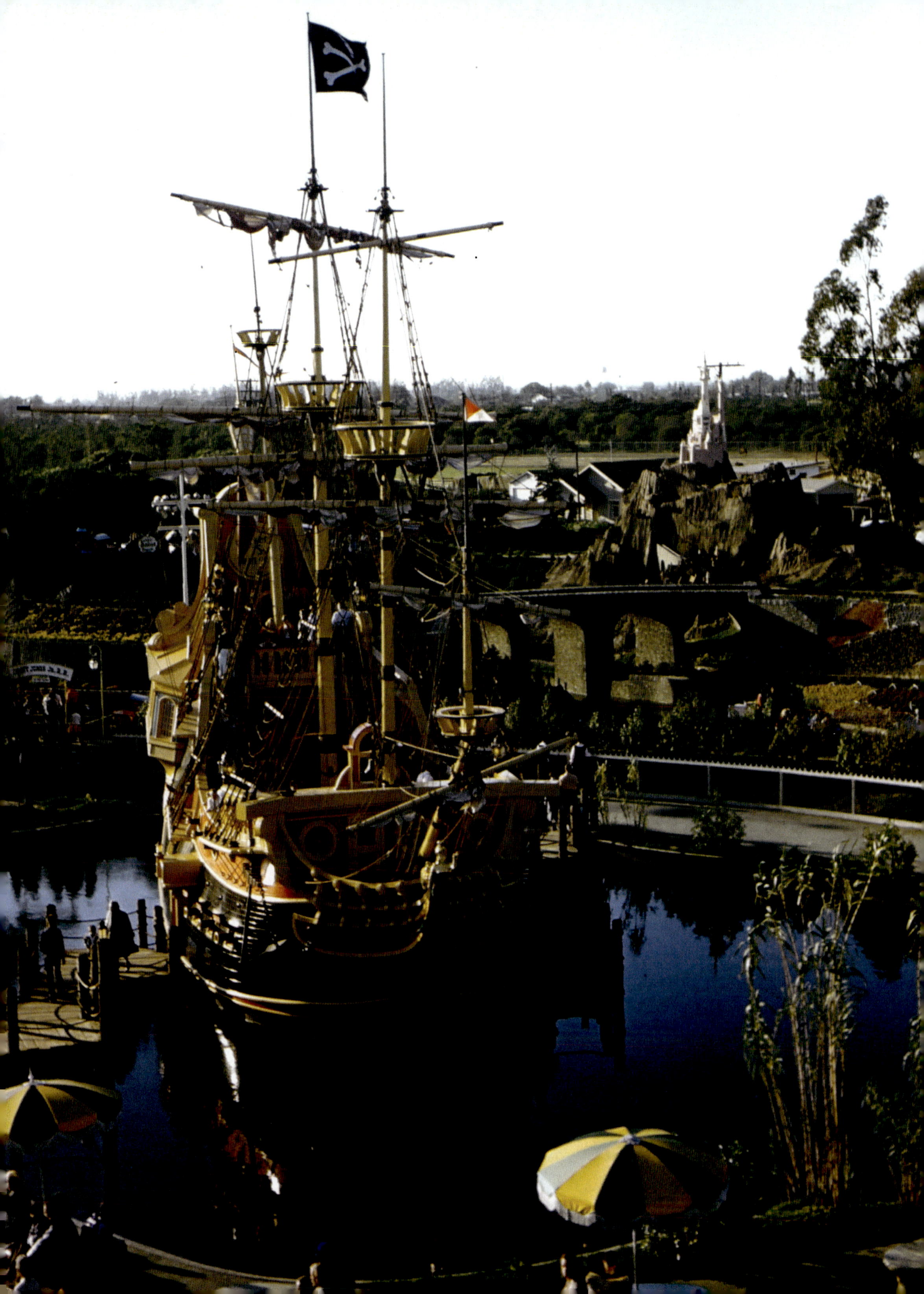

"Located in the heart of Fantasyland, just beyond the towering castle, you'll find a real, full-sized Pirate Ship gently riding at anchor in a small lagoon.

This exciting ship is over 75 feet long, and you can enter its hold over a gangway, under cover of cannon looming out of the portholes. Up on the forecastle another big cannon is likely to boom out your welcome as you come aboard.

The skull and crossbones of the Jolly Roger are flying high on the 65-foot mast, above the colorful full-rigged canvas sails. It's too dangerous to climb the rigging, but you can explore the rest of the ship from stern to stern. Examine the beautiful details of the blonde mermaid figurehead on the bow. Aft, on the poop deck, you can spin the helmsman's wheel as you command a deck just like the ones where many bloody battles were fought in days of old!

The intricately designed blonde mermaid figurehead was modeled in clay at Walt Disney Studios. It was then cast in plastic and painted in full color before it was mounted on the ship."

—***Independent Press Telegram***, July 15, 1955

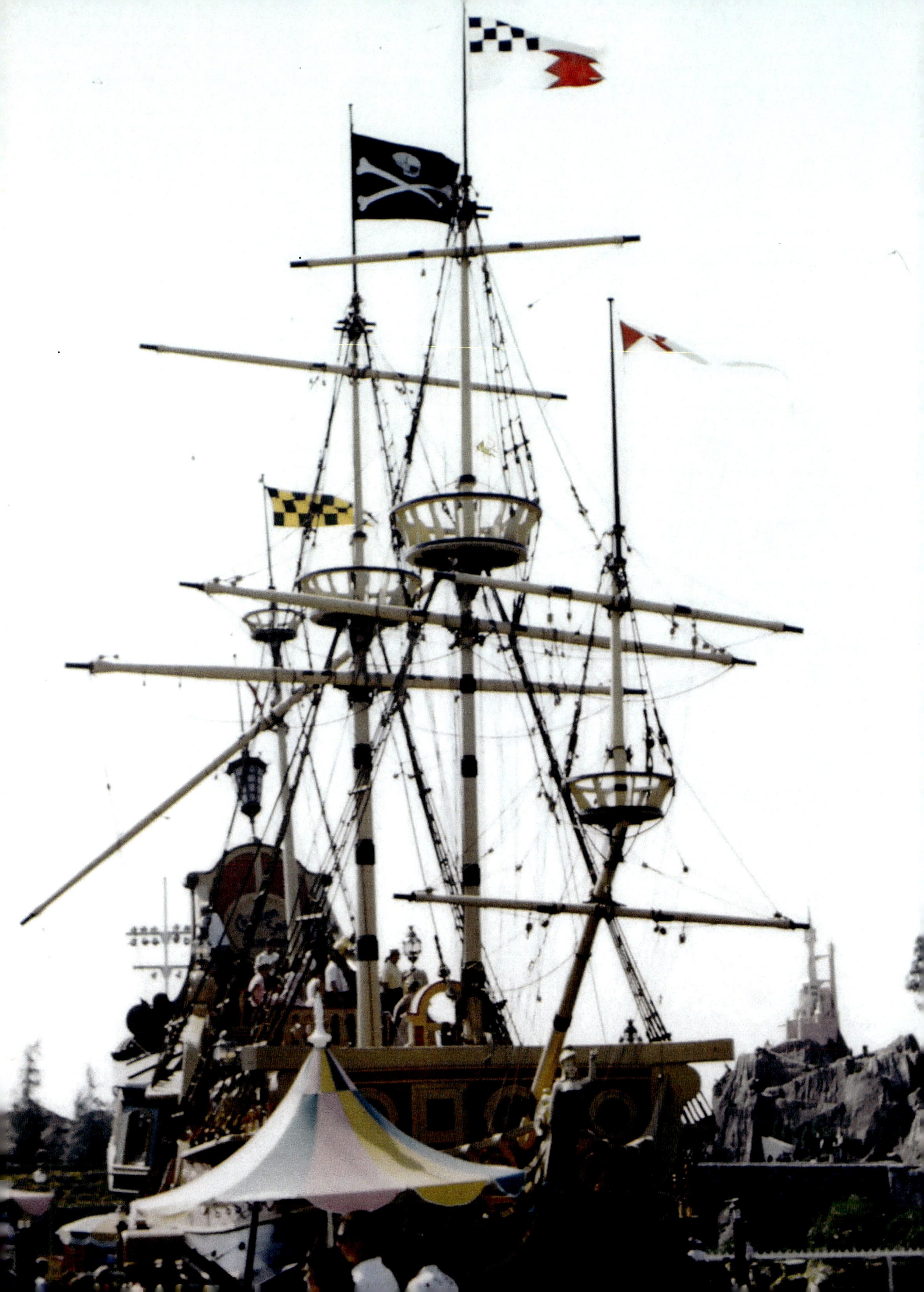

"Riding gently at anchor in the heart of Fantasyland, the CHICKEN OF THE SEA Pirate Ship Restaurant is a magic must for meals or snacks, when you visit Disneyland. Here in the world's most colorful cafeteria designed by Walt Disney, you will enjoy both the food and fun offered by the greatest name in sea foods, Chicken of the Sea."

—***Los Angeles Times***, July 15, 1955

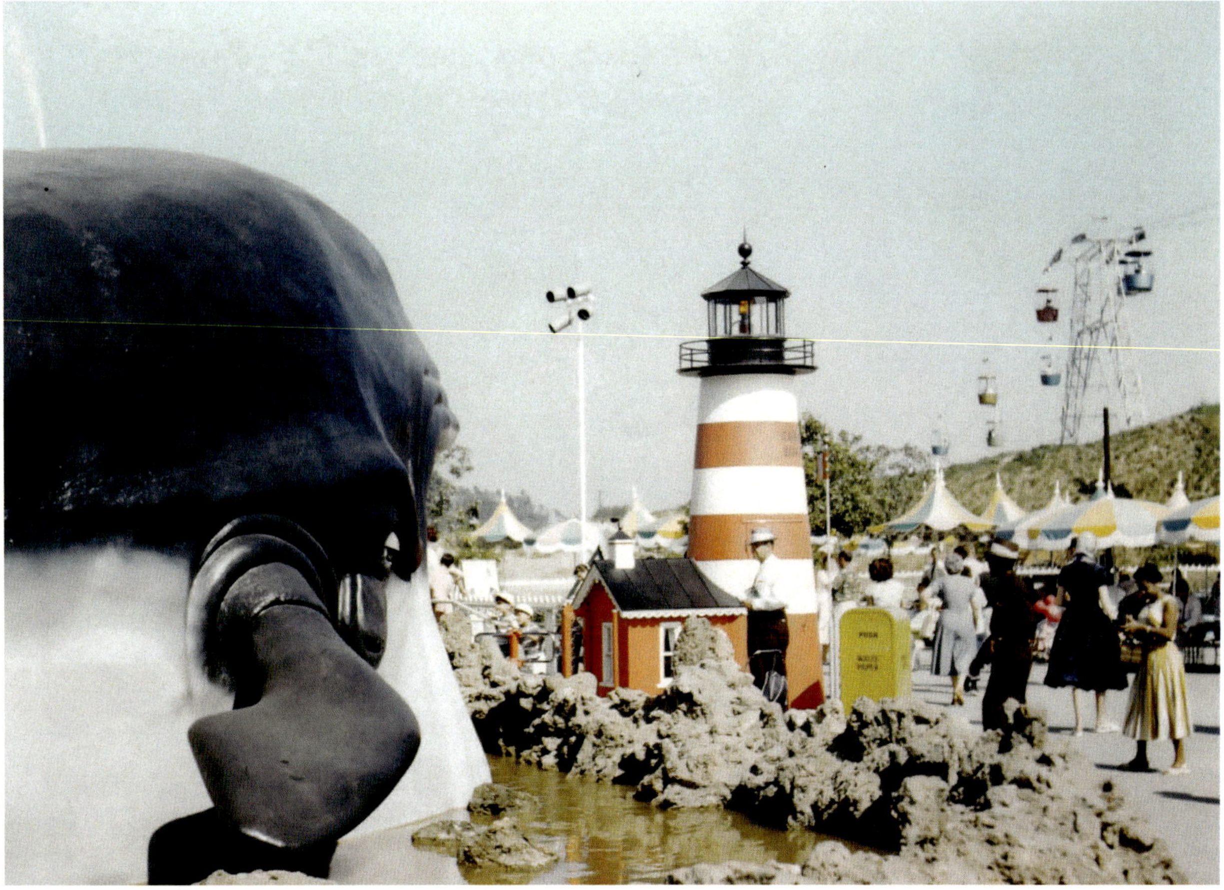

The waterway for the Storybook Land Canal Boats contains 1,000,000 gallons of water and has a gunite bottom; it is 1,000 feet long, 4 feet deep, and 25 feet wide.

(Photo not from opening day)

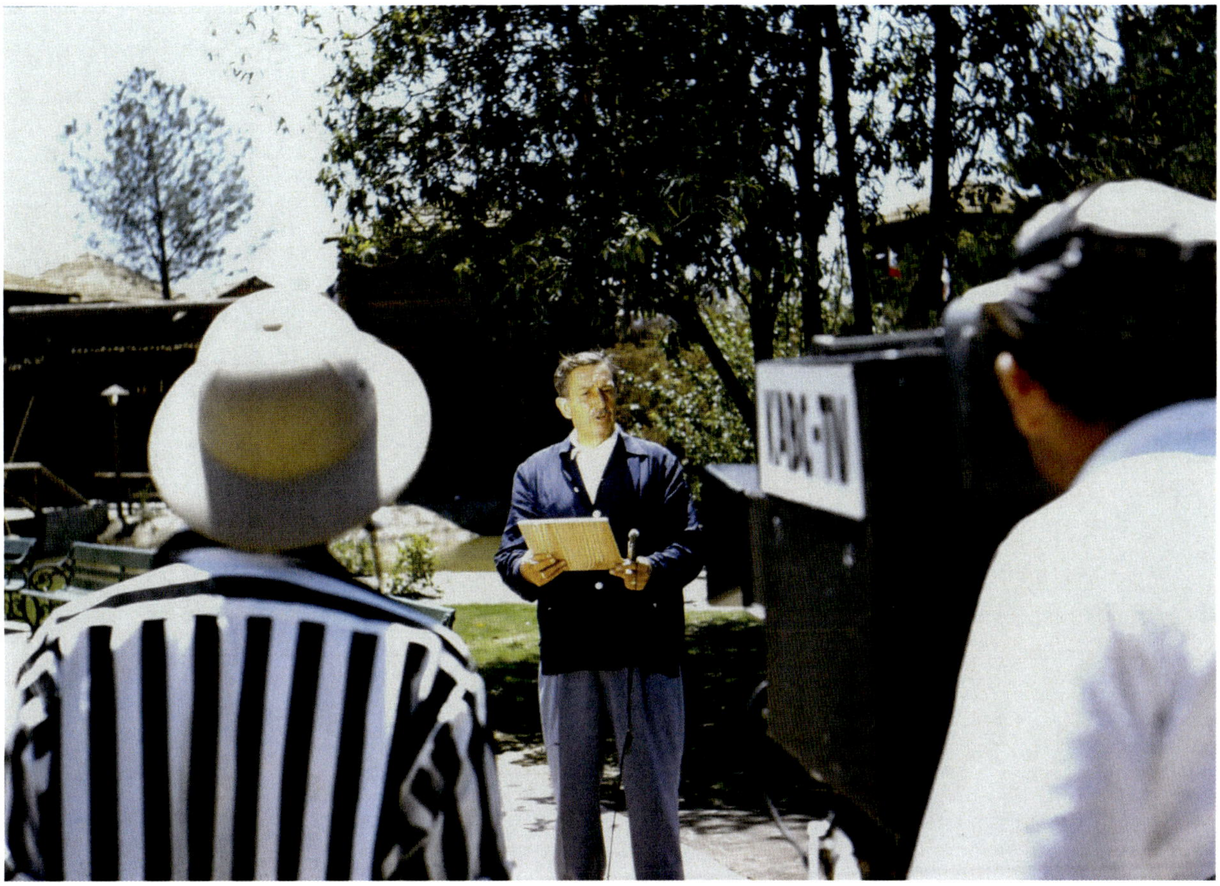

"Somehow, I can't believe there are many heights that can't be scaled by a man who knows the secret of making dreams come true. This special secret, it seems to me, can be summarized in the four C's. They are Curiosity, Confidence, Courage, and Constancy, and the greater of these is Confidence. When you believe in a thing, believe in it all over, implicitly and unquestioningly."

— Walt Disney, "From the Wisdom of Walt Disney," **Wisdom**, Volume 32, December 1959

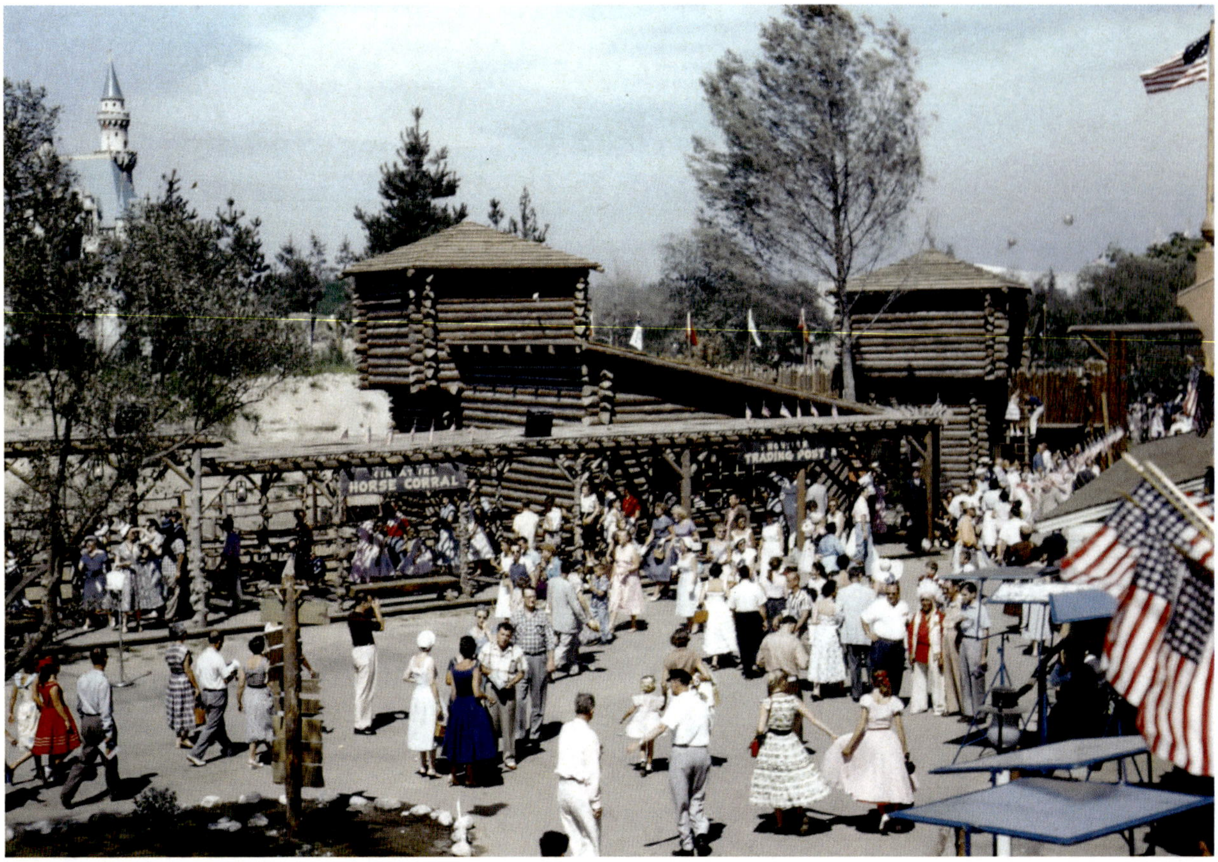

"The logs for the stockade and log cabins in Frontierland were cut in the Arrowhead region, then specially picked men hewed them by hand. The only power tools used was a gasoline chainsaw. In Frontierland some of the gnarled pine posts were picked up by Disney on a trip to the Jackson Hole country in Wyoming. He spotted the logs because of the unusual burls growing on them and had about 60 shipped to Disneyland."

Los Angeles Evening–Citizen News, July 16, 1955

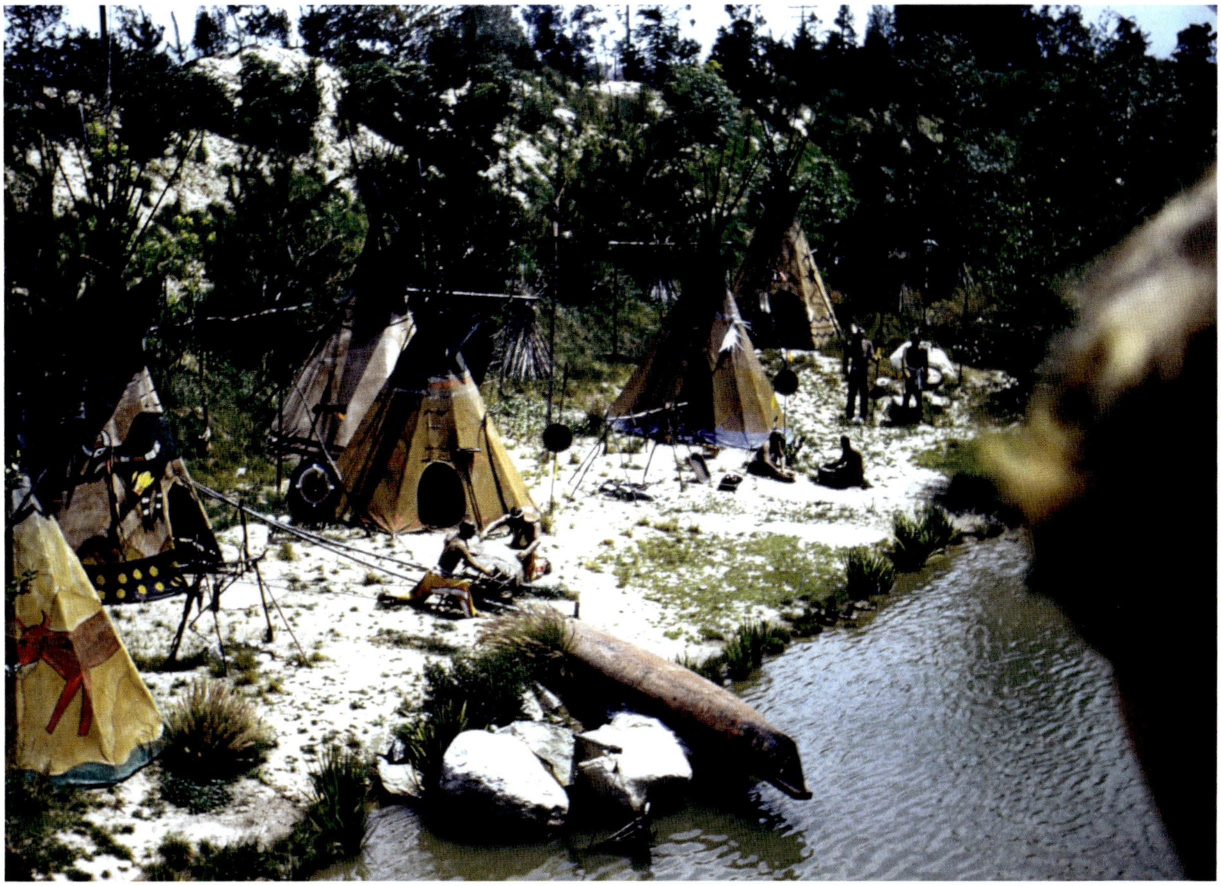

"Dedicated to the ideals, the dreams and exploits that created our country, Frontierland recreates America of the past—our strength and inspiration for the good things of life we enjoy today. Entering Frontierland through the gates of an old log fort, you'll see frontiersmen and Indians of many tribes, and trod board sidewalks to shop in stores and buildings reminiscent of the old west. Visit the Davy Crockett museum, assay office, the general store or watch ponies being shod at the blacksmith shop. At the Western railroad station, you can board the 1860 Santa Fe and Disneyland freight train for a ride around Disneyland."

—***Los Angeles Times***, July 15, 1955

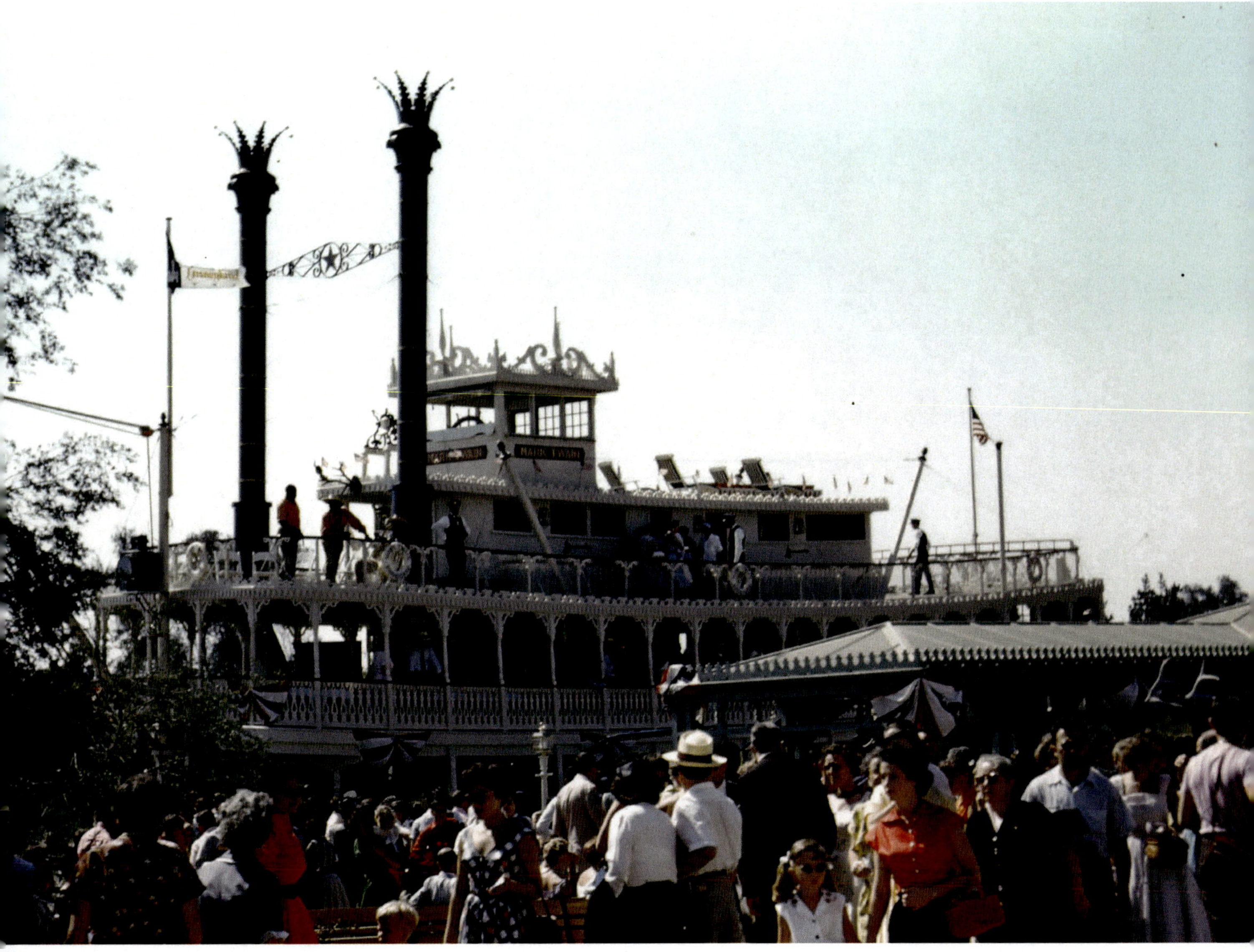

On the opening day broadcast, actress Irene Dunne, a personal friend of Walt Disney's, christened the ***Mark Twain*** using a bottle filled with water from the major rivers across America. She mentioned that her father was supervising General of Steamships in the United States and her grandfather used to build them. Dunne even noted on television that the boat seemed to be listing. She was correct in her observation; the ***Mark Twain*** was packed with so many passengers that it did list and began to take on some water on one side.

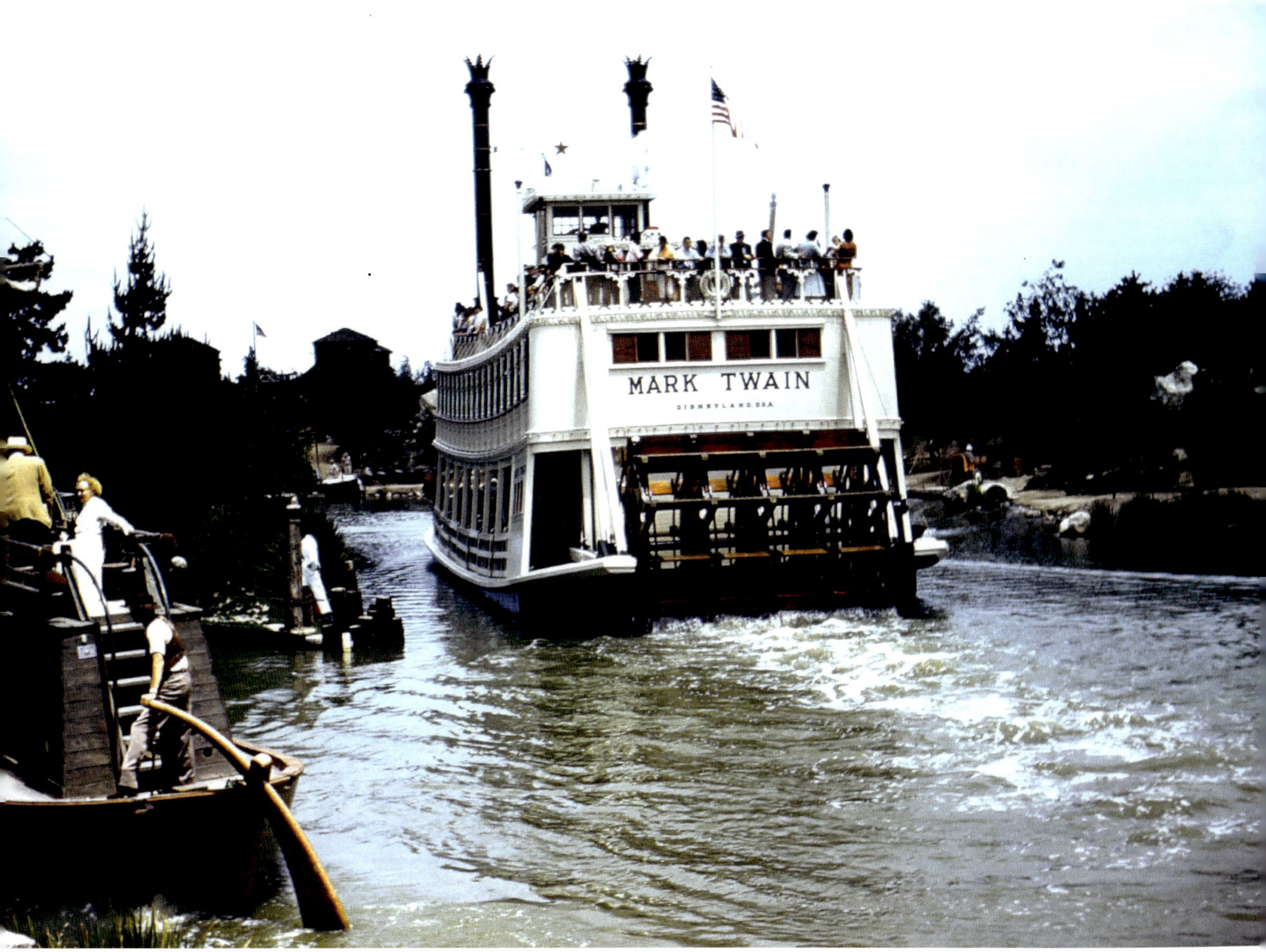

"Disney has been working with scripts for years, and there's no stopping him now that he's in the amusement park business. In the pilot's cabin of the Mark Twain sternwheeler, there's a list of typewritten instructions for the captain. It tells him what phrases to sing out, and when and includes the admonition: 'Finish spiel last turn before dock.'"

— ***Star Tribune***, December 23, 1956

(Photo not from opening day)

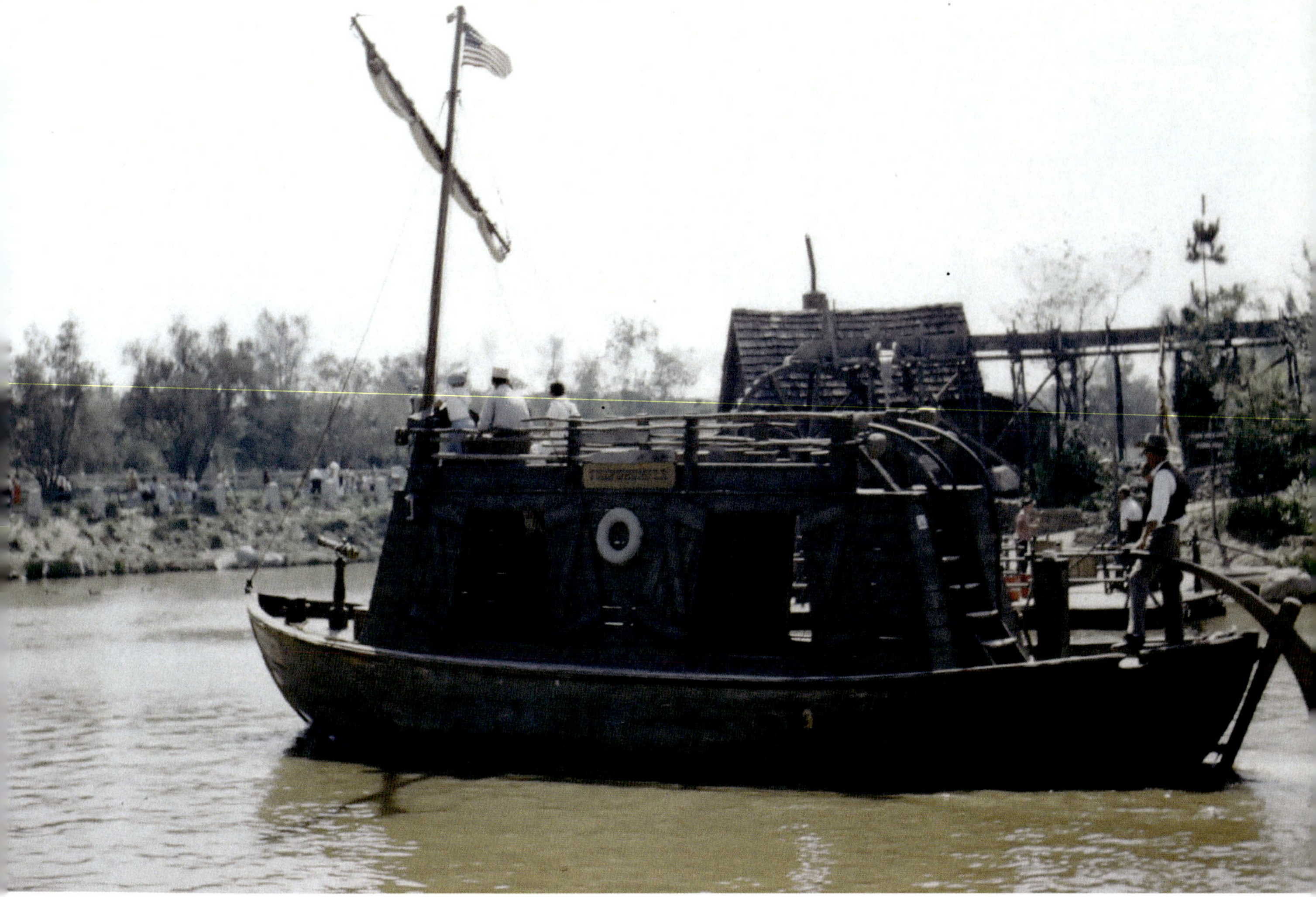

The Mike Fink Keel Boats were the actual boats used in the Walt Disney ***Davey Crockett*** movie and television series. The two boats, ***Gullywhumper*** and ***Bertha Mae***, navigated around Tom Sawyer's Island on the Rivers of America. Unlike the ***Mark Twain***, the Mike Fink Keel Boats did not operate on a guide rail.

(Photo not from opening day)

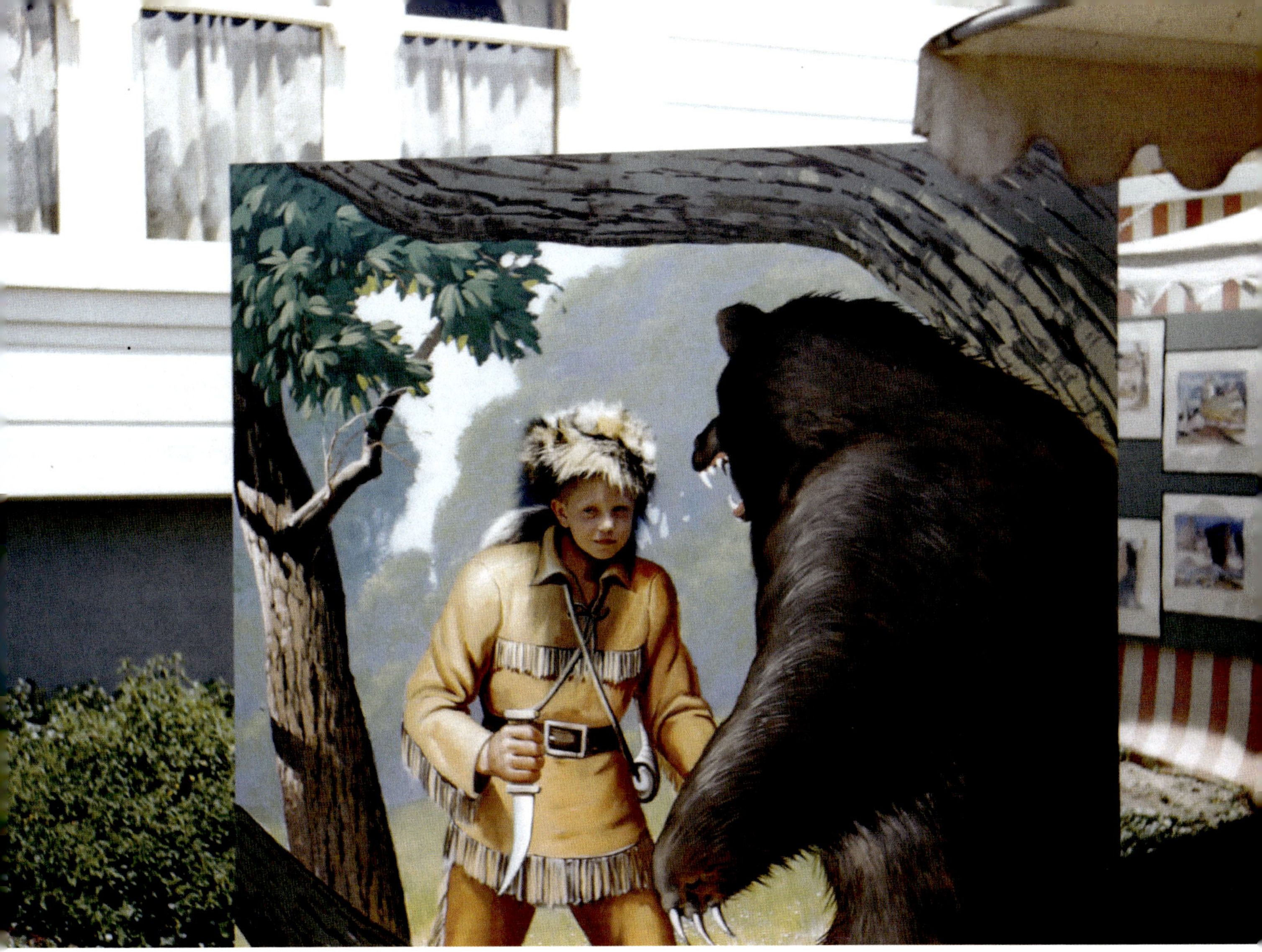

"For a child, encouragement from a grown-up can be a thrilling thing with lasting consequence. It can help fix his objectives, give him confidence to drive unswervingly toward his goal, spell the difference between failure and success."

— Walt Disney, "From the Wisdom of Walt Disney,"
Wisdom, Volume 32, December 1959

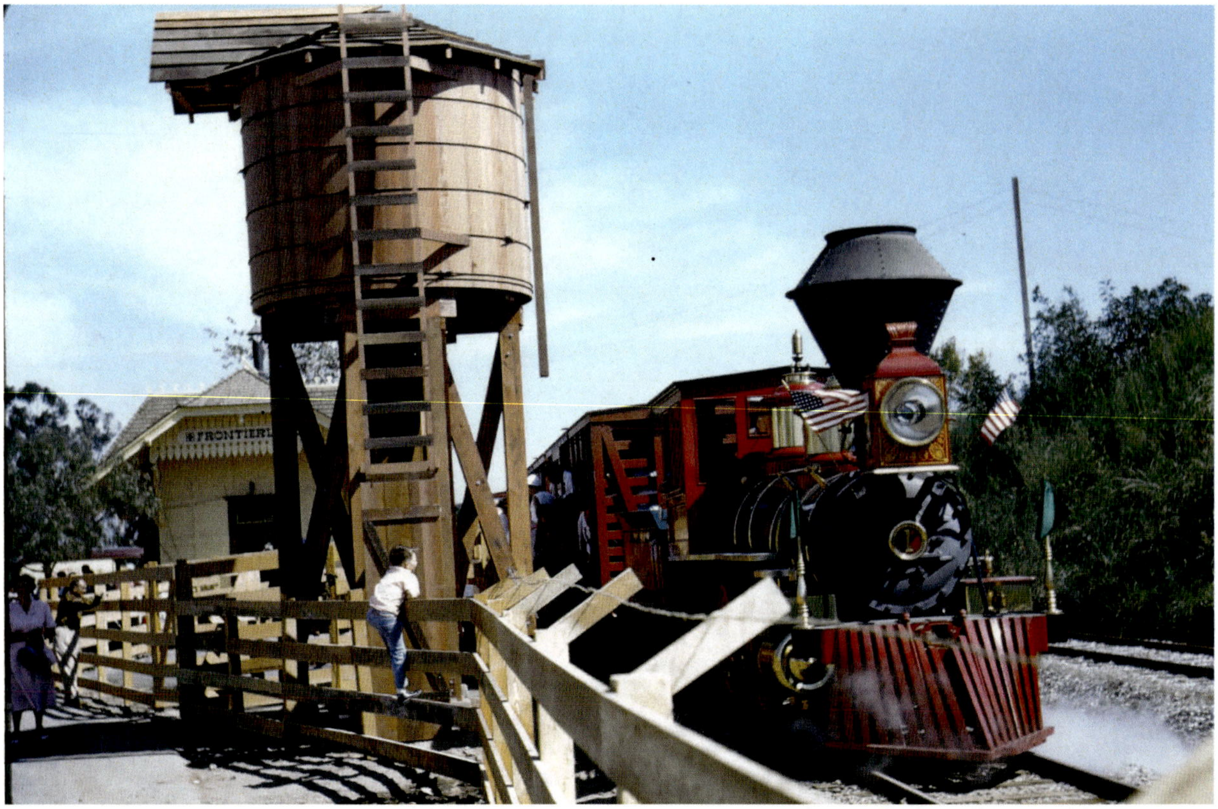

"A brand-new railroad, The Santa Fe and Disneyland, 'ride size' (five-eighths normal size) for child and grownup alike, was announced today for Walt Disney's fabulous magic kingdom now being built at Anaheim, 22 miles southeast of downtown Los Angeles.

Disneyland will open to the public on July 18. Two trains, one passenger and one freight, will be operated over the Santa Fe and Disneyland Railroad. Both will carry passengers, and visitors to Disneyland may realize a lifetime of ambition to ride in the cupola of a caboose if they desire.

An enthusiastic railroad fan, Walt Disney has decreed that the Santa Fe and Disneyland line will be authentic in every respect save size. It will compromise a mile and a quarter of 36-inch gauge railroad and approximately 9000 feet of trackage including sidings, laid along the perimeter of the 64-acre Disneyland."

–***Boston Globe***, June 5, 1955

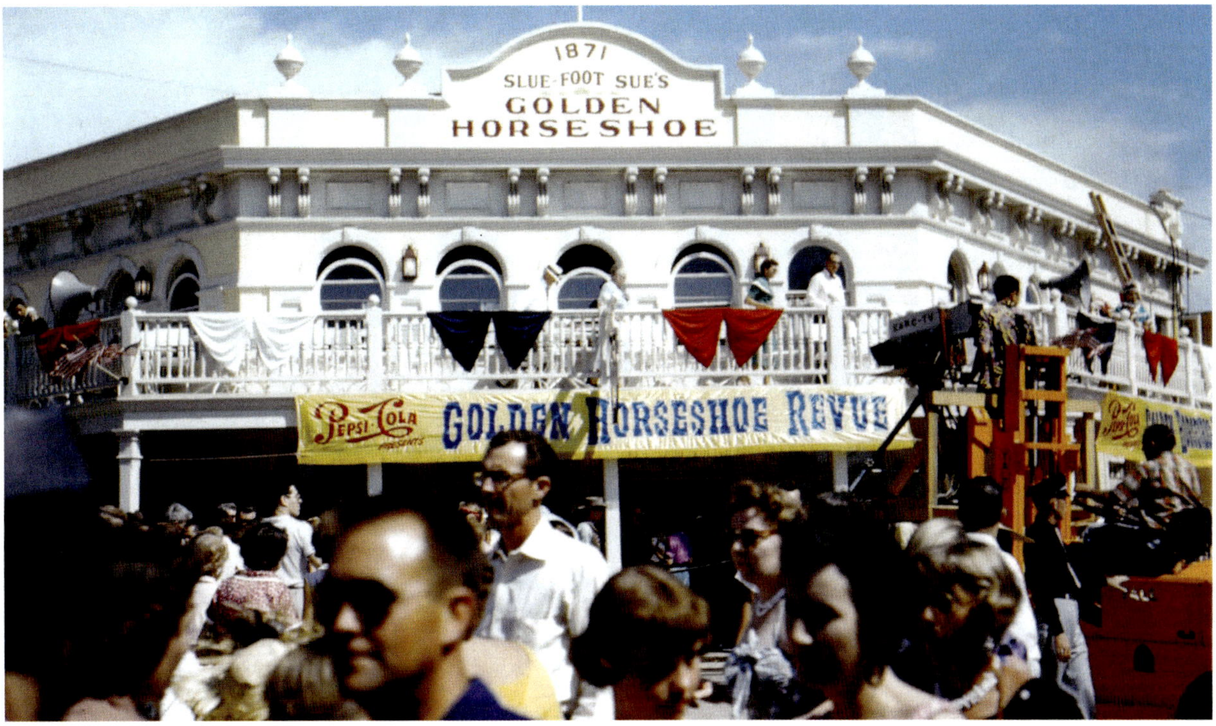

On July 13, 1955, Walt and Lillian Disney celebrated their thirtieth wedding anniversary with 250 of their closest friends and family members at the Golden Horse Shoe. Hedda Hopper, the former actress and infamous gossip columnist for the ***Los Angeles Times***, was in attendance that evening. She gave a glowing review of Walt's Disneyland and the Golden Horse Shoe.

"In the Slewfoot Sue Golden Horseshoe Saloon we all ate a marvelous dinner and watched some old-time entertainment. A buxom blonde played the piano and sang all the old songs; Donald Novis brought the house down with his Irish tunes; and a line-up of girls did the can- can. Then the biggest wedding cake in history was wheeled out. Toasting the Disneys were the Edgar Bergens, Kay Kysers, Norman Chandlers, Buddy Ebsens, Leigh Battsons, Mrs. Bob Cummings, the Jules Steins, Bill Pereiras, Peter Godfreys, Hernando Courtright and his fiancée Marcella Cuillery.

But I saw no big brass from CBS or NBC. Both networks refused to meet Walt's terms for his TV show and thereby lost out on it and a chance to get in on Disneyland. But ABC was smarter and got in on the gold mine. Neither of the other networks has been able to create a show that can take the attention away from Disney's time. He's got a monopoly on the American public on Wednesday nights.

Mervyn LeRoy called it [Disneyland] 'the eighth wonder of the world'. I'll add, 'it's the ninth, tenth, eleventh and twelfth.' When you congratulate the modest Walt, he grins and says, 'All it took was money, Hedda, and fortunately my partners were very generous with that folding stuff.'"

—***Los Angeles Times***, July 16, 1955

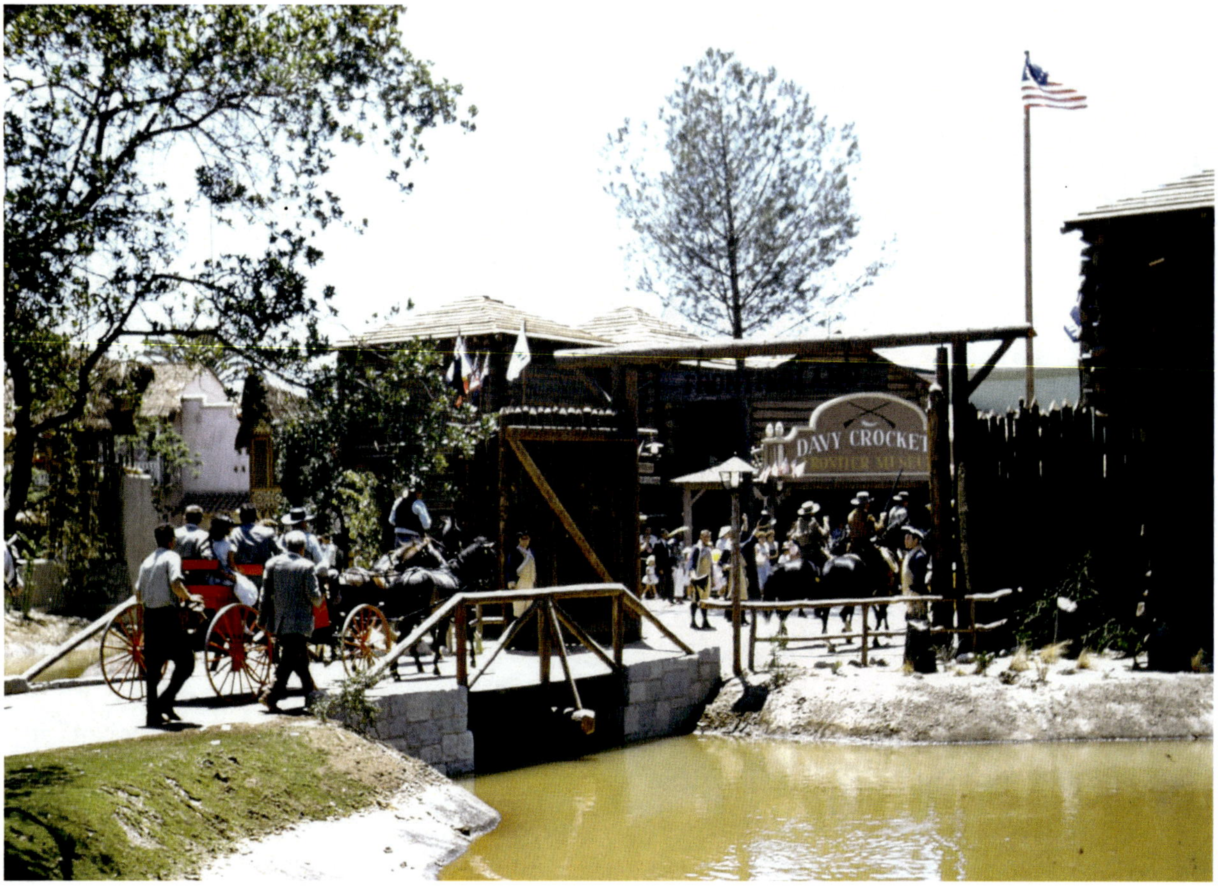

"In Frontierland, you can 'live' America's colorful past.

Entering through the great gates of an old log fort, you will glimpse the yesterday of Davy Crockett, Paul Bunyan, Pecos Bill, Daniel Boone, John Henry and Johnny Appleseed—giants of American Folklore and history.

Pasadena residents will meet Indians of many tribes, watch ponies being shod, and ride almost every kind of conveyance known to the old West. They also will see the amazing Golden Horseshoe, with its frontier days floor show.

These and many other exciting activities await you when you 'meet America of the past—out of whose strength and inspiration came the good things in life we enjoy today.'"

—***Pasadena Independent***, December 18, 1955

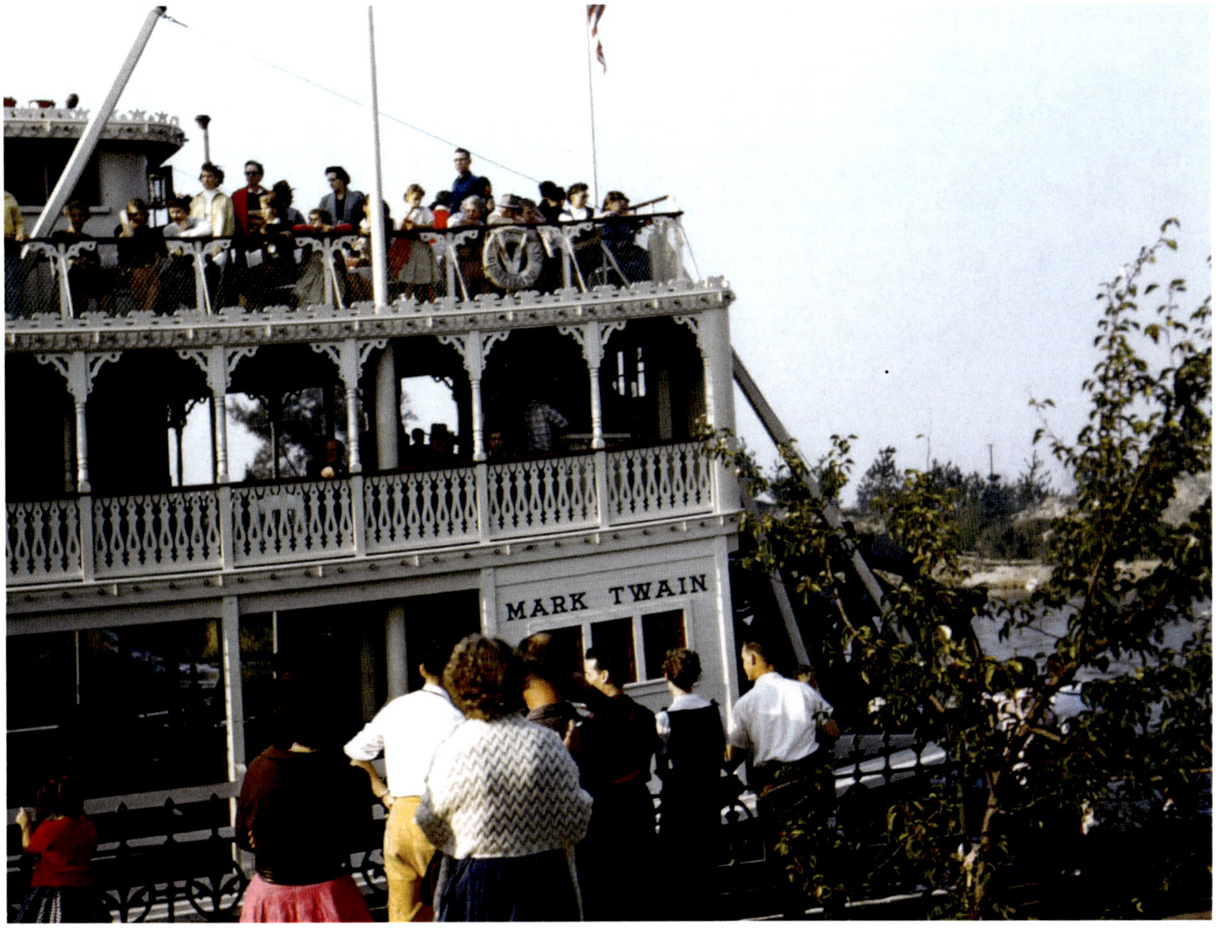

"The Mark Twain, first paddle wheeler built in America in 50 years—travels the 'rivers of America' at Disneyland. Walt Disney's Mark Twain is a 105-foot replica of the romantic old vessels that opened American river traffic into a western wilderness.

The 100-ton riverboat is divided into five watertight compartments and built to 5/8 scale. It travels four knots per hour over its own Disneyland waterway and carries 300 passengers.

In outfitting the Mark Twain, an extensive search was made for gimble lights, smoke bells, and running lights of the period and size required.

Firefighting buckets and their racks had to be made up specially because of the round bottom pails used in earlier days. Reason for the round bottoms was simple one—since these buckets wouldn't stand upright, it prevented the deck hands' taking them for purposes other than firefighting—and leaving empty racks.

The hull and 9-ton paddle wheel were made by Todd Shipyards. The superstructure was built at Disney Studio in Burbank and then brought to Anaheim and assembled."

—***Long Beach Independent,*** July 15, 1955

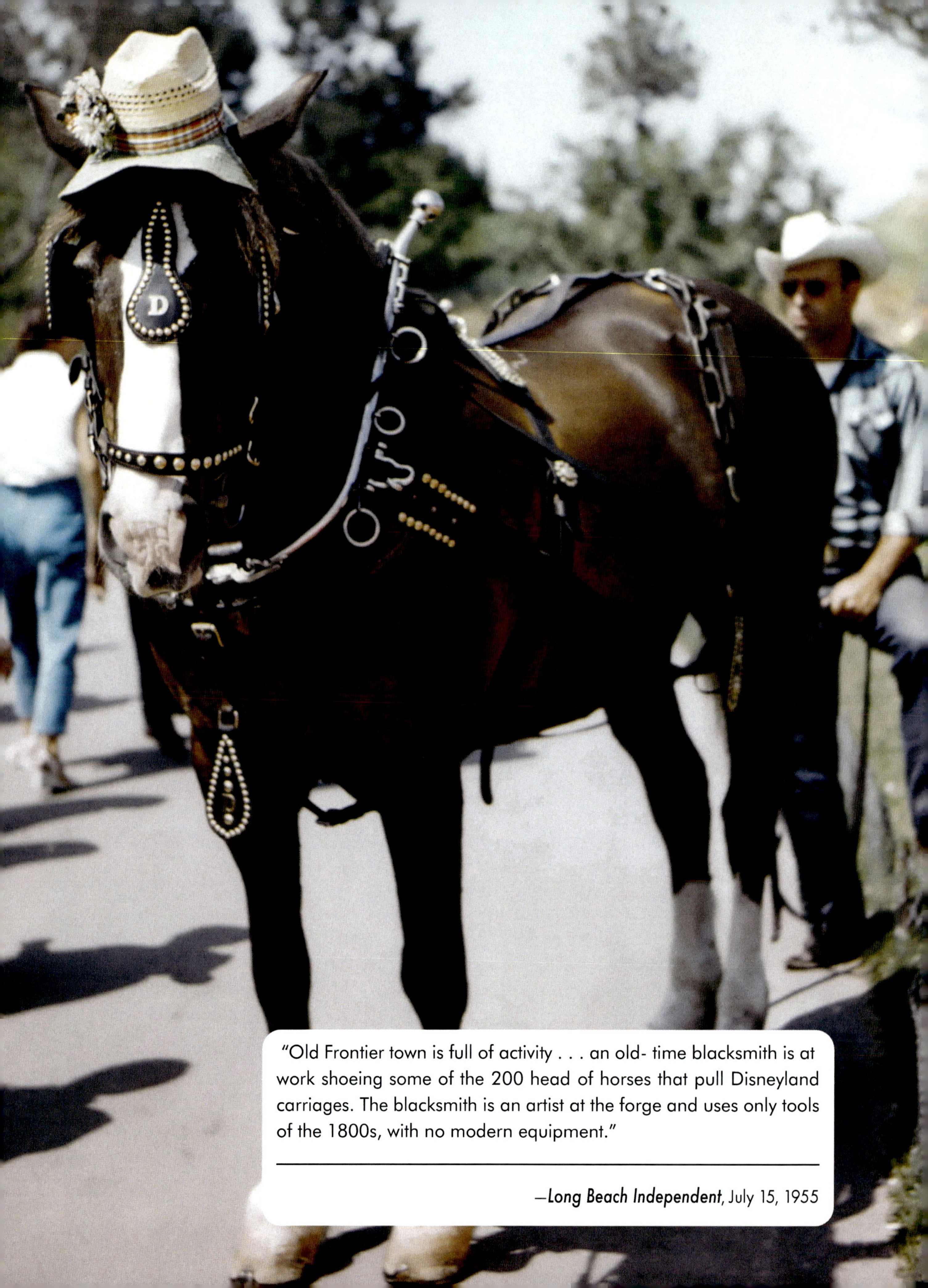

"Old Frontier town is full of activity . . . an old- time blacksmith is at work shoeing some of the 200 head of horses that pull Disneyland carriages. The blacksmith is an artist at the forge and uses only tools of the 1800s, with no modern equipment."

—***Long Beach Independent***, July 15, 1955

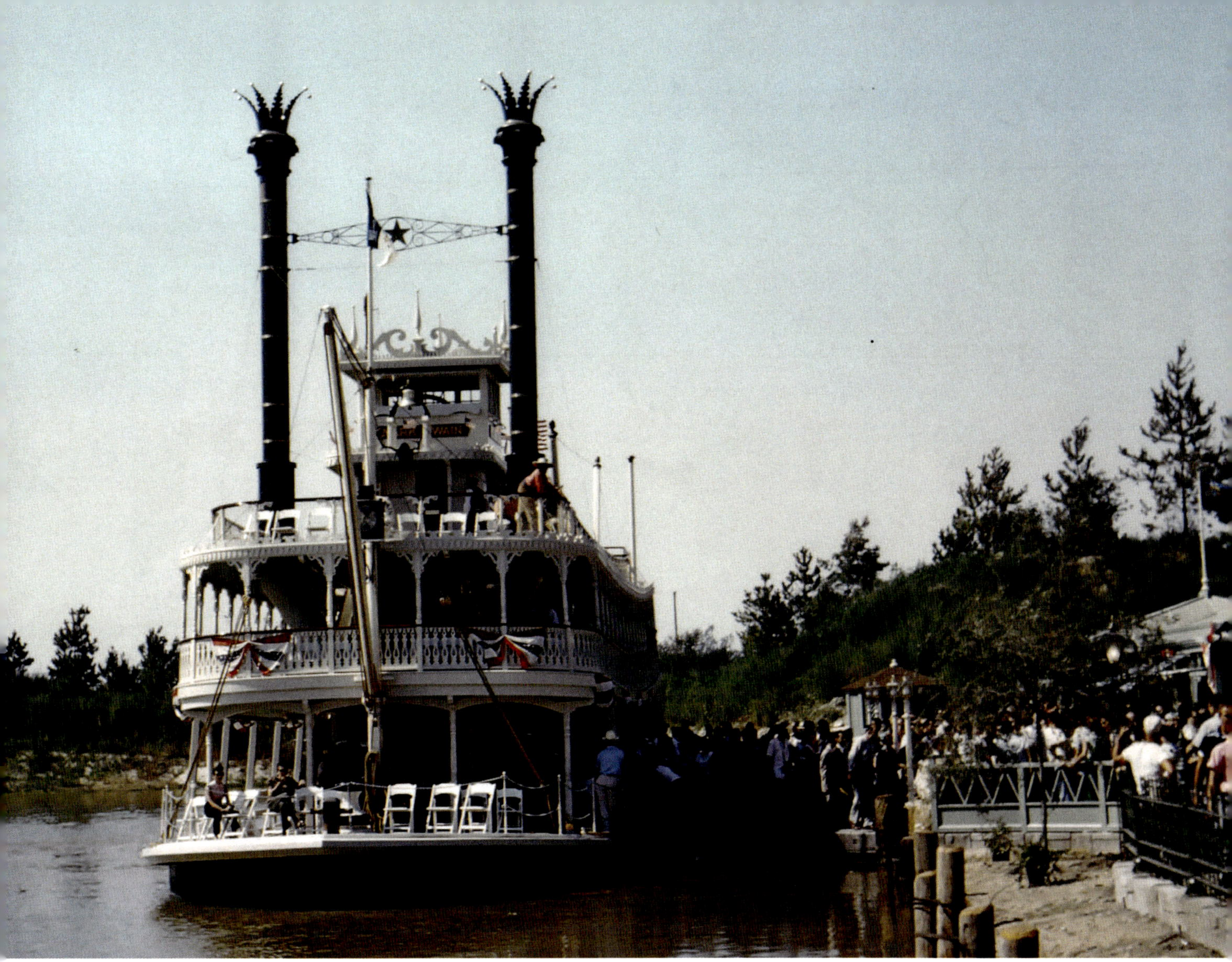

"The Mark Twain was designed and the superstructure built at the Walt Disney Studio, while the hull was built at Todd Shipyards in Long Beach, California. The entire boat was assembled and completed at Disneyland under the supervision of Rear Admiral Joseph W. Fowler, U.S.N. (ret).

Overall length: 105ft
Height: keel to pilot house: 28 ft
Draft: 2ft 3 in
Beam: 27 ft 6 in.
Displacement: 125 tons.

The Mark Twain is powered by its two huge stream engines which operate the stern wheel, it runs on a rail 2,450 ft. long."

—Walt Disney Productions materials

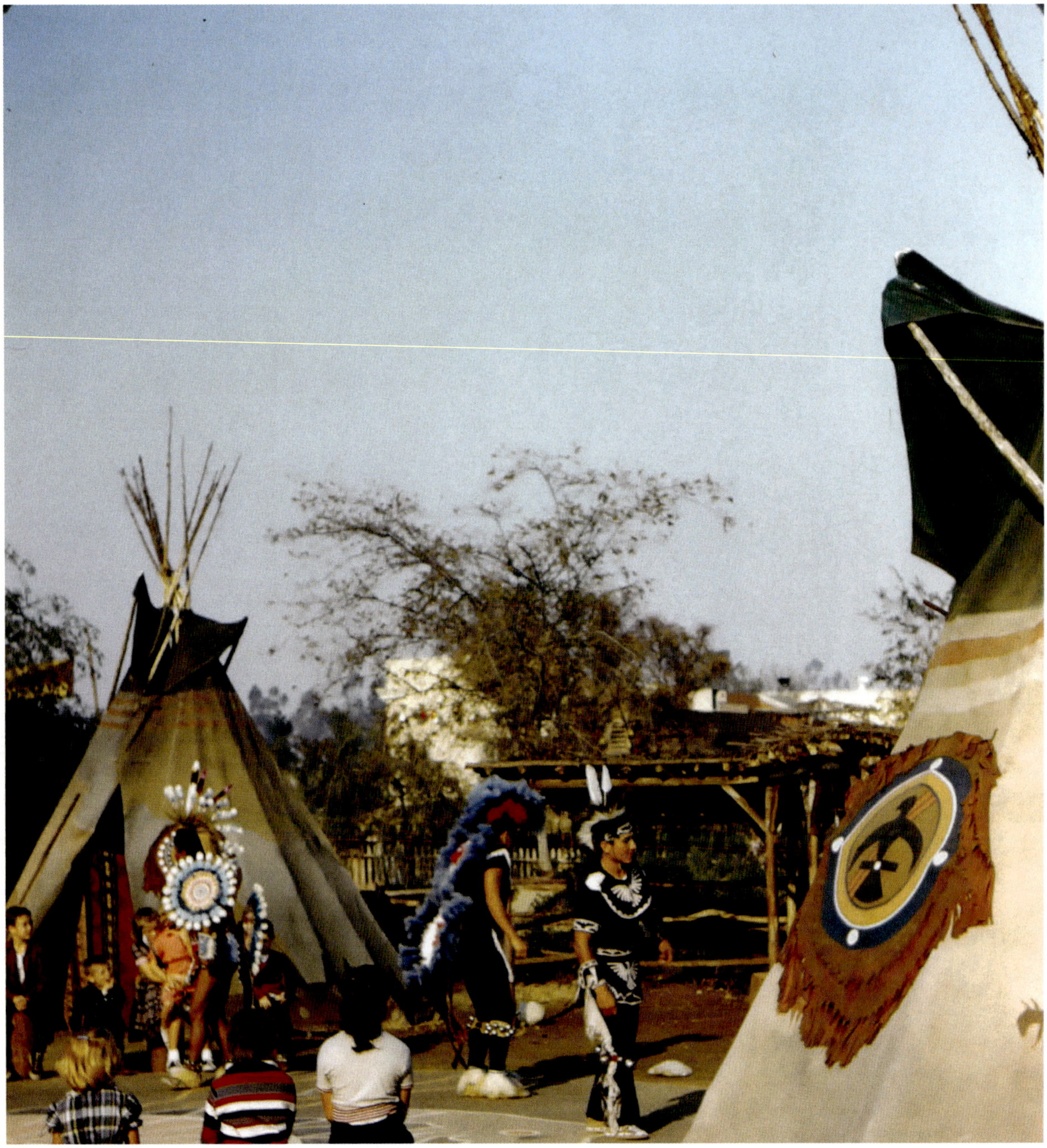

"People who have worked with me say I am 'innocence in action.' They say I have the innocence and unselfconsciousness of a child. Maybe I have. I still look at the world with uncontaminated wonder, and with all living things I have a terrific sympathy. It was the most natural thing in the world for me to imagine that mice and squirrels might have feelings just like mine."

— Walt Disney, "From the Wisdom of Walt Disney," ***Wisdom***, Volume 32, December 1959

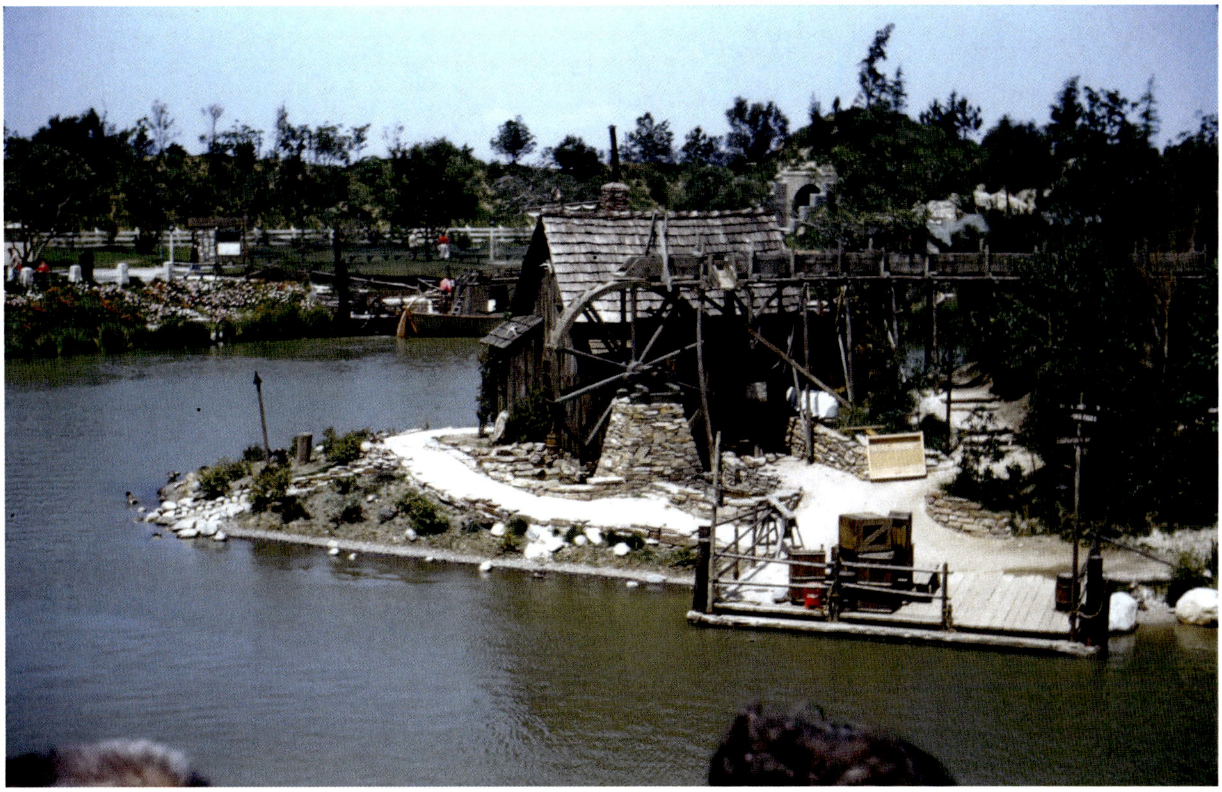

"They brought a little bit of Missouri here to be installed in Disneyland on the newly finished Tom Sawyer Island and Missouri has asked that the island remain Missouri territory.

Gov. Phil Donnelly sent a letter along in which he asked Gov. Goodwin Knight to 'take appropriate action which will cause the Tom Sawyer Island in Disneyland, California, to be deeded to the Sovereign State of Missouri, the only true and rightful possessor of any and all Tom Sawyers in the world.'

Two youngsters came from Hannibal, Mo., to participate in the dedication. Chris Winkler, 12, was chosen by the Hannibal Chamber of Commerce to represent Tom Sawyer, and Perva Lou Smith was named to represent Becky Thatcher.

The two of them planted a box of Missouri soil taken from Jackson's Island, at the foot of the Tom Sawyer Island pier. Then they used a bottle of water from the Mississippi river to christen the Tom Sawyer raft used in connection with the island.

After the dedication ceremonies, they were guests of Walt Disney and Gordon Richmond, assistant to Governor Knight, at a fish fry."

—***Kansas City Times***, June 27, 1956

(Photo not from opening day)

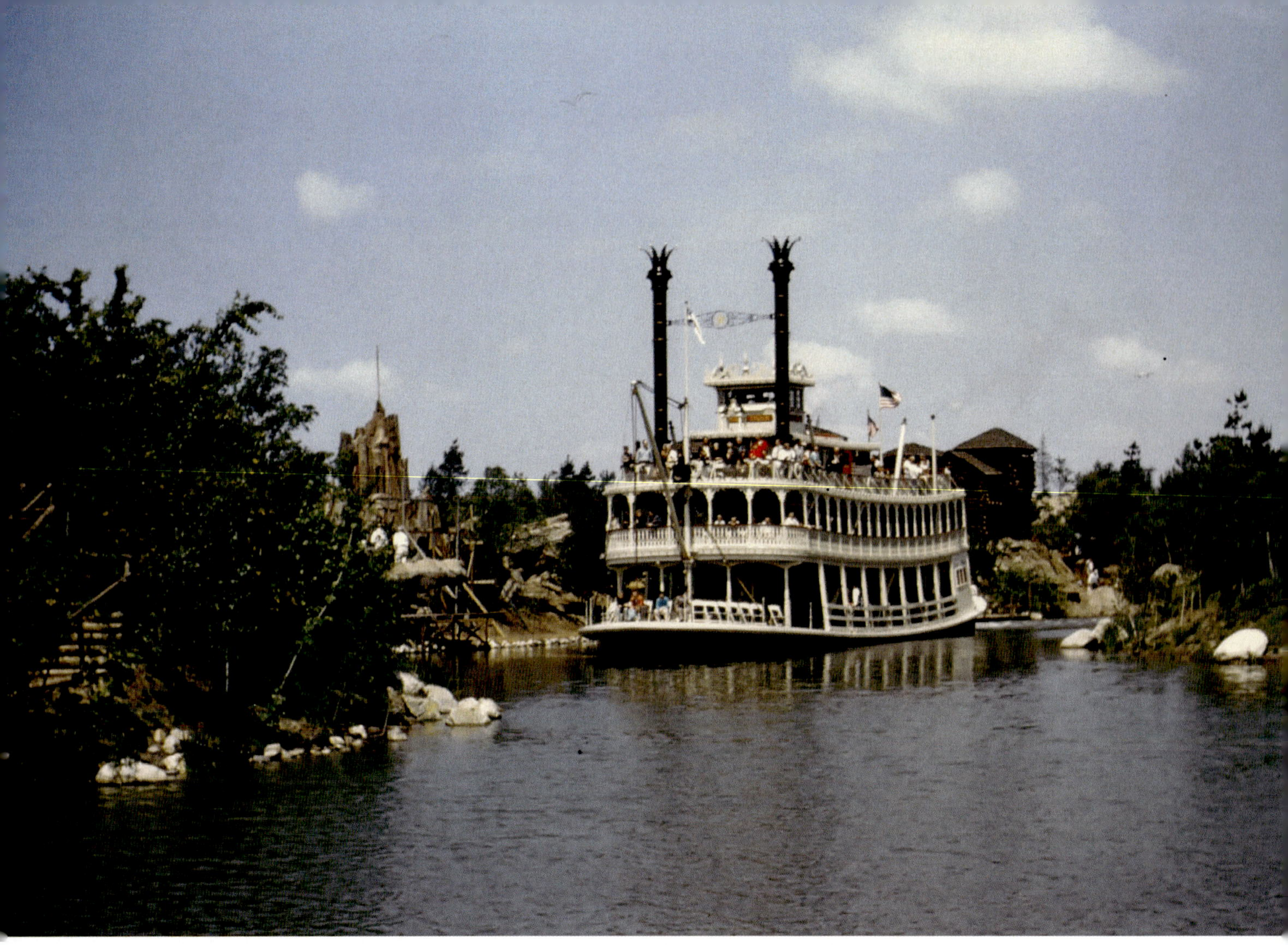

"Walt's invitation read: 'Come to the fish fry and dedication of Tom Sawyer's Island and fish to your heart's content.' So, I did, and found Walt himself, rod and reel in hand but nothing much happening. 'We deposited 1,200 bluegills and some thousands of catfish from the Mississippi.' He grinned. 'but the fish aren't biting yet. It generally takes a couple days for them to become acclimated.'

Walt has just returned from a trip to New Orleans, where he picked up some authentic African spears, shields and headdresses that were being sold at auction. 'Hate to tell you what I paid for them, but they're worth it. Should look just right for Adventureland.'"

—Eve Starr, ***Ledger-Enquirer,*** June 28,1956

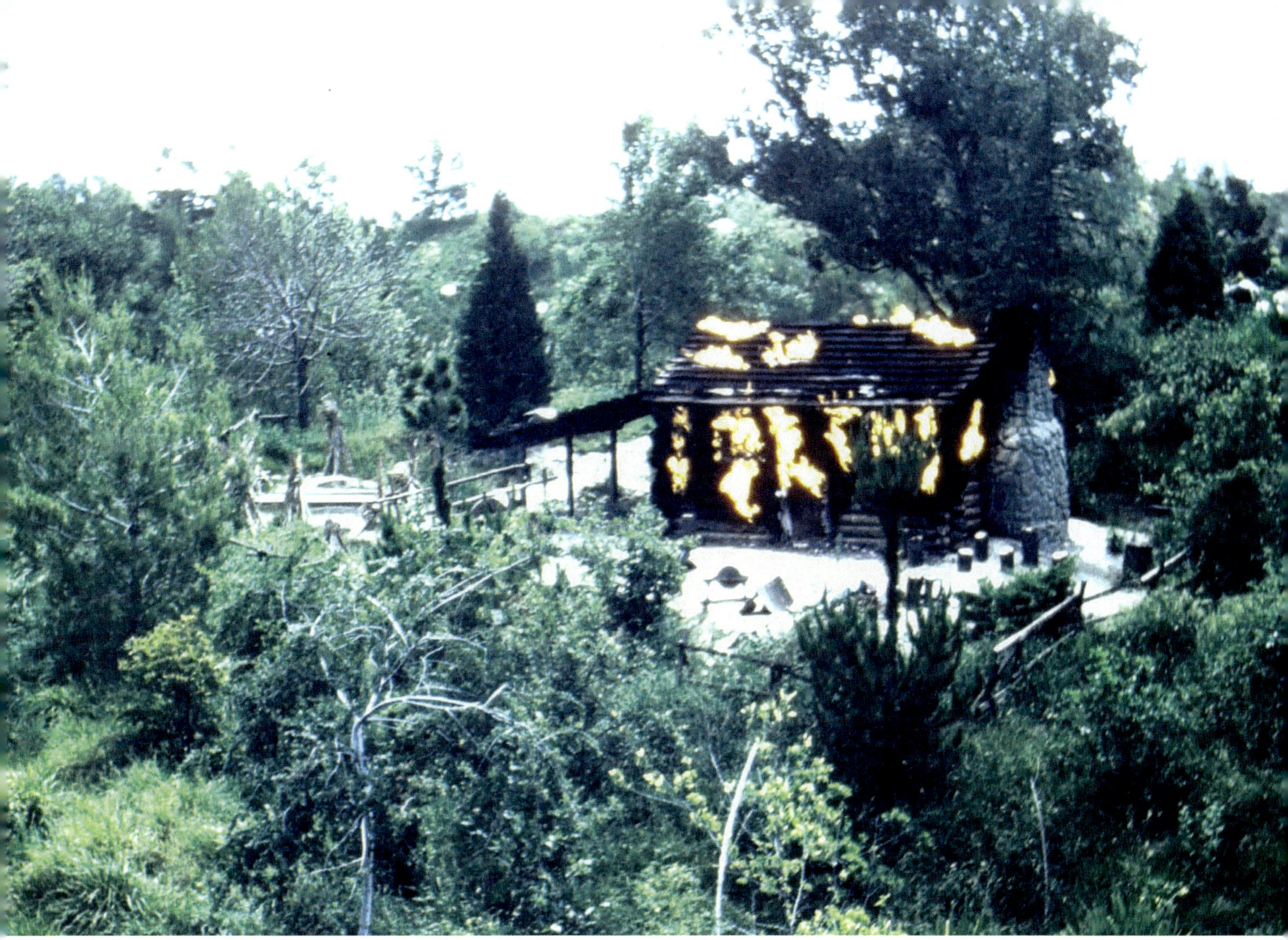

"Cross the river on a raft . . . explore Injun' Joe's Cave . . . walk the suspension bridge . . . visit Fort Wilderness . . . see the Burning Settlers Cabin. Relive exciting days out of America's lusty past. Explore all the magical mysteries of an island built just for fun! Whatever you want to do, you will find fun and excitement for the whole family at this Newest Disneyland attraction—Tom Sawyers Island.

The happiest place on earth is growing . . . adding new acres of smiles . . . new laugh-a-minute rides."

Los Angeles Evening Citizen, June 18, 1956

(Photo not from opening day)

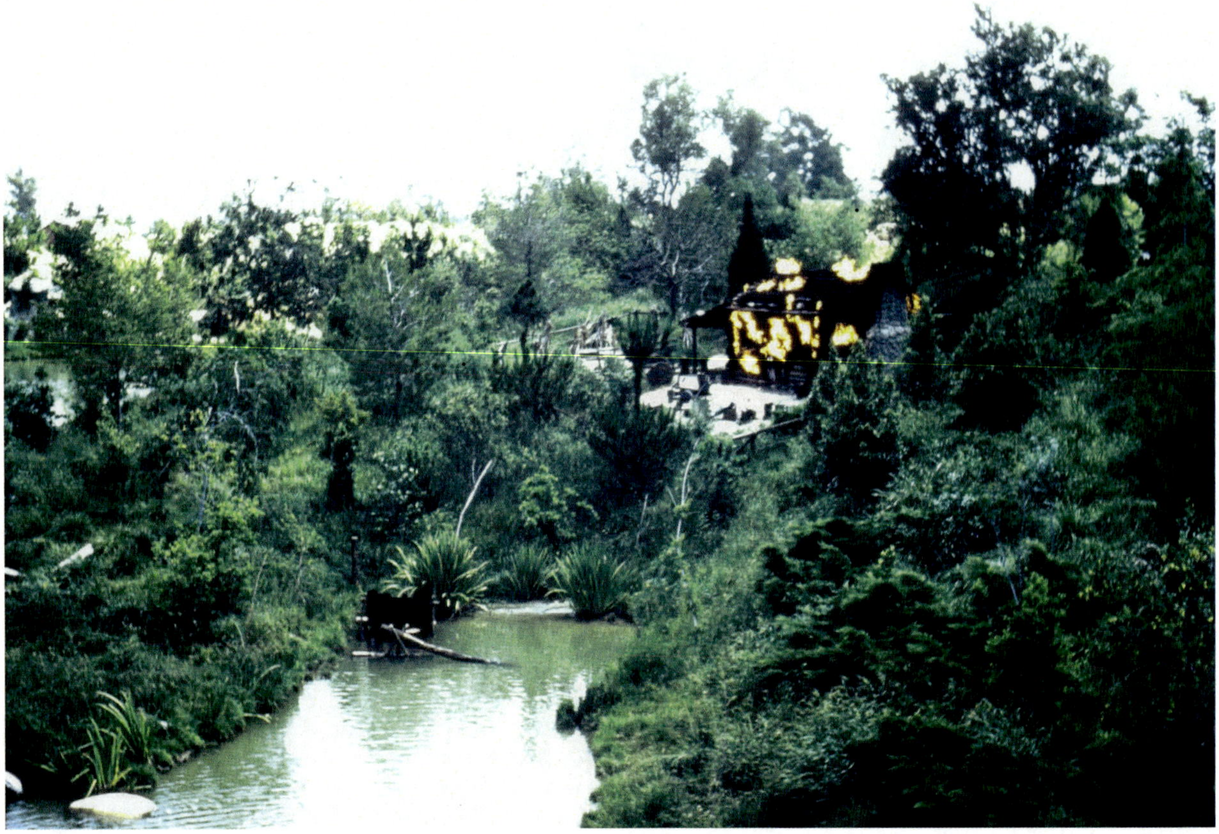

"Among the sights past which the steamboat cruises—a sight also available from the Disneyland trains—is a frontier log cabin in flames. It burns perpetually, being made of a special material unaffected by the flames from hidden gas jets. Lying in front of it is a corpse (plastic) of an old settler done in by the Indians.

Just beyond this sobering sight is the camp of the plastic Indians themselves. There was much concern aboard the *Mark Twain* the day I made my voyage, when some real people were spotted in the Indian camp. A guy and a couple of girls in 20th-century clothes were skulking among the tepees. They hid as the boat approached. Soon as the boat landed, a scout was dispatched to the Indian camp. He came back with word that the intruders were the comedian and a couple can-can girls from the Golden Horseshoe, another Disneyland attraction. They were visiting the Indian camp, with permission, on a picture-taking expedition. But why did they hide when the boat approached? 'We didn't want to spoil the illusion for the people on the boat,' one explained."

—***Star Tribune***, December 23, 1956

(Photo not from opening day)

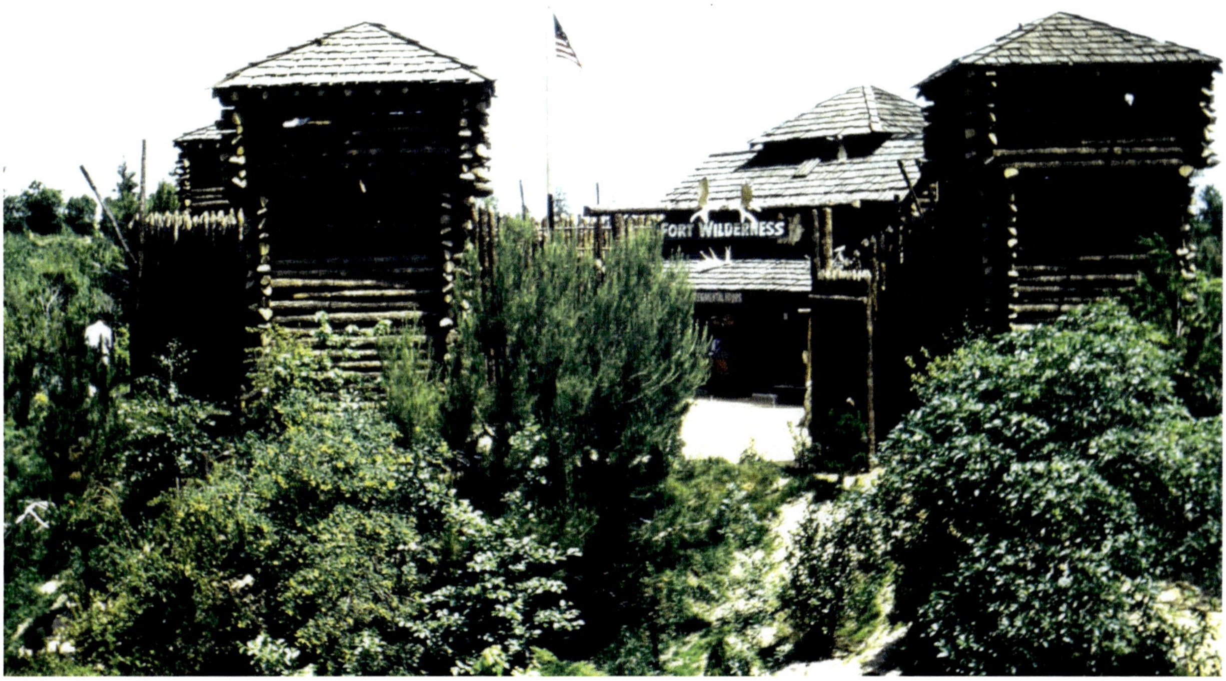

"Disneyland is now past the half-way point in a spring construction program that will add 1½ million dollars in new rides and amusements to Walt Disney's Magic Kingdom in Anaheim.

Major areas of activity are Frontierland and the Tom Sawyer Island in the Rivers of America. More than $250,000 is being spent to make the island a 'playland out of a youngsters dream.' On the island—named for and dedicated to the most famous youngster in American folklore—will be docks for fishing, hills to climb, caves to explore and an authentic replica of an old western log fort named Fort Wilderness by Disney for one that actually stood guard on America's frontier more than two centuries ago."

— ***Long Beach Press Telegram,*** May 13, 1956

(Photo not from opening day)

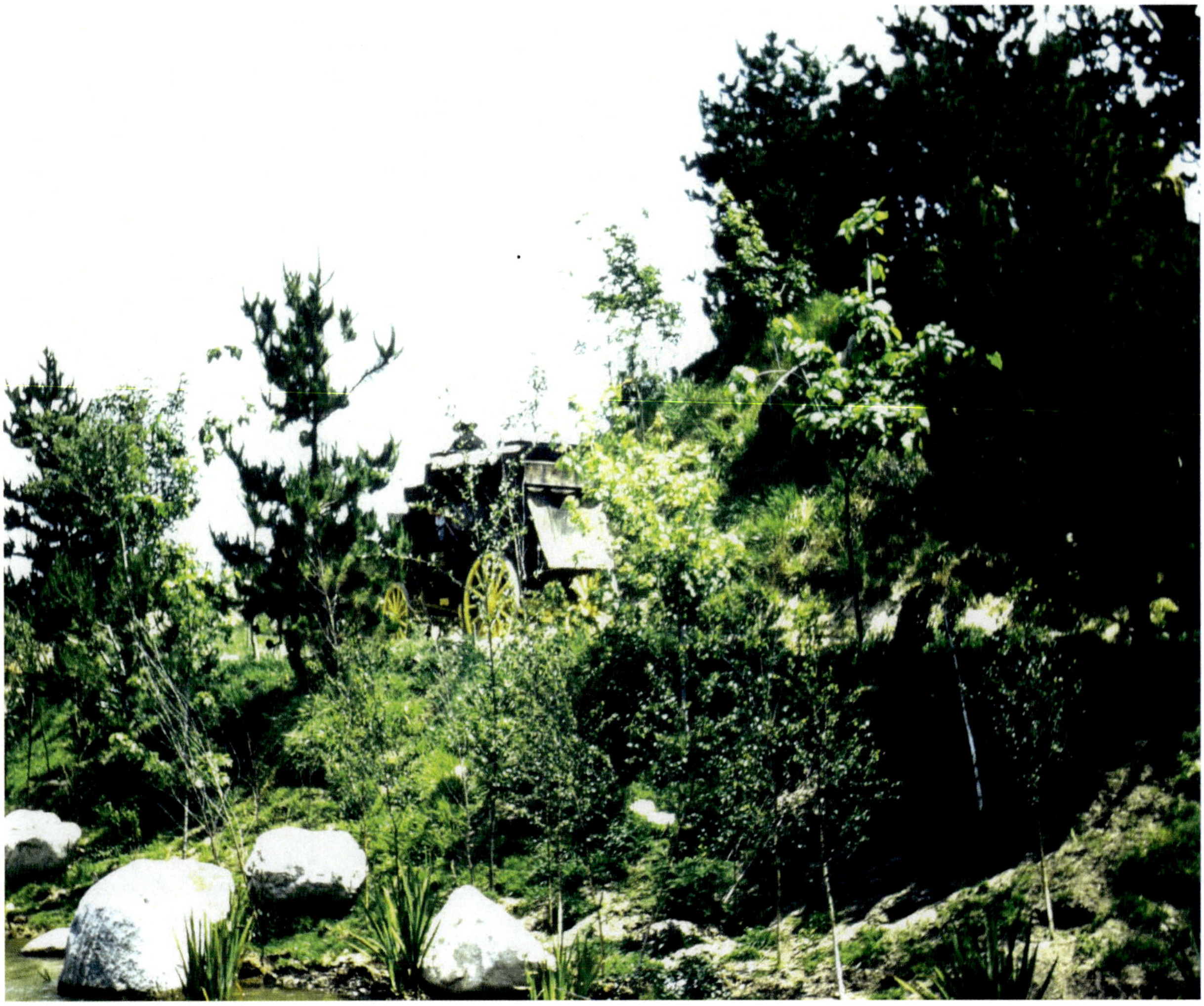

"You will ride the Conestoga Wagon in Frontierland—one of the most picturesque and vital vehicles in history.

It was the Conestoga, not the covered wagon that developed the West. The great wagons were first built in the Conestoga Valley of Pennsylvania, with water-tight bottoms that permitted safe crossings of rivers.

You will also see and ride authentic stagecoaches, pack trains, and buckboards in this remarkable re-creation of the old West."

– ***Pasadena Independent***, December 18, 1955

(Photo not from opening day)

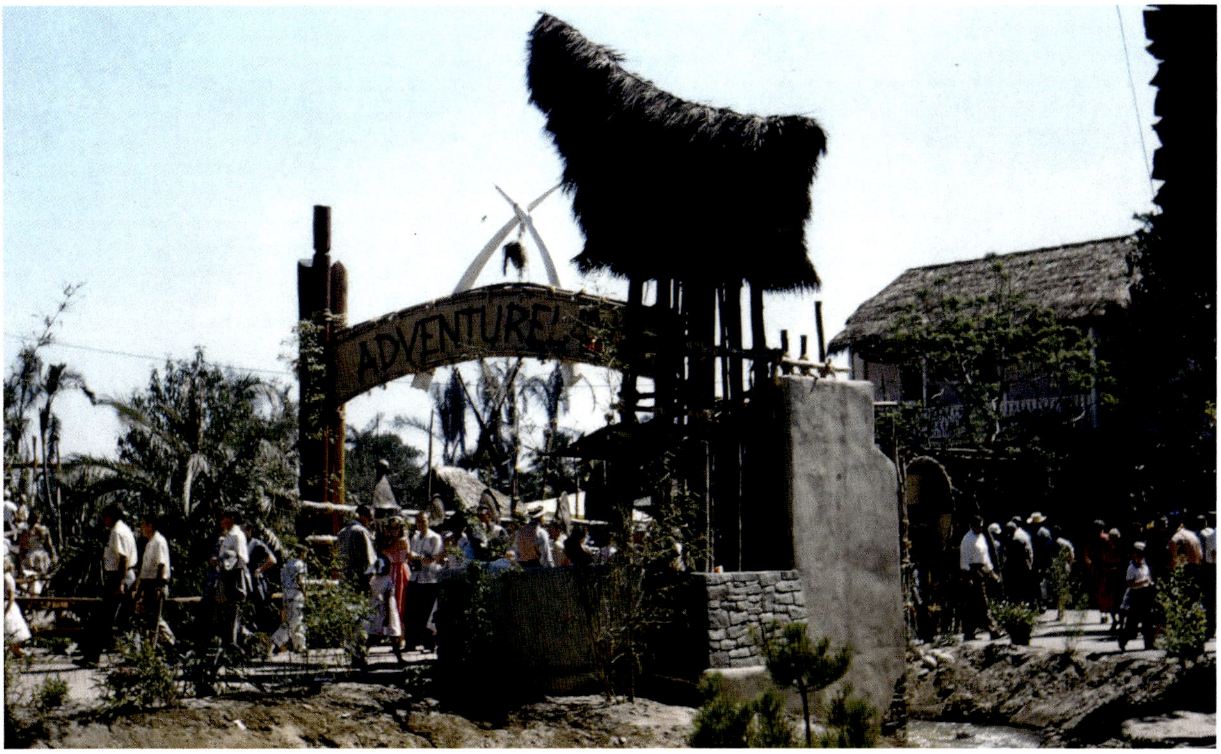

"Walk beneath crossed elephant tusks from a long-ago safari . . . pass between tribal war shields . . . and cross a small river, here is Adventureland.

And here Pasadena area residents will find the sounds, the savagery, the strange peace of the jungle.

The voices of a hundred birds crisscross the tropical rivers of the world. A snarling lioness guards her kill on shore. A real giraffe raises her head to gaze with mild interest at your passing explorers boat.

You will watch chattering monkeys disturb the tranquility of a dying Indo-Chinese pagoda. Alligators slip menacingly thru dark waters, a monstrous hippopotamus rears suddenly from the Nile and white war paint head hunting natives appears now and again amid tropical vegetation that has come from all over the world.

Pasadena delegates to Disneyland have agreed with Walt Disney's description of Adventureland: '. . . a wonderland of Nature's own design, featuring her wild creatures, her settings, her fabulous plan of life.'"

—***Pasadena Independent***, December 18, 1955

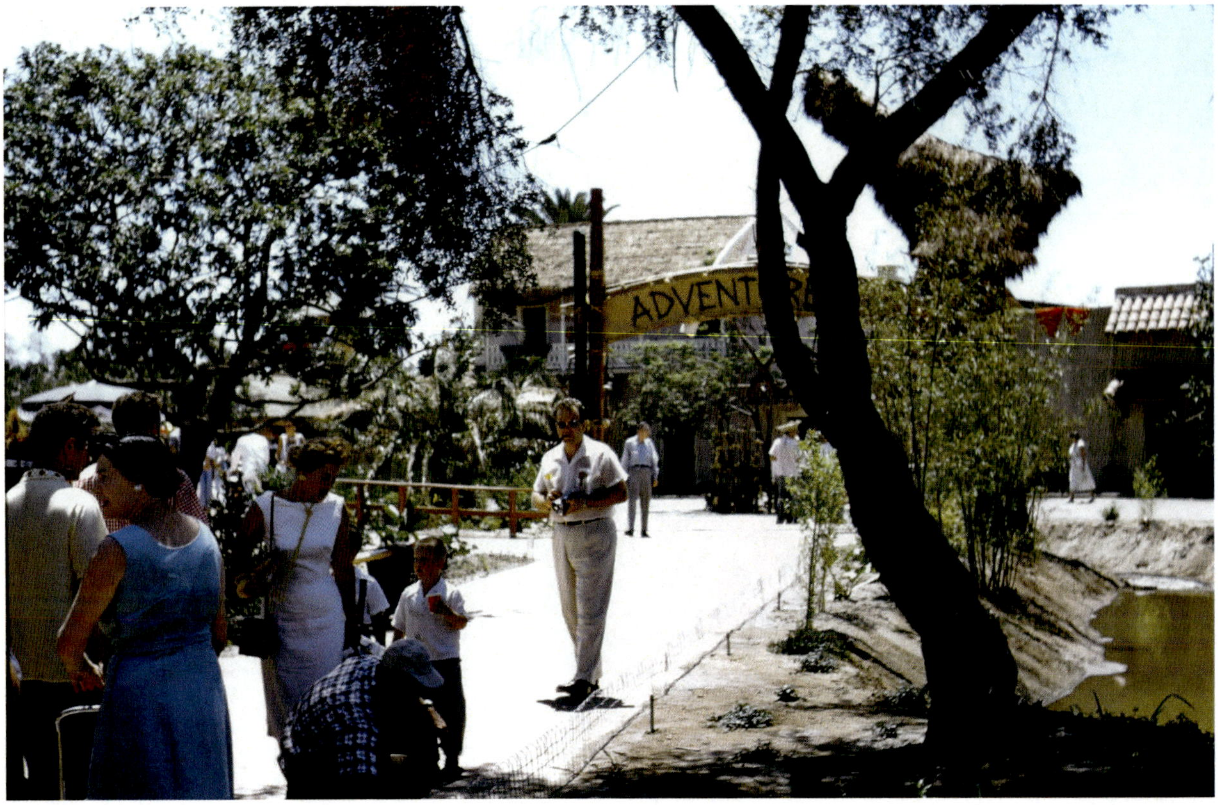

"In transplanting approximately half a million dollars worth of trees and shrubs, vitamins, hormones, peat moss and a solution of nitro-humus had to be supplied to Disneyland's sandy soil to lessen the shock to the plants.

Trees from Australia, New Zealand, South Africa, South America, China and Japan ranging in age from 30 to 50 years, were imported for Adventureland."

—***Los Angeles Evening Citizen News,*** July 16, 1955

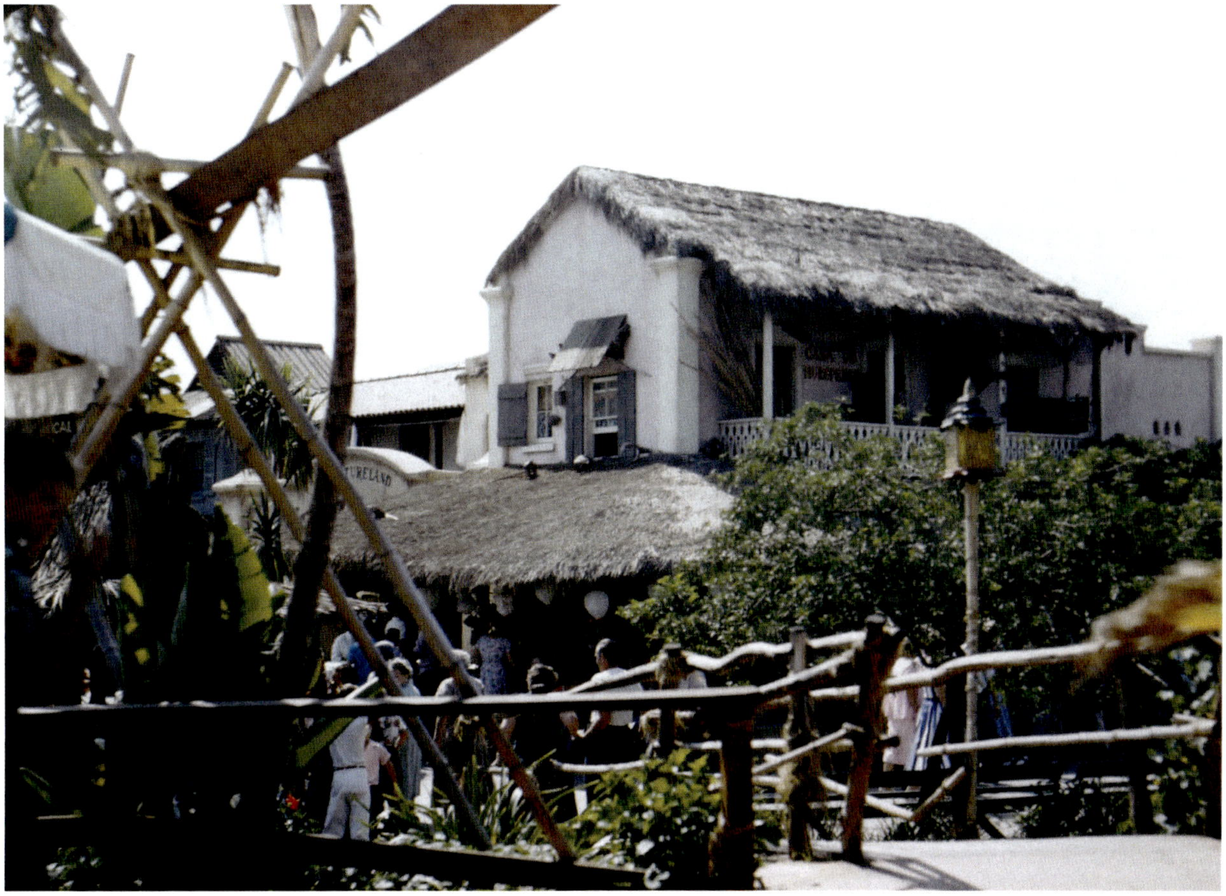

Evans and Reeves Landscaping Inc. were the official landscape architects for Disneyland. After the park opened, the firm ran advertisements that stated, "If you do not notice how we made a jungle out of an orange grove . . . the hills and rivers that never existed before and are now covered with forests . . . or the way we planted an unknown planet . . . If it all looks as if it had always been here . . . then we have achieved the perfect landscaping for Disneyland! Because that is the way it was planned to be!"[12]

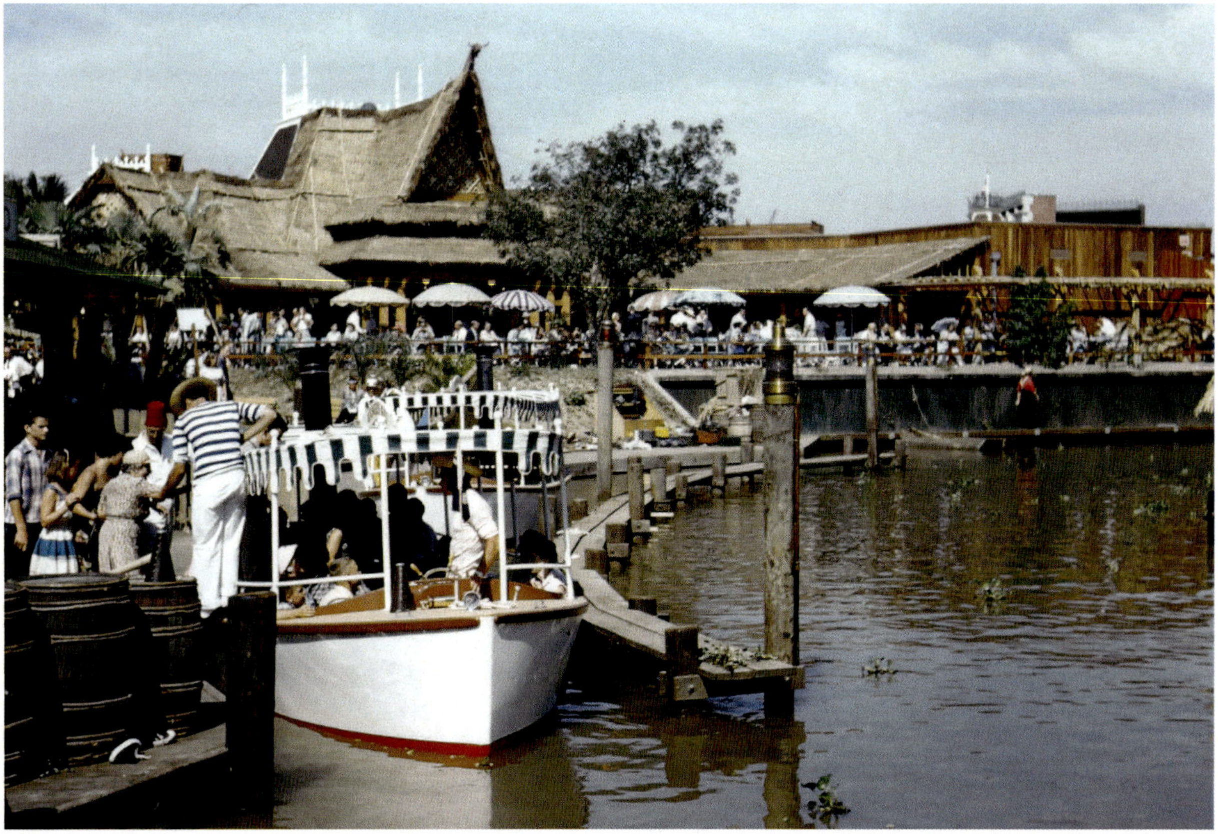

"The wonderland of Nature's own design, featuring her animal creature, her natural settings, her fabulous plan of life. From Adventureland, you will take an explorers boat on a voyage down tropical rivers of the world where lifelike animals, reptiles and jungle natives add thrill to your trip at every river bend.

Adventureland helps fulfill Walt Disney's promise that Disneyland will be a place for parents and children to share pleasant times together; a place for teacher and pupils to discover greater ways of understanding."

—***Los Angeles Times***, July 15, 1955

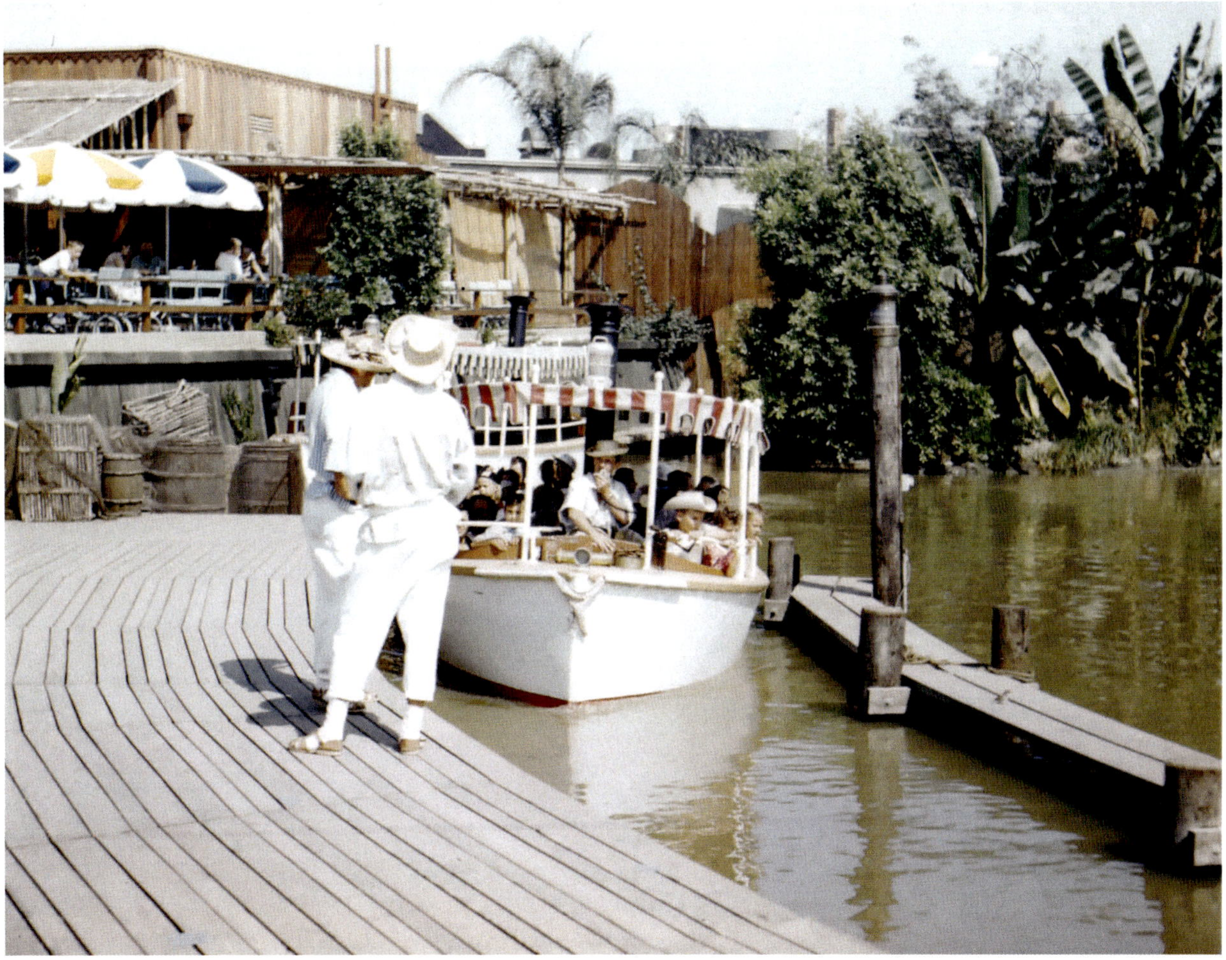

Jungle Cruise Boats operated with Gray Marine engines on a 1,640-foot-long guiderail. Each boat had a capacity of thirty-five people, including their guide. The overall length of the vessel was twenty-seven feet, with a beam of nine feet.

The animals and natives found throughout the cruise were designed and built by WED Enterprises. They operated via electronic and hydraulic devices and were built at the Walt Disney Studios.

The sound effects heard throughout the attraction were tape recordings of actual animals and their natural habitat.

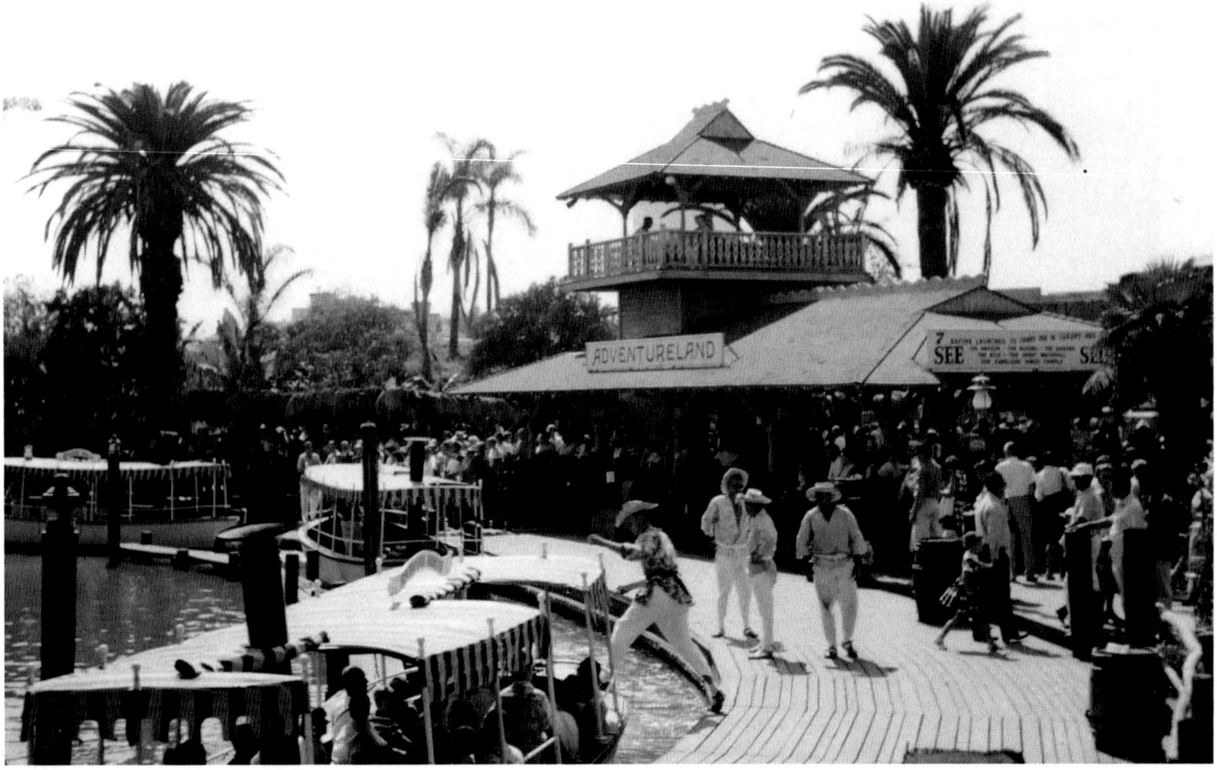

"An exotic Tahitian settlement, home port for the tropical explorers' boats, is the threshold of Adventureland. Beautiful jungle flowers, bright-hued birds, fish, shells and native handicraft from the South Seas. Africa and South America are all displayed in Adventureland's outdoor bazaar for your pleasure and enjoyment."

—***Los Angeles Times Supplement***, July 15, 1955

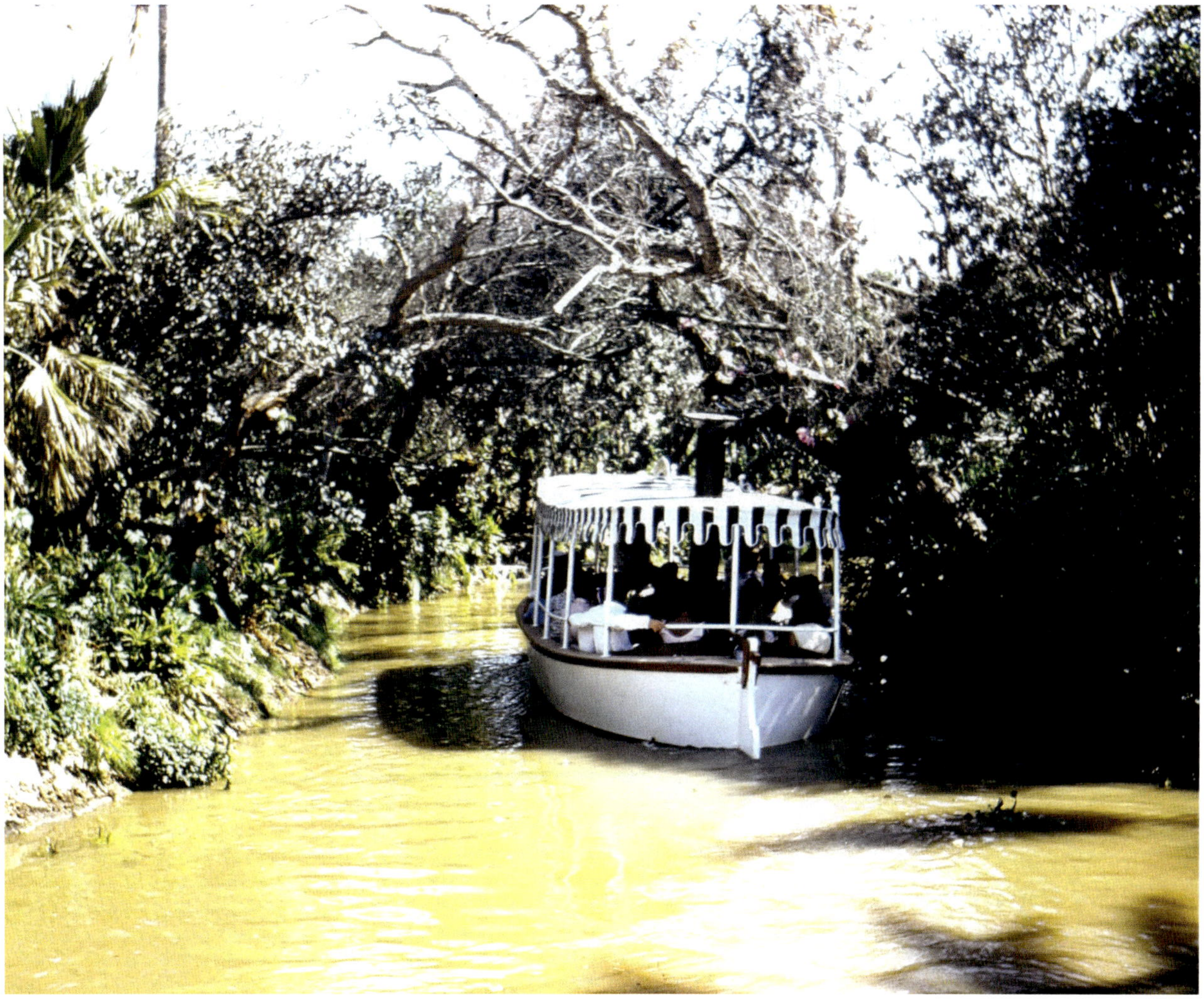

"No fears for Adventureland visitors since each Explorers Boat 'skipper' is armed with a .38 revolver. Guns are used on need during the popular jungle rides."

—***Pasadena Independent***, December 18, 1955

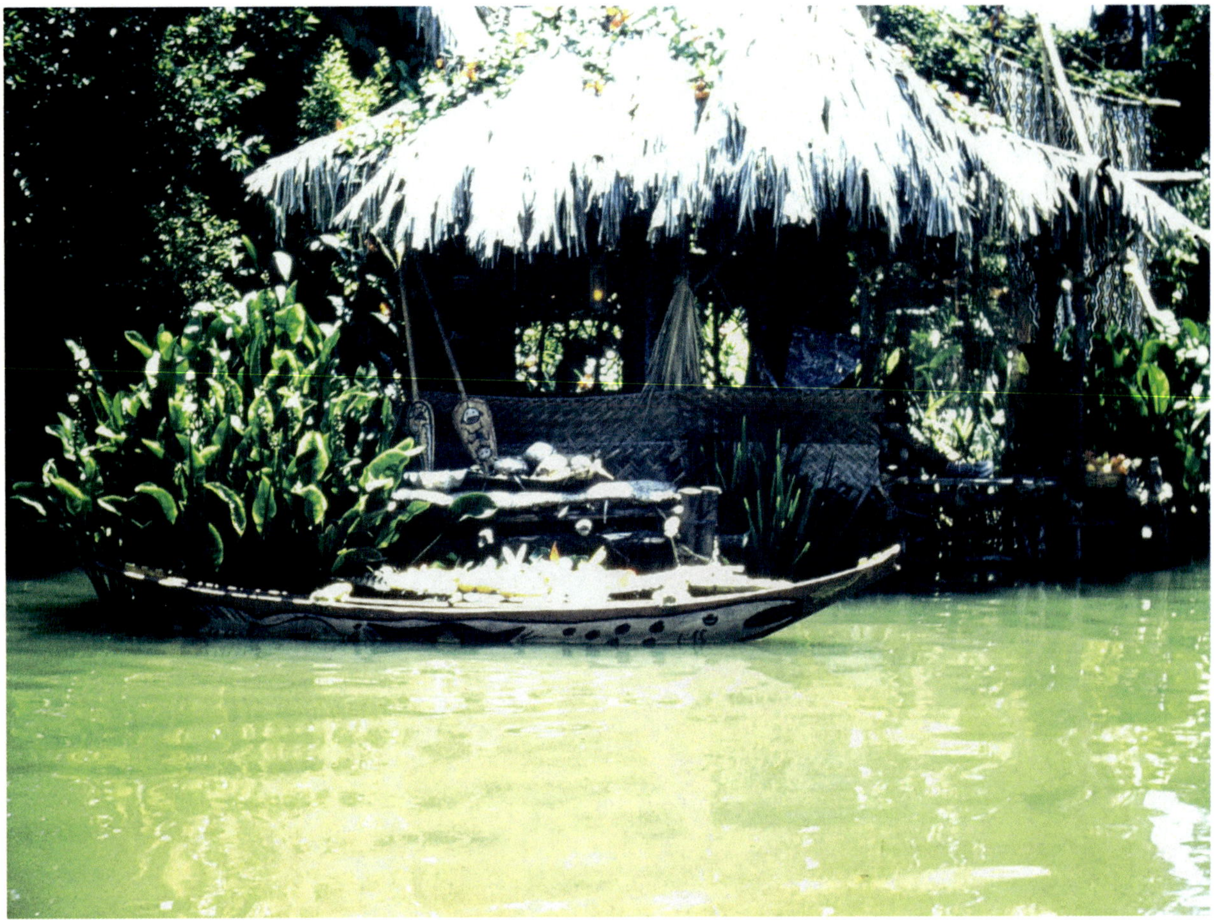

"'One of our biggest problems was to obtain the full-grown big trees and then get them planted. There weren't enough full-matured specimens in Southern California nurseries. Bill and I spent hundreds of hours during the year scouring old gardens in Southland for trees.'

[Jack] Evans and his brother tell of their experiences in spotting trees on old ranches and private estates, negotiating for their purchase, and in many cases being donated the tree in exchange for digging it up and taking it away. Frequently a caravan of several trucks with 90-foot booms to carry their tree-load would solemnly roll into Disneyland during the day.

The 'big-tree-caper' did not end until the trees were planted. Evans estimates 90 percent of them were planted by giant cranes which dropped them into position. Other special equipment was required and devised to handle problems of planting, where there was no precedent to follow in doing the job."

—***West Los Angeles Independent***, July 17, 1955

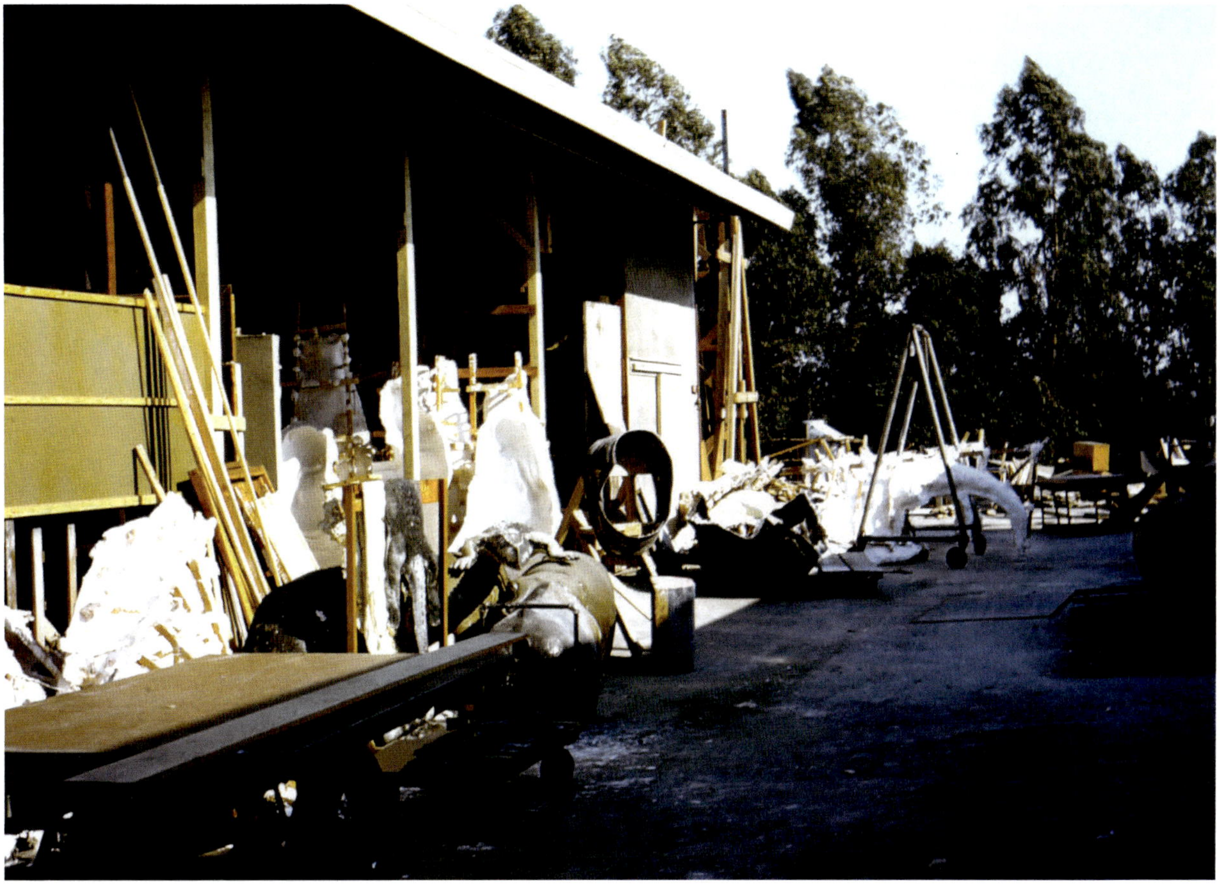

"Disney remarked that the explorer boats in Adventureland have proven the most popular feature in the park. That's the river ride that has wild animals jump up at you. It cost $400,000 to create"

—***Pomona Progress Bulletin***, September 15, 1955

(According to Tom Morris, this photo shows the lumber storage building-turned-makeshift staff shop, which was located at the Disney studio and not at Disneyland.)

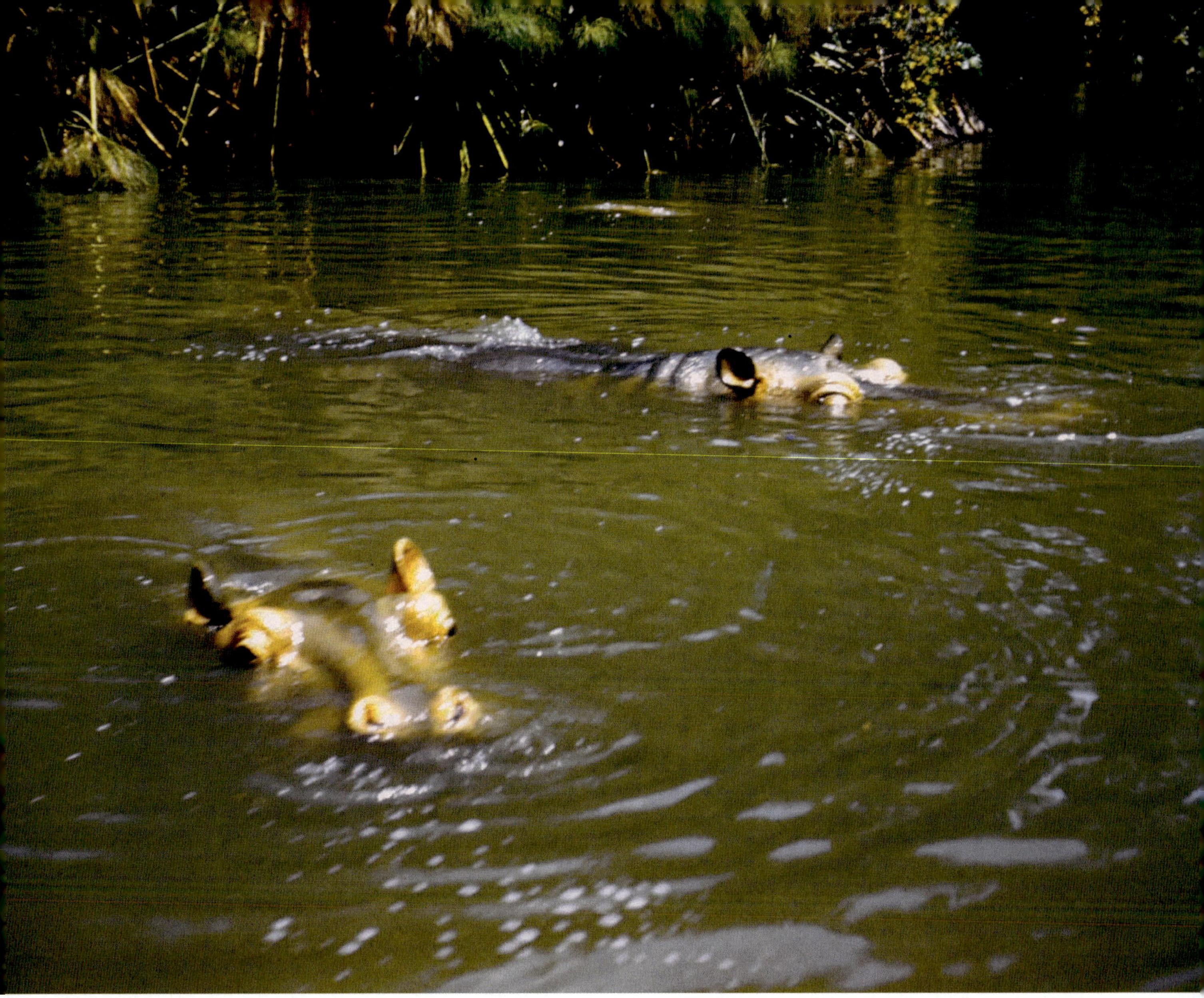

"On the lush banks of the river are rhinos, hippos, elephants, and lions that grunt, trumpet and roar and move about. They're the creations of Bob Mattey, who built the giant squid for Disney's '20,000 Leagues Under the Sea.'"

—***Orlando Sentinel***, August 14, 1955

Decades after mechanizing the squid for ***20,000 Leagues Under the Sea*** and the animals for Disneyland's Jungle Cruise attraction, Robert A. Mattey created the three sharks used in the production of the film ***Jaws***.

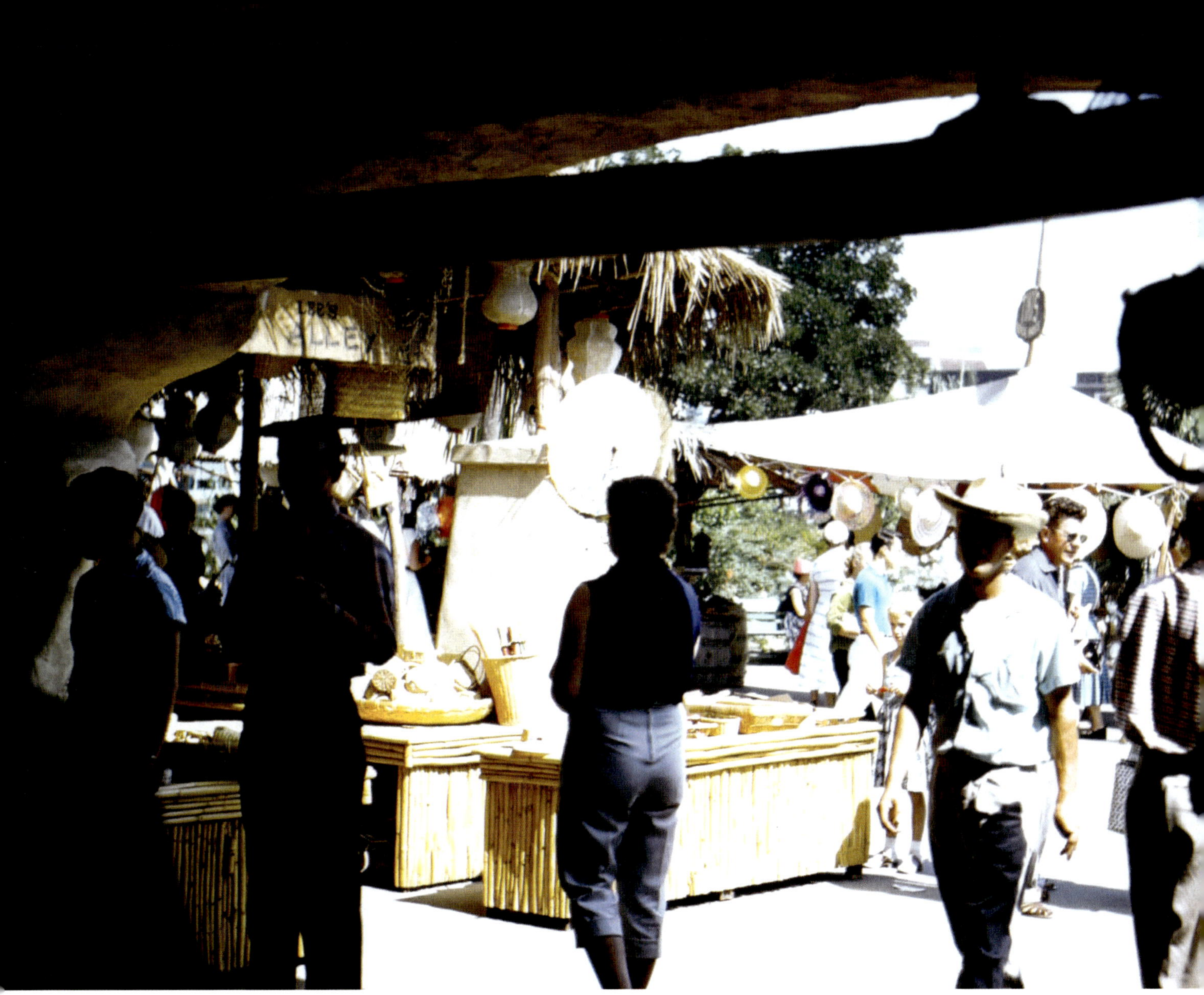

"Adventureland in Walt Disney's magic kingdom is a land of natural wonders and primitive savagery—a land of exotic beauty where the romance of the tropics prevails. Entrance to this tropical paradise is made through a Tahitian Village where bazaars offer merchandise of the South Seas, India, and Africa. Victorian architecture blends into the thatched roofs of Polynesia and the village itself appears to have had its share of tropical storms."

—***Long Beach Independent***, July 15, 1955

(Photo shows General Lee's Bamboo Alley)

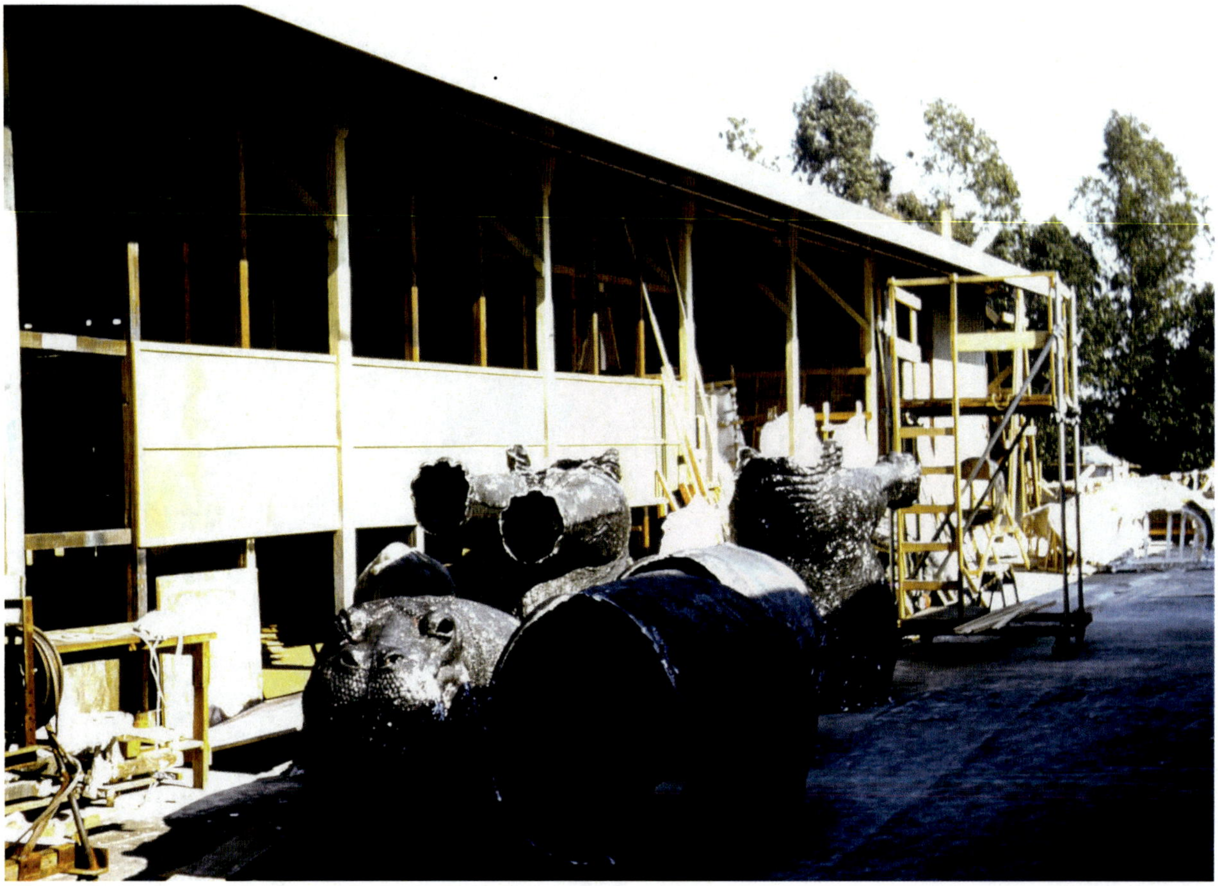

"From the very beginning of Disneyland, Evans and Reeves Landscaping faced new kinds of problems. One incident involved a colorblind bulldozer operator. Jack Evans earmarked some of the orange trees for removal with red streamers, and those few which stayed where they were with green streamers. One bulldozer operator uprooted a dozen trees before somebody realized he was color-blind."

—***West Los Angeles Independent***, July 17, 1955

(According to Tom Morris, this photo shows the lumber storage building-turned-makeshift staff shop, which was located at the Disney studio and not at Disneyland.)

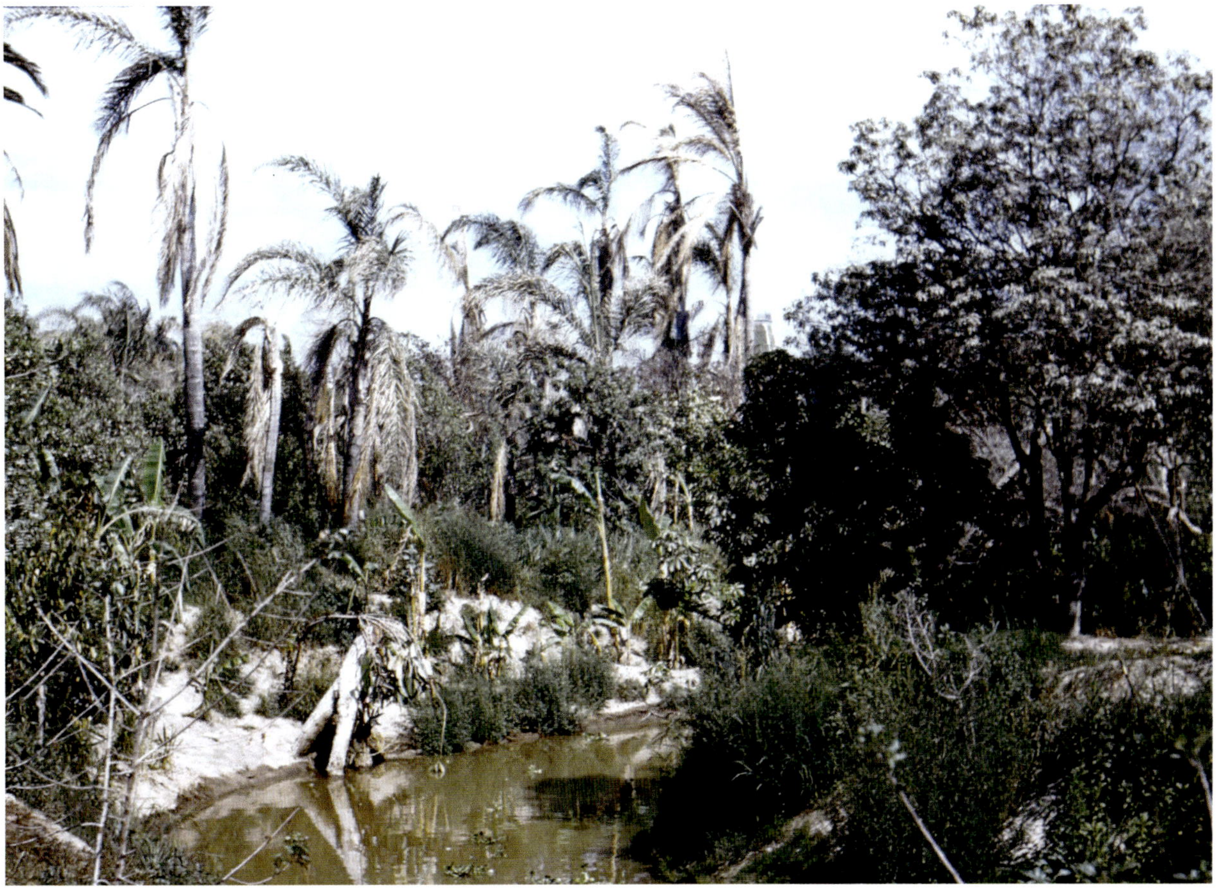

"More than 6,000 trees ranging from 6 to 60 feet, now grow in the park and represent all parts of the world. Some of the more familiar trees in Disneyland are Brazilian Peppers, Magnolia, Rubber, Palm, Pine, Elm, Sandalwood, Oak and Pittosporum.

Epiphytic and terrestrial type orchids bloom in Adventureland's Amazon section and Bougainvillea plants present a blaze of beauty. The Gunnera Plant, or Bog Plant, with its six-foot leaves grow at the edge of the tropical 'river' in this section.

The Congo is represented by Lilies of the Nile and by Nile and Papyrus grasses. The Bushman 'Poison Plant' whose juices are used to make poison darts, is a native of the African Congo and is grown in the Congo area of Adventureland.

Banana trees from Ethiopia grow in Adventureland, as does the Cycador Sago Palm, one of the oldest forms of plant life in the world. This latter is a transitional plant—from the Paleozoic age when ferns began to acquire arborescent character. Here, too, is found the Dragon Tree which actually 'bleeds' a red fluid if wounded.

The Taro Plant from Hawaii used to make the staple food called poi, is also grown in Adventureland."

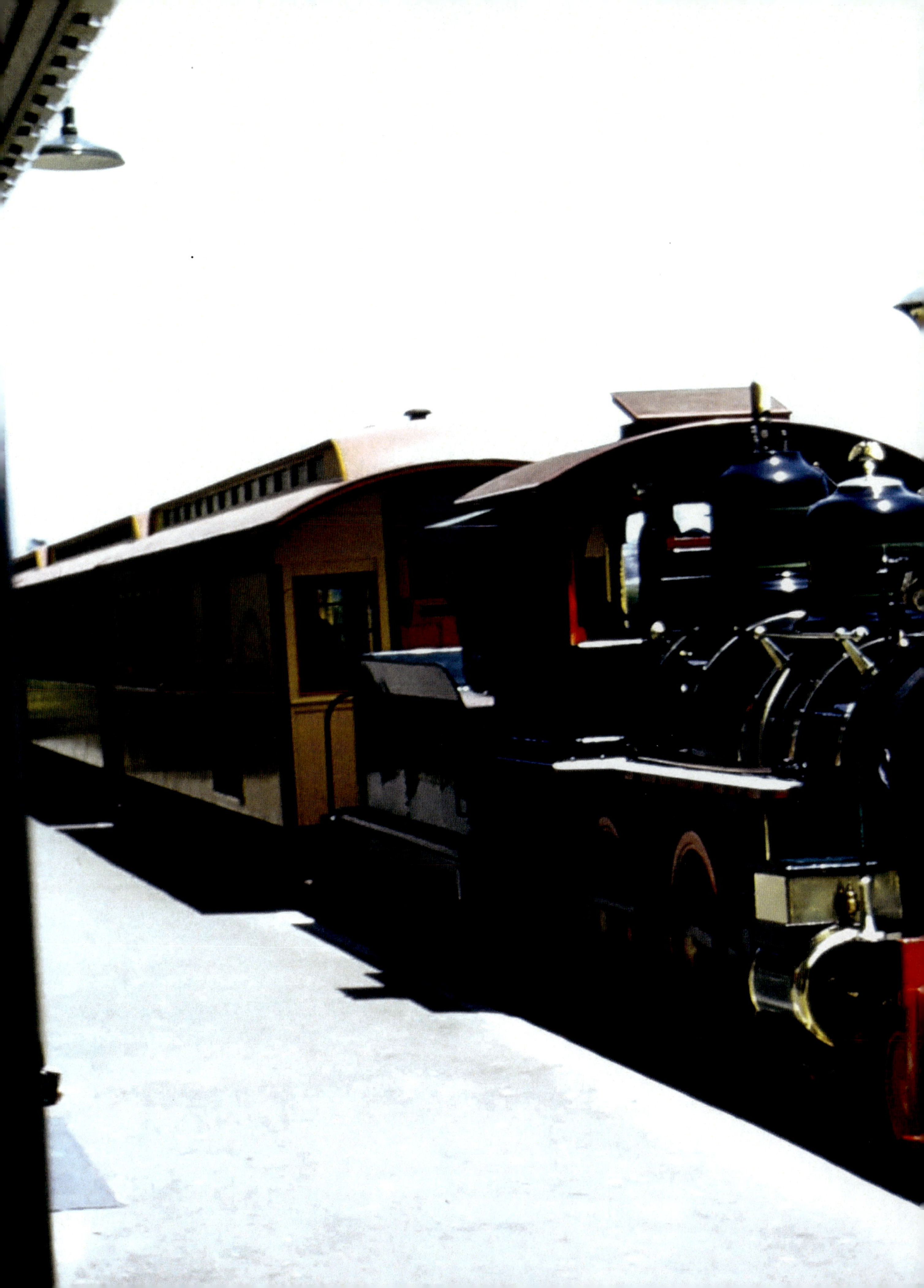

"Equipment for the two trains is now being built. The passenger cars, decorated in the fashion of the Gay Nineties, will be of the wooden type used in early-day railroading except for steel underframes and modern air brakes. Disneyland today is thunderous with the roar of machinery as excavators move 200,000 cubic yards of earth, to form mountains, hills, rivers and roadbeds for the SF&D."

—*Pomona Progress Bulletin*, May 27, 1955

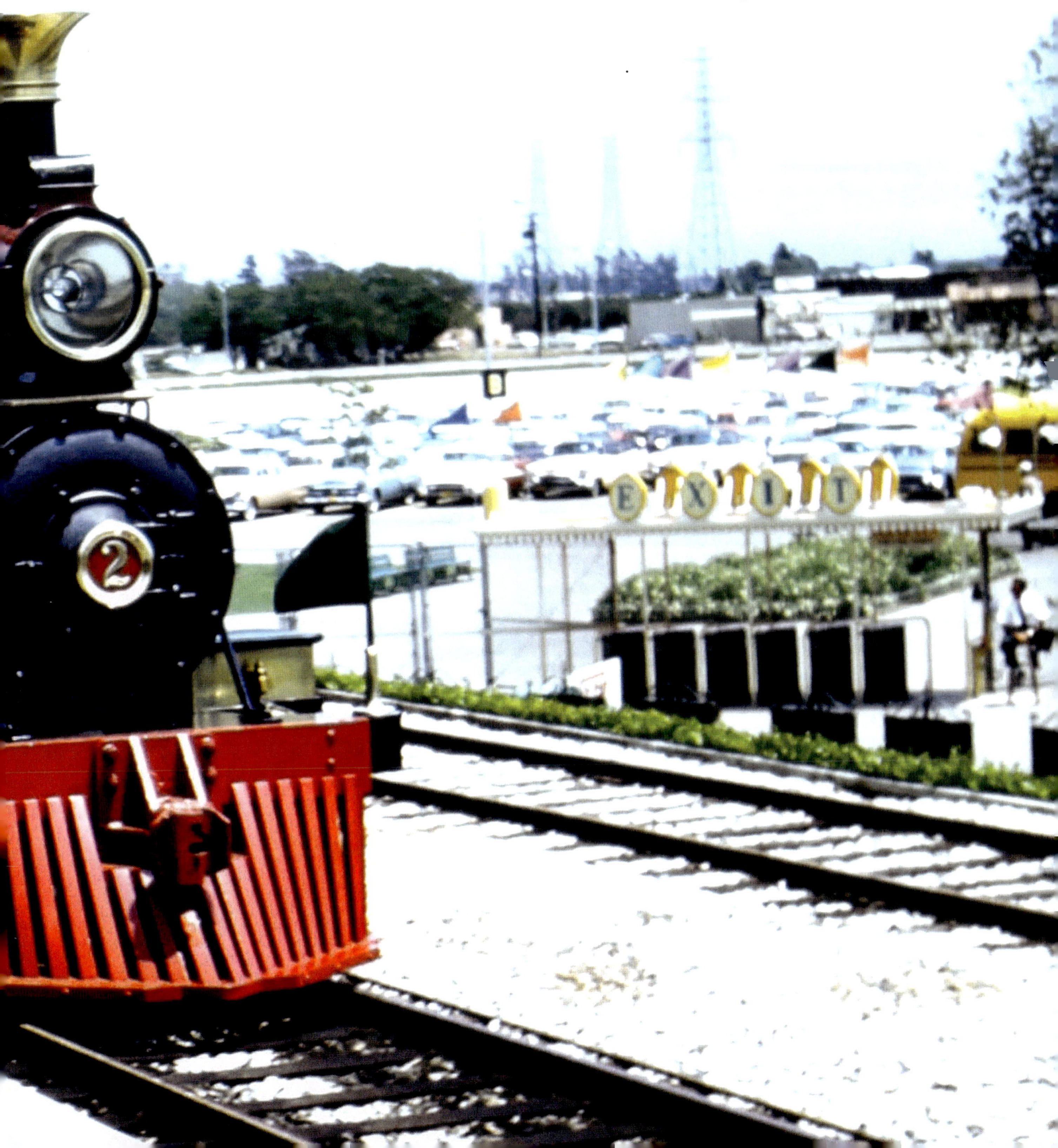

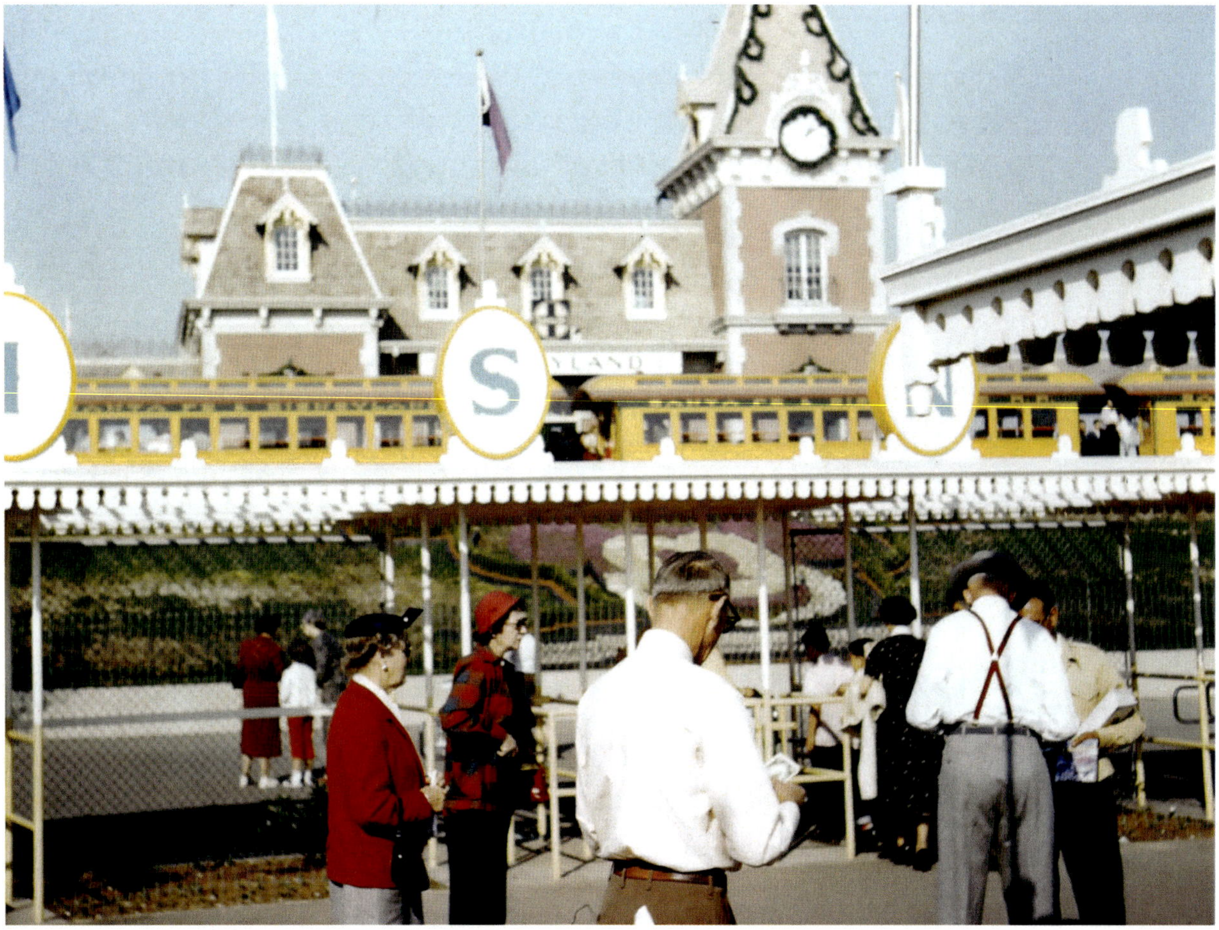

"Announcement of a new 'Day at Disneyland' ticket book plan, effective October 11th through November 23rd was made today by the management of the park in Anaheim.

The new ticket book plan offers Disneyland visitors their choice of 8 rides and amusements and includes admission to Disneyland, all for a fixed price. The ticket plan books will only be sold at Disneyland's box office.

According to C.V. Wood, Jr., Vice President and General Manager of Disneyland, the plan has been developed as a 'convenient way for individuals and families to plan a day's entertainment at Disneyland and know beforehand what their expenditure will be.'

The ticket book was also developed to encourage Southern California residents to visit or revisit the Park during the 'low-tourist months.'

With more than 1,200,000 people having visited Disneyland since its opening, statistics compiled at the Park show that children average approximately 7 rides or amusements on a visit, with adults averaging approximately 6 rides."

—***Tustin News,*** October 20, 1955

(Photo from Christmas time 1955, not opening day)

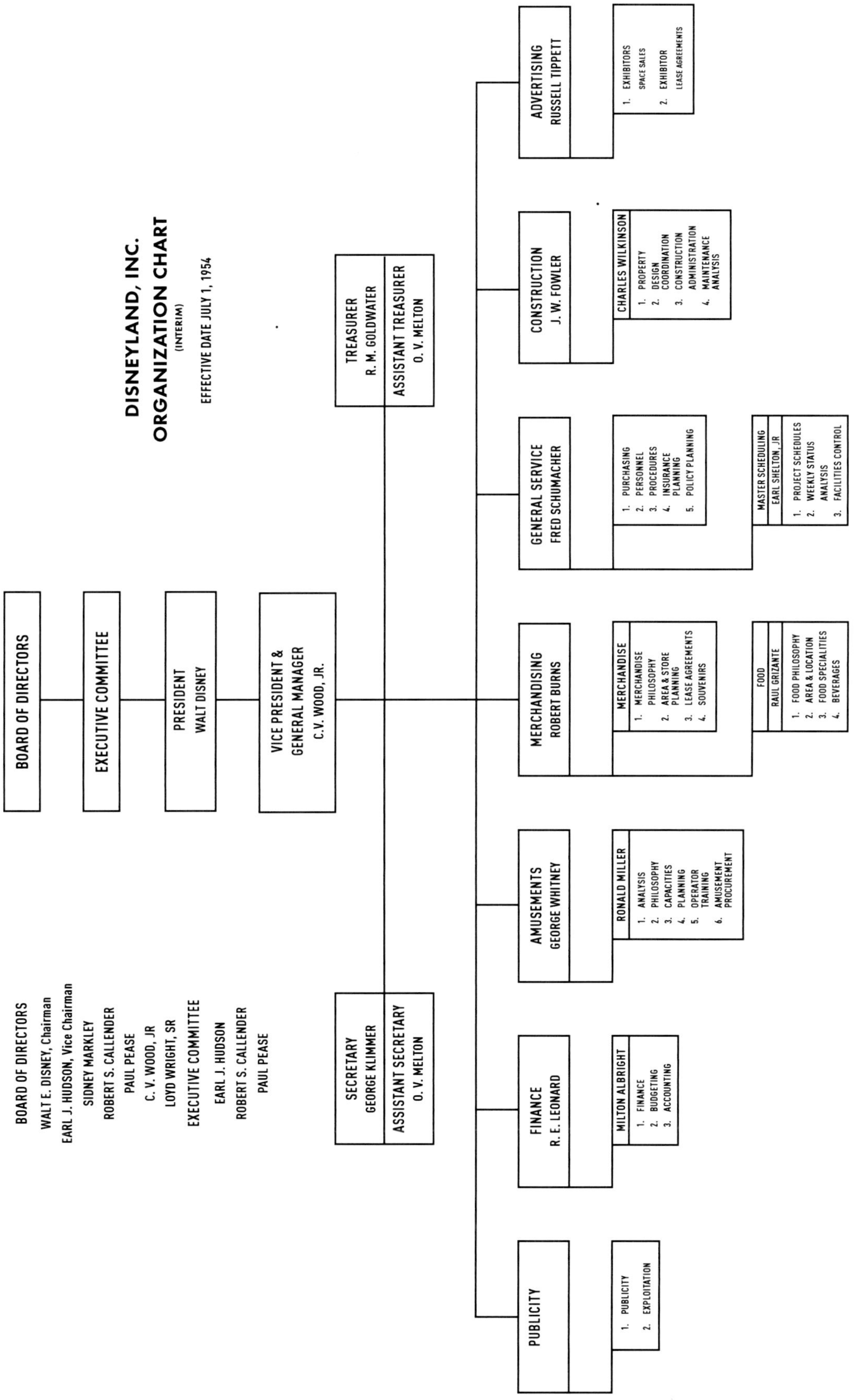
DISNEYLAND, INC.
ORGANIZATION CHART
(INTERIM)
EFFECTIVE DATE JULY 1, 1954
BOARD OF DIRECTORS
WALT E. DISNEY, Chairman
EARL J. HUDSON, Vice Chairman
SIDNEY MARKLEY
ROBERT S. CALLENDER
PAUL PEASE
C. V. WOOD, JR
LOYD WRIGHT, SR
EXECUTIVE COMMITTEE
EARL J. HUDSON
ROBERT S. CALLENDER
PAUL PEASE
BOARD OF DIRECTORS
EXECUTIVE COMMITTEE
PRESIDENT
WALT DISNEY
VICE PRESIDENT &
GENERAL MANAGER
C.V. WOOD, JR.
TREASURER
R. M. GOLDWATER
ASSISTANT TREASURER
O. V. MELTON
SECRETARY
GEORGE KLIMMER
ASSISTANT SECRETARY
O. V. MELTON
PUBLICITY
1. PUBLICITY
2. EXPLOITATION
FINANCE
R. E. LEONARD
MILTON ALBRIGHT
1. FINANCE
2. BUDGETING
3. ACCOUNTING
AMUSEMENTS
GEORGE WHITNEY
RONALD MILLER
1. ANALYSIS
2. PHILOSOPHY
3. CAPACITIES
4. PLANNING
5. OPERATOR TRAINING
6. AMUSEMENT PROCUREMENT
MERCHANDISING
ROBERT BURNS
MERCHANDISE
1. MERCHANDISE PHILOSOPHY
2. AREA & STORE PLANNING
3. LEASE AGREEMENTS
4. SOUVENIRS
FOOD
RAUL GRIZANTE
1. FOOD PHILOSOPHY
2. AREA & LOCATION
3. FOOD SPECIALITIES
4. BEVERAGES
GENERAL SERVICE
FRED SCHUMACHER
1. PURCHASING
2. PERSONNEL
3. PROCEDURES
4. INSURANCE PLANNING
5. POLICY PLANNING
MASTER SCHEDULING
EARL SHELTON, JR
1. PROJECT SCHEDULES
2. WEEKLY STATUS ANALYSIS
3. FACILITIES CONTROL
CONSTRUCTION
J. W. FOWLER
CHARLES WILKINSON
1. PROPERTY
2. DESIGN COORDINATION
3. CONSTRUCTION ADMINISTRATION
4. MAINTENANCE ANALYSIS
ADVERTISING
RUSSELL TIPPETT
1. EXHIBITORS SPACE SALES
2. EXHIBITOR LEASE AGREEMENTS

"We allow no geniuses around our studio. If anybody gets highbrow around the studio— out he goes."

— Walt Disney, "From the Wisdom of Walt Disney," ***Wisdom***, Volume 32, December 1959

The blurb about Disneyland changing over to a ticket book features a quote from C. V. Wood. Wood was part of the early planning committee for Disneyland, and as the park came to fruition, he was named Vice President.

Cornelius Vanderbilt Wood (C. V.), was a colorful personality and a piece of the Disneyland story. As the quote above alludes to, Walt had little tolerance for egos and personalities that he thought could be out of step with his own views and his company's. Contrary to the previous quote, Walt's organization did allow one genius—himself.

Walt's and C. V.'s personalities just didn't work well together, causing the two to clash. During Disneyland first year of existence, Wood was relieved of his duties.

But that wasn't the last time Walt would hear about Wood.

In May of 1960 Walt Disney filed suit against C. V. Wood and Marco Engineering Company.

"Walt Disney asked a Los Angeles court Tuesday to restrain C.V. Wood from claiming that Disneyland was Wood's idea. Disney's suit said that Wood and the Marco Engineering Company have been telling people that they 'conceived the idea for Disneyland,' or designed, engineered or constructed Disneyland.

The representations were made, Disney said, in promoting Disneyland-like amusement parks including Circusland at Sanford, Fla; International Recreations Corps Freedomland, Bronx, New York City and Magic Mountain in Denver.

Wood was once manager of Disneyland, but Disney says he was an operating manager only and did not make decisions on creative matters."

—***Charlotte Observer***, May 18, 1960

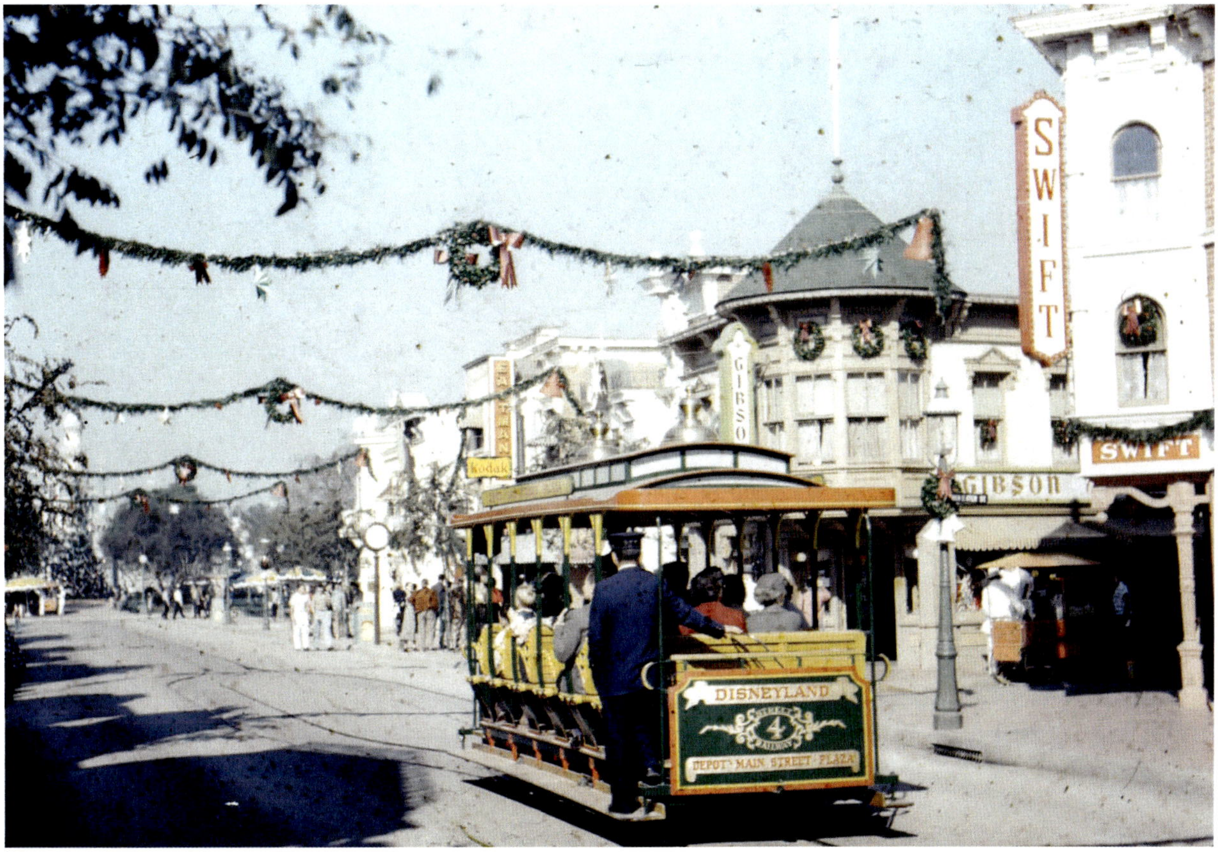

"The first annual 'Christmas as Disneyland' festival will open at Walt Disney's 'magic kingdom' on Thanksgiving Day, it was announced yesterday by Disneyland officials.

Highlighting the six-week celebration will be the premiere of the 'Mickey Mouse Club Circus,' a complete full scale hippodrome attraction personally produced by Walt Disney at a cost in excess of $300,000. Making their first public appearance will be the Mouseketeers, stars of Disney's Mickey Mouse Club TV series. Wild animal acts, a complete menagerie and trapeze and acrobatic acts have also been chosen by Disney for his first circus production.

Other features of Disneyland's Christmas festival will be a Yule decoration theme highlighted by Christmas decor in keeping with the 'lands' of Disneyland. A 'Christmas Bowl' adjacent to Disneyland's Plaza, is being designed where church choral groups, youth organizations and others will daily present musical entertainment in the Christmas season tradition for Disneyland visitors.

More than 60 musical groups, from as far away as Oklahoma, have already been scheduled to appear in Disneyland's 'Christmas Bowl.'"

— ***Pasadena Independent***, November 9, 1955

(Photo not from opening day)

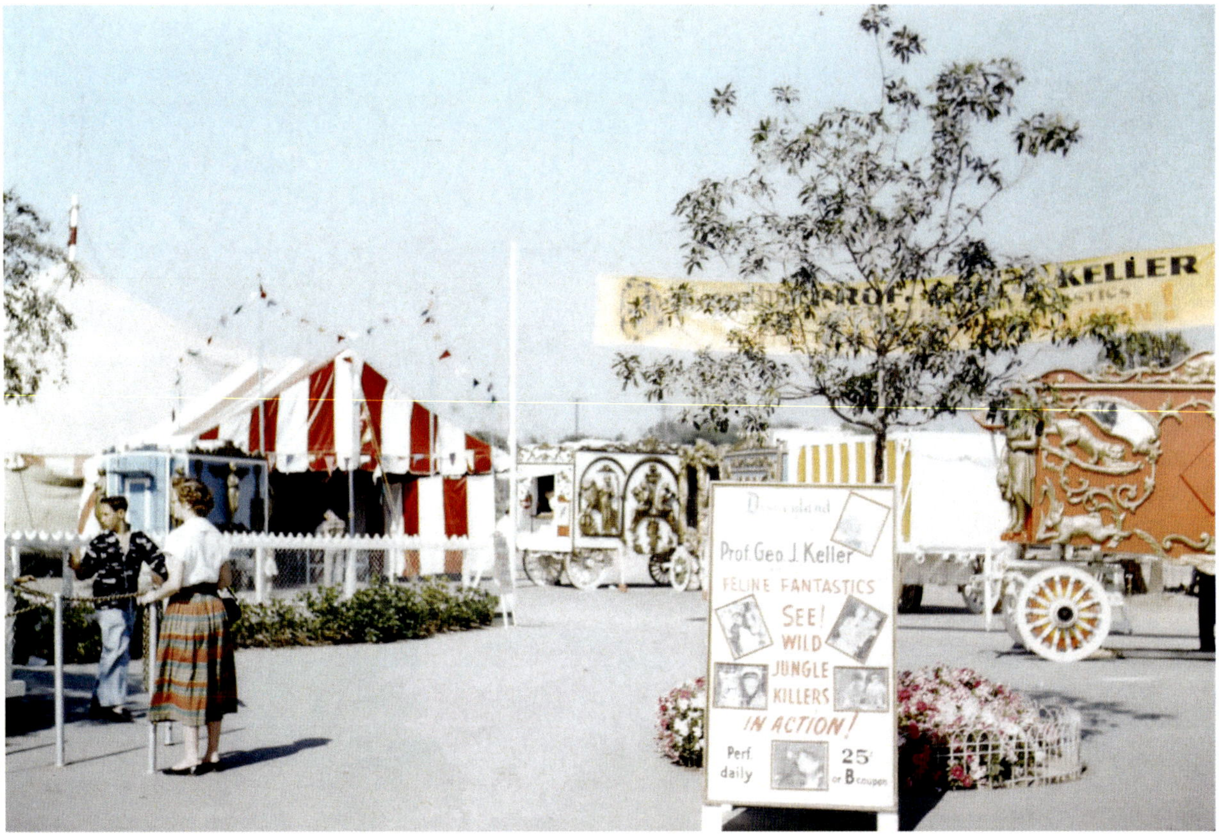

"Walt's latest venture marks his first entry into the circus field, the show promises to be one the greatest things he has done. Titled the Mickey Mouse Club Circus, it will present animal acts and aerialists, clowns and elephants and introduce the public, for the first time in person, to the Mickey Mouse Club Mouseketeers, including Jimmy Dodd, the Grand Mouseketeer as Ringmaster and Roy Williams, the 'Big Mooseketeer' as the Circus Strong Man.

The Mouse Club Circus will boast a menagerie of more than 80 animals, a talent roster of over 70 performers picked by Walt personally from the best circus talent available in the world. Some of these star attractions include Professor George Keller's Feline Fanatics, wild animals act fresh from engagements with Ringling Bros. and the Ted De Wayne troupe of acrobats and gymnasts. DeWayne's troupe has appeared in 46 states and 32 foreign countries with its sensational trampoline, tumbling and human pyramid gyrations.

Actions will get underway Thanksgiving Day with an old time Circus parade up Main Street. The entire Circus cast—animals, acrobat clowns and Mouseketeers—will march or be pulled in magnificent, original circus wagons. The parade will be climaxed by the official lighting of Disneyland's 'Old Fashioned Christmas' displays and the entire Main Street will sparkle from the illumination of colored lights on every building and in every shop window.

Immediately following the ceremony, the circus will have its premiere showing. Seats for 2500 persons will be available under Disneyland's 'Big Top' to be located in Holidayland and reached through Fantasyland. General admission prices are 50 cents for both adults and children. Reserved seats will also be available at $1 for children and adults.

The show itself is to be a fast paced presentation that will last about 75 minutes, twelve major acts headline the bill. Leading off will be Professor George Keller's amazing Feline Fanatics. Thirteen jungle animals, including lions, pumas, ocelots, leopards and tigers headline Keller's big cat act. His unique presentation—he works without whip, gun or chair—has sent chills through every audience he has played.

After the professor's act, clowns will ease the tension and then Walt's own Mouseketeers will take over center stage with a breathtaking aerial ballet, specially created for presentation here. Trained ponies, dogs, and seals enter next, followed by Kinko the Clown and his miniature auto. Performing Camels and Llamas make up the sixth act. After the animals is Ted DeWayne's troupe of acrobats and gymnasts will enliven center ring.

Special effort is being made to make this one of the most visual circuses ever seen. The 'Big Top' is being built to order for Disneyland at a cost of more than $30,000, and inside arrangement of the tent will assure a good view of the action from every seat.

The Big Top itself will be a major holiday attraction because of its gay red and white stripes. Measuring some 185 feet by 130 feet, it will be the largest striped Circus tent in the world. Seats will be permanent and sturdily reinforced. Another feature, a heating installation will make it the world's only heated surface tent. More than 200,000 people are expected to see the Mickey Mouse Club Circus during its holiday season run at Disneyland."

–Disneyland News, November 1955

Walt Disney loved the circus from the time he was a young boy. He figured his Disneyland guests would love it as well. As it turned out, the circus was a flop. Despite providing top-notch, exciting entertainment, perhaps it was actually a bit too banal alongside his Park, as visitors preferred to visit Disneyland over the circus.

The Mickey Mouse Club Circus didn't make another appearance after its first season and joins the Phantom Boats as two of Disneyland's shortest-lived attractions.

(Photo not from opening day)

"The switchboard at Disneyland, according to the telephone company, had an average of 900 calls per hour during peak construction periods. This amounted to 42,000 incoming calls a week figured on an 8-hour day, 6 days a week."

— ***Beach Independent***, July 15, 1955

(Photo not from opening day)

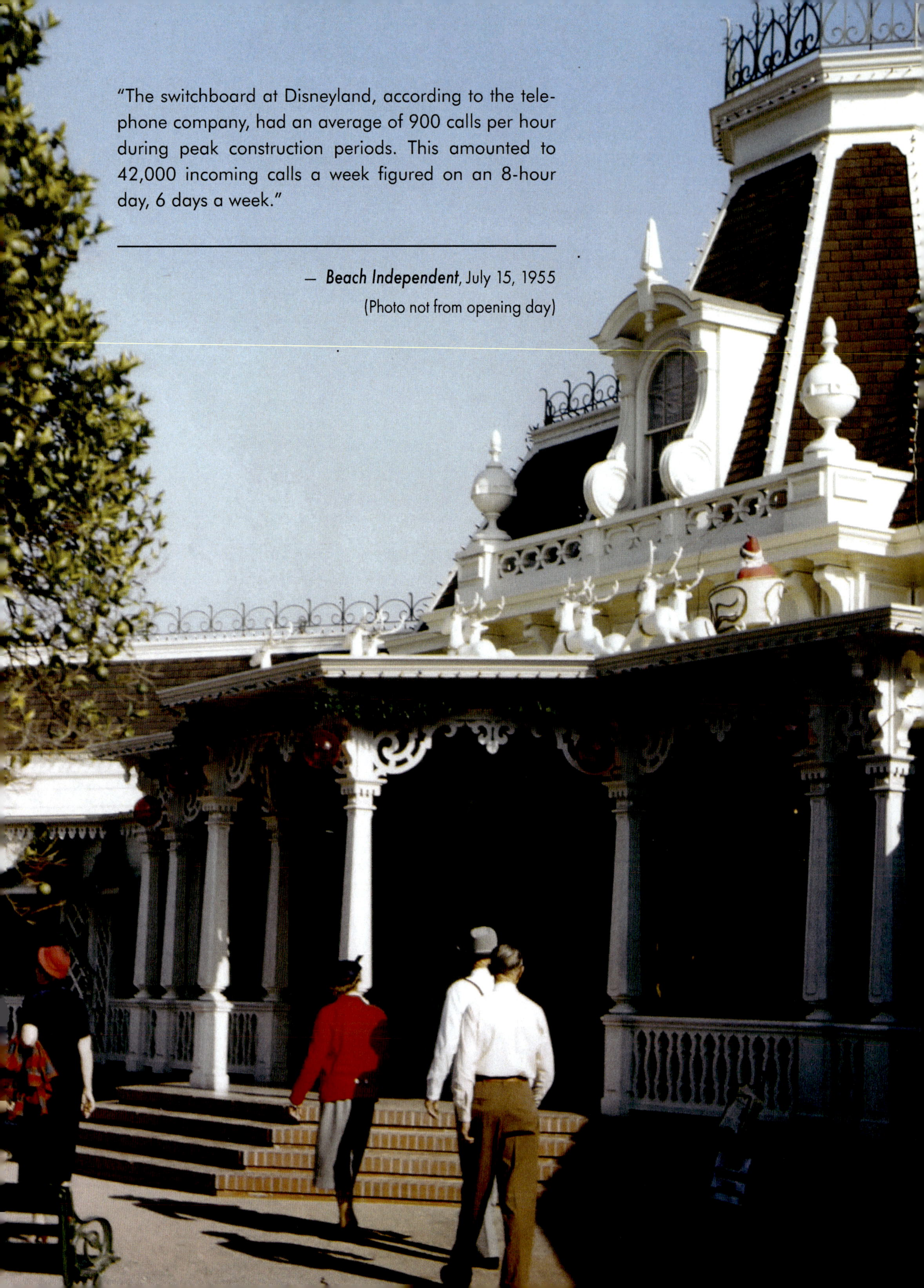

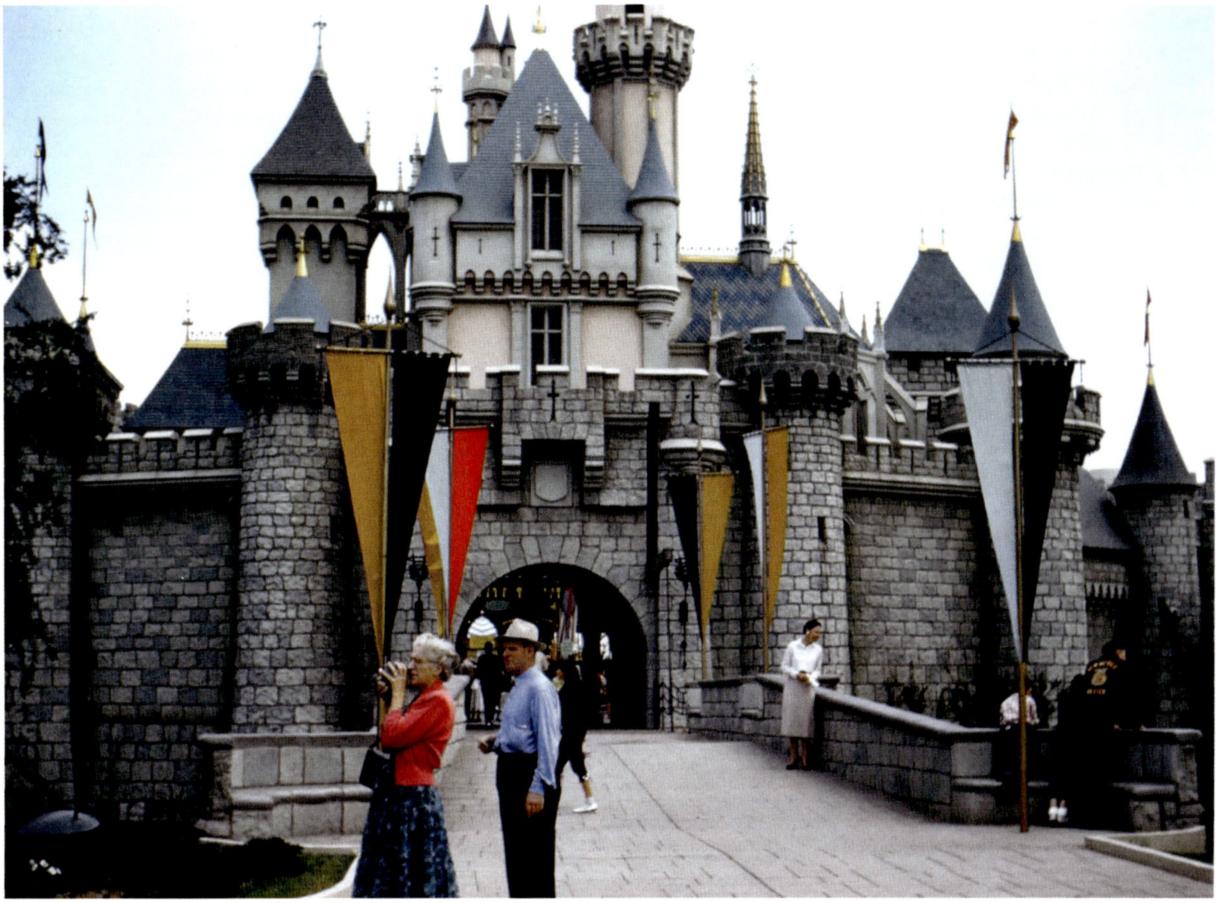

"'Right now we've [Disneyland] got a lot of bills to pay. We found a million dollars worth of bills we didn't know we had. We'll certainly have a profitable operation, but we won't have the full picture until we've had a year's cycle. We're learning all the time.'

A surprise so far: 70 percent of the patrons are adults. Does he [Walt Disney] have any disappointments? He said he hadn't, but admitted that his enjoyment of a project was more in its planning than the operation."

— ***Progress***, September 15, 1955

(Photo not from opening day)

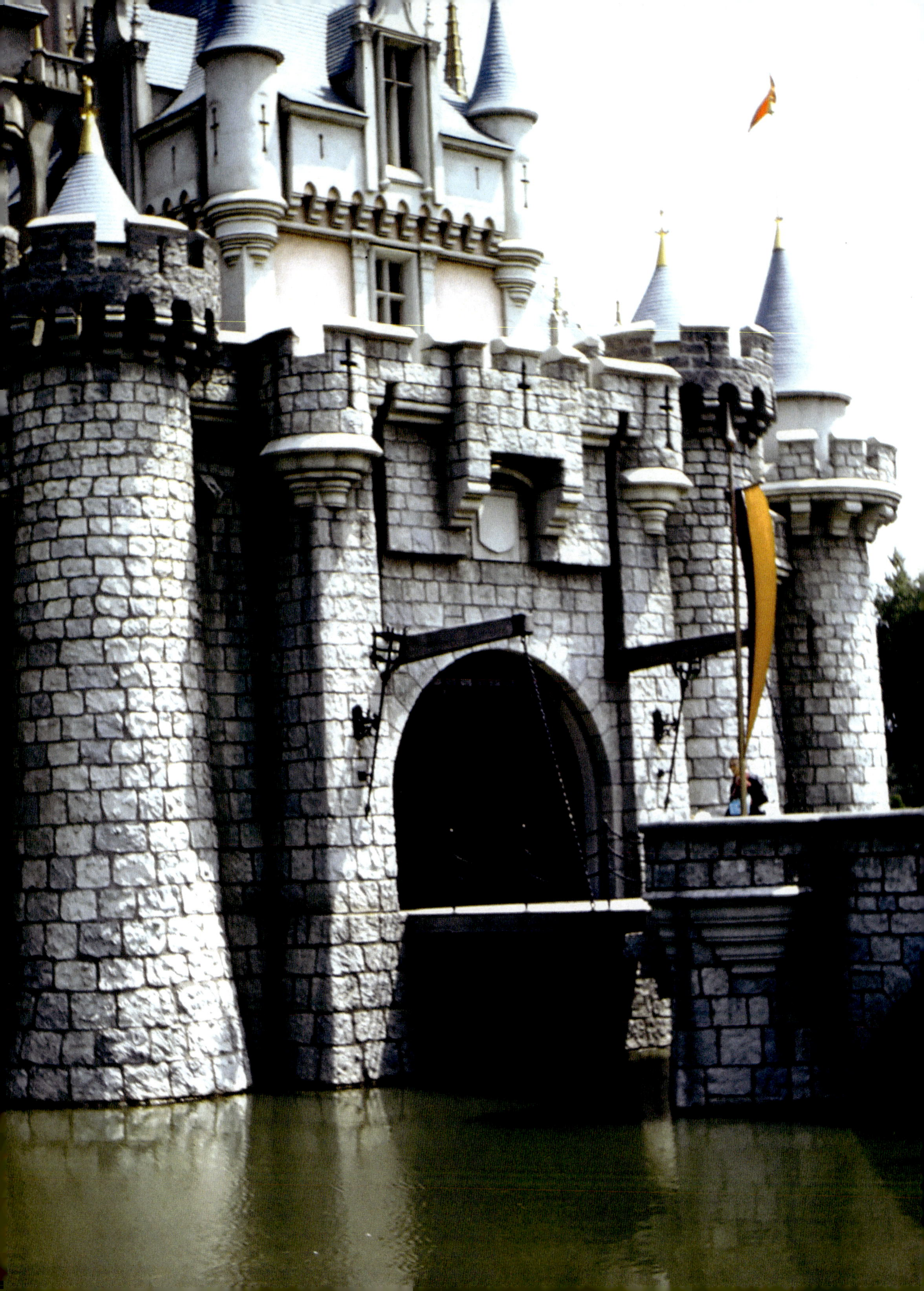

"I've never called my work an 'art.' It's part of show business, the business of building entertainment."

— Walt Disney speaking about Disneyland from Walt Disney Productions Tencennial Press Clippings
(Photo not from opening day)

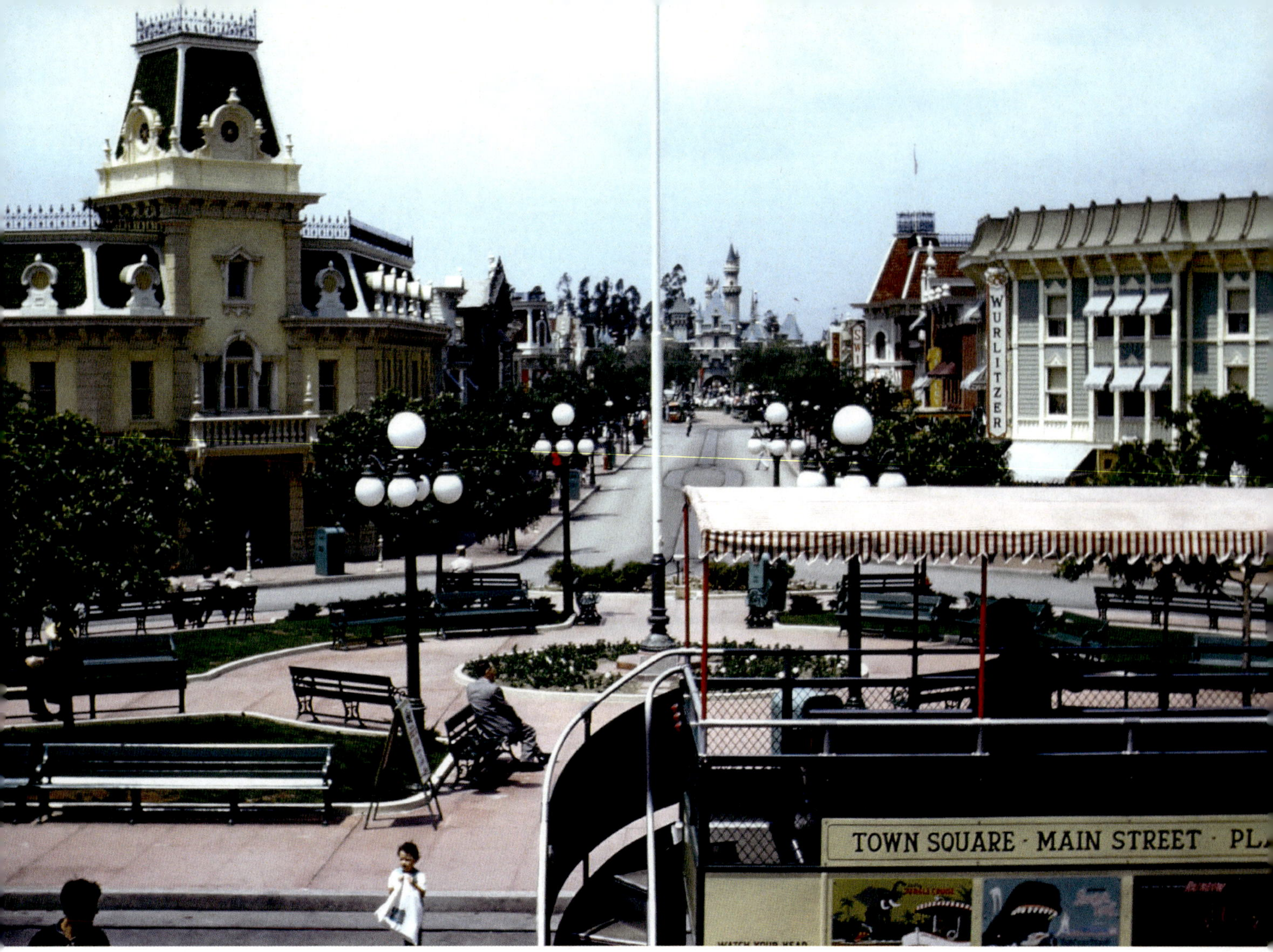

"Is it a success? 'Oh yes. No doubt about it. Attendance has been very satisfactory. Our only problem is adjusting the attendance so crowds don't pile up at one time and thin out at others . . .'"

— ***Pomona Progress,*** September 15, 1955

(Photo not from opening day)

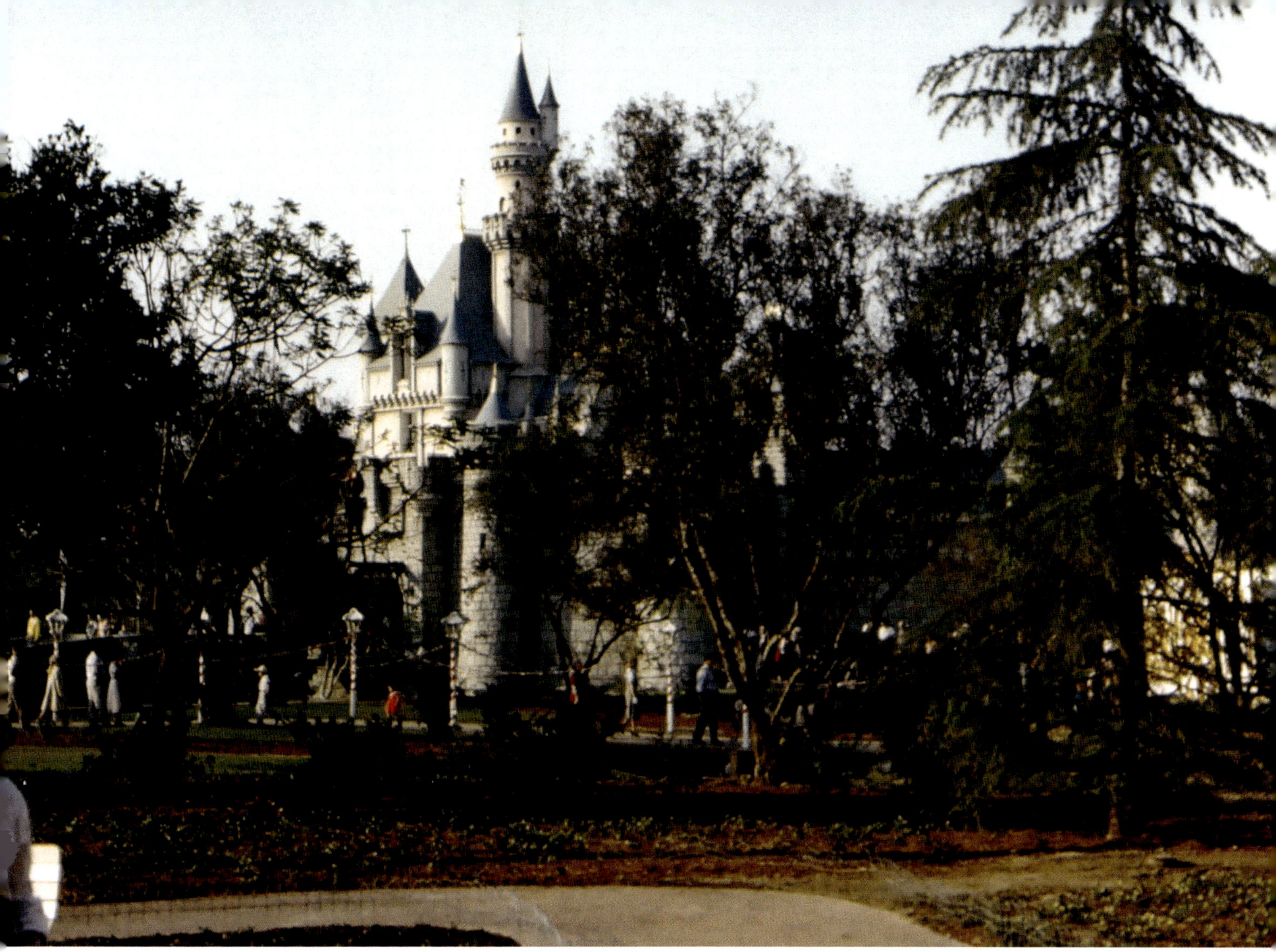

"Aside from the practical horticultural aspects of Disneyland landscaping, [Jack] Evans points out that a major consideration for the landscape architect was the 'photographic' quality of the setting.

'Disneyland is sure to become one of the most photographed places in America. When we designed and planted each area, we had to keep this constantly in mind. Every time a section was planted, or in preliminary stages, we would go out and stand at various camera distance angles to look at it. If we found a tree blocking the view, or if it was possible to see a palm tree planted in the tropical area from the section devoted to Main Street in the 1890s, we did something about it.'

Landscaping with a camera-eye may not be in the usual landscape architect's repertory but it meant that Disneyland's landscape architects sometimes had to 'forget the plans and just eyeball-it-in.'"

—***West Los Angeles Independent***, July 17, 1955

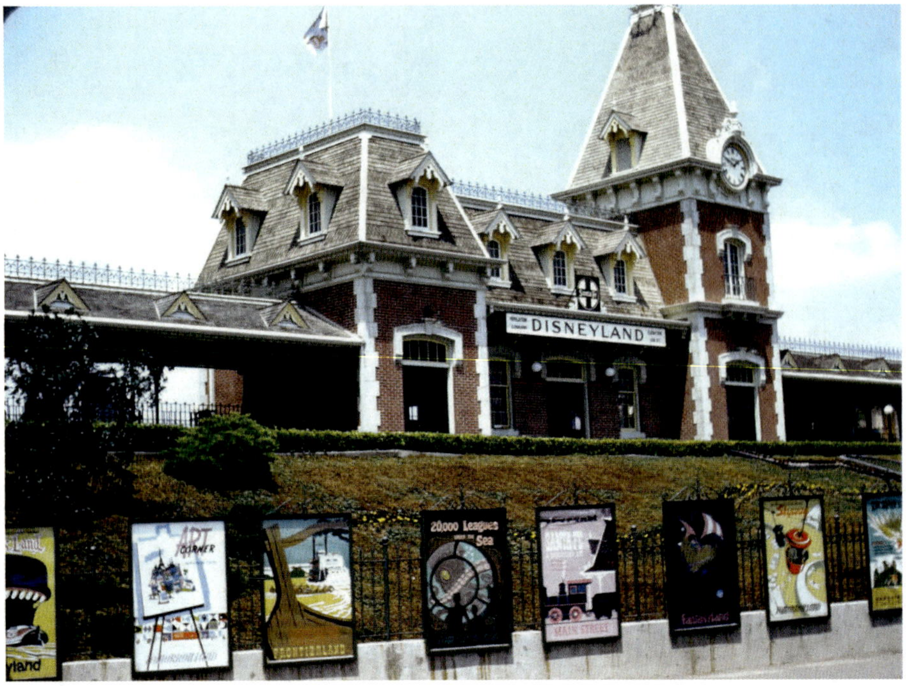

"Interesting contrast in brotherly characteristics is the successful Disney team. Walt—the creator, the artist—is seldom concerned about financial affairs. Roy is the treasury watchdog, the business member of the duo.

Roy was entertaining a group of the newly appointed directors of Disneyland in the studio commissary. Walt was sitting at the lunch counter munching a sandwich, reading a script when they came in.

'I have some bad news for my brother,' said Roy. 'I've got to go over and tell him that our budget on 20,000 Leagues Under the Sea has gone from the original two and-a-quarter-million dollar estimate to four million.'

Roy strolled over, interrupted Walt with the bad news. Walt looked up dreamily from his script for a moment and replied, 'Is that right?' and went back to his reading."

—*Valley Times,* June 21, 1954

"I love being an innovator. Money is something I understand only vaguely, and think about only when I don't have enough to finance my current enthusiasm, whatever it may be. All I know about money is that I have to have it to do things. I don't want my bank dividends, I'd rather keep that money working. I regard it as a moral obligation to pay back borrowed money. When I make a profit, I don't squander it away; I immediately plow it back into a fresh project. I have little respect for money as such, regard it merely as a medium for financing new ideas. I neither wish nor intend to amass a personal fortune. Money—or rather, the lack of it to carry out my ideas—may worry me, but it does not excite me. Ideas excite me."

— Walt Disney, "From the Wisdom of Walt Disney,"
Wisdom, Volume 32, December 1959
(Photo not from opening day)

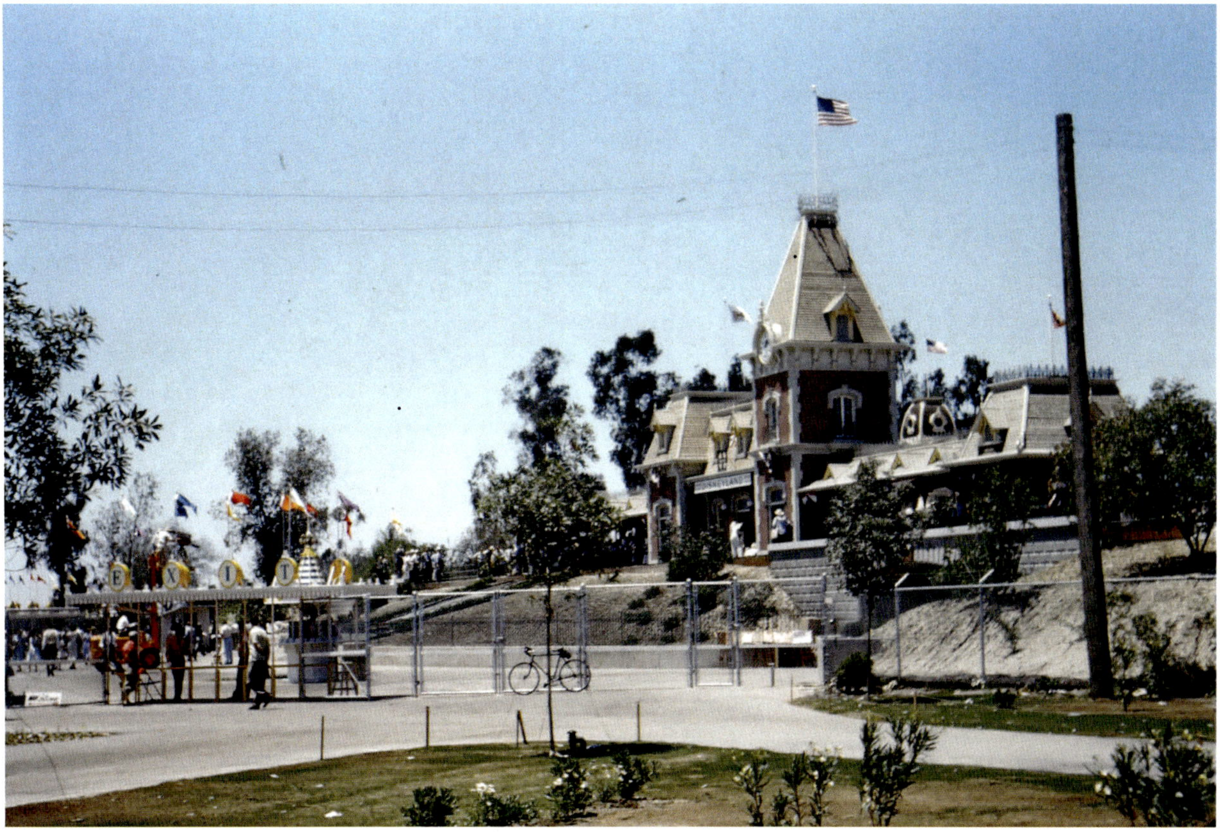

"Will Disneyland be duplicated elsewhere? 'I don't think so. You have to have a year-round business to make money from such a large investment. The only other place it would be possible is Florida.'"

—***Oakland Tribune***, May 8, 1955.

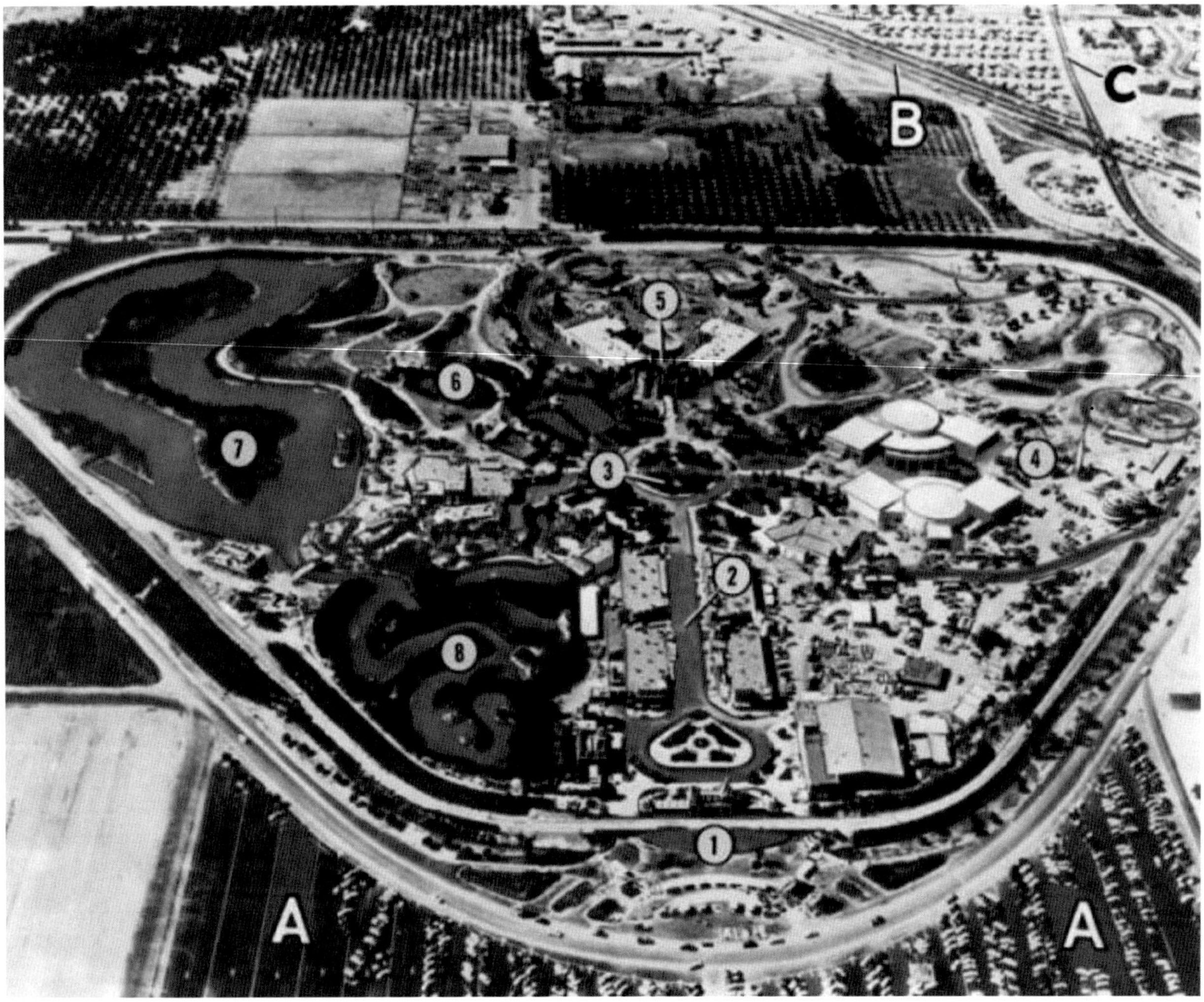

1955 aerial photo

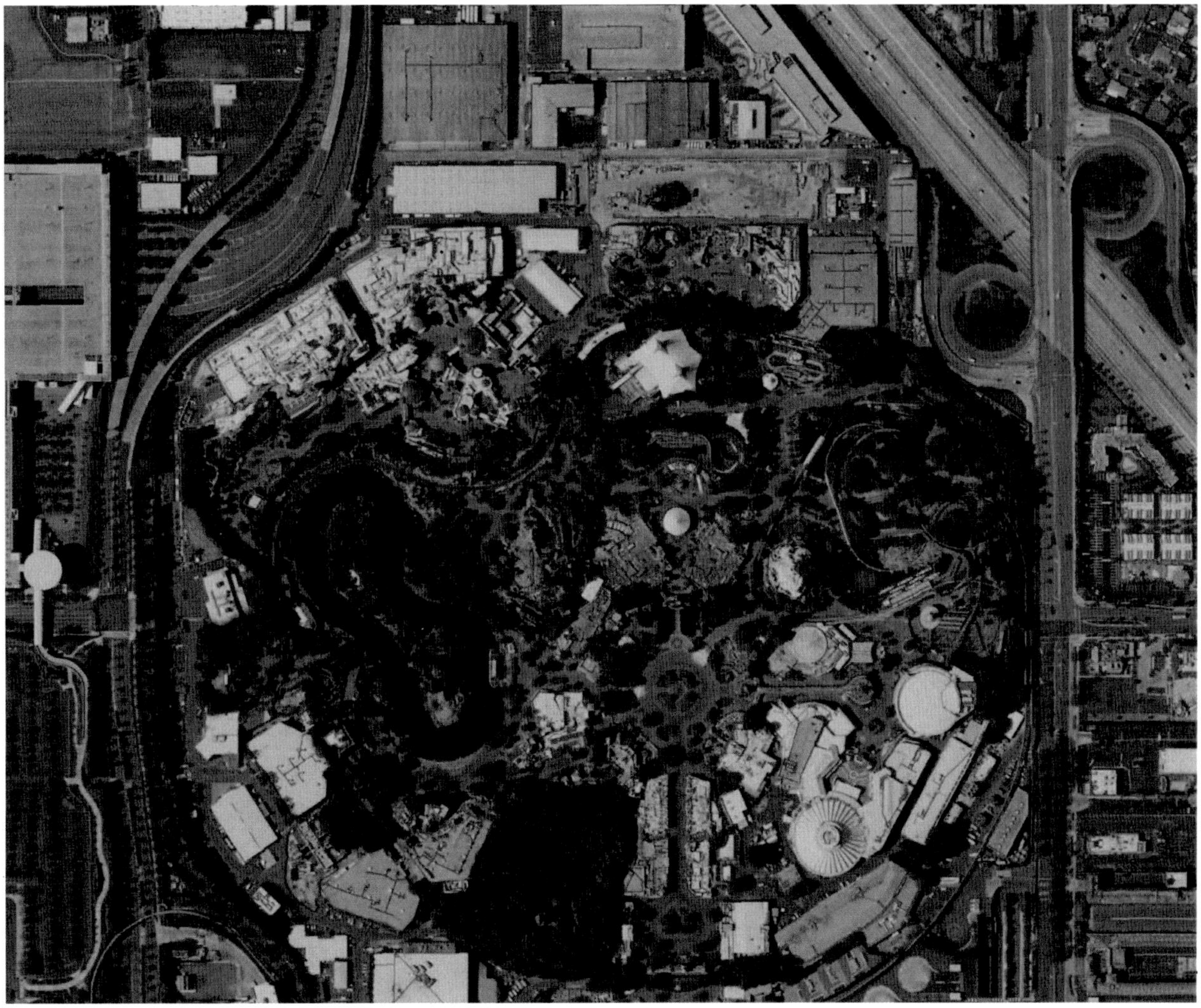

2020 aerial photo

Endnotes

1. *Independent Press Telegram*, Long Beach, California, July 15, 1955
2. *Oakland Tribune*, Oakland, California, May 8, 1955
3. Valley Times, North Hollywood, California, September 4, 1952
4. Laura Staloch, "Feeling low? Take a walk down memory lane. Study says nostalgia improves psychological well-being," Psypost, October 30, 2022
5. Arlin Cuncic, "What Is Nostalgia?" Very Well Mind, May 23, 2022
6. Nicholas J. Kelley, et.al, "Nostalgia confers psychological well-being by increasing a uthenticity," Journal of Experimental Social Psychology, Volume 102, September 2022
7. "Disney A to Z: Firehouse Five Plus Two," D23.com, 2023
8. Coos Bay Times, Coos Bay, Oregon, January 12, 1957
9. North County Times, San Diego, California, July 19, 1990
10. Randy Bright, Disneyland: Inside Story (New York: Harry N. Abrams, 1986)
11. Associated Press, May 8, 1955
12. West Los Angeles Independent, Los Angeles, California, July 17,1955

About Aaron

In the simplest terms, I'm a fan of all things Disney, just like you're probably a fan of some aspect of the Walt Disney Company. I just took my fandom to the next level!

I am University of Pennsylvania alumnus, from which I graduated with a bachelor's degree and a master's degree in anthropology. Looking back on my trajectory, perhaps on a subconscious level I wanted to finally make use of my degrees post-college, so I began to research Walt Disney and his creations. This led me to write and publish several books about Walt, his theme park, and his creations, both on the small screen and big screen.

I'm proud to say some of my books have won multiple awards, hit bestseller status, and are carried in-store by major booksellers across the country—pretty remarkable feats for a small publisher like myself.

Over the years, I have guest authored a story about Disney for the Library of Congress, and I've been interviewed regarding Disney by the *New York Times*, the *Wall Street Journal*, *CNN*, *NBC News,* the Los Angeles Times, the *Orlando Sentinel*, and the *San Francisco Chronicle*, to name a few!

More Great Books By Aaron!

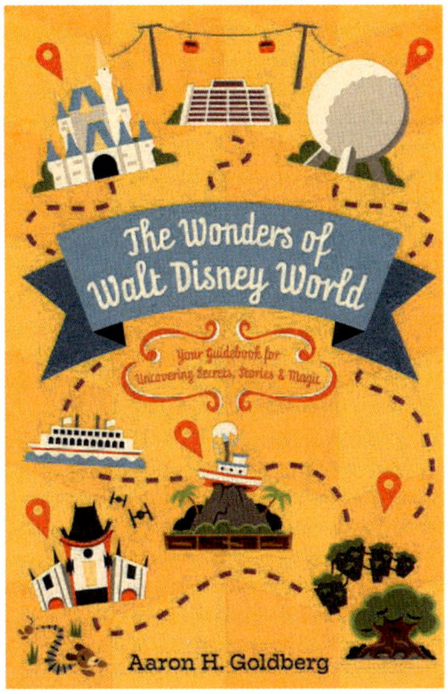

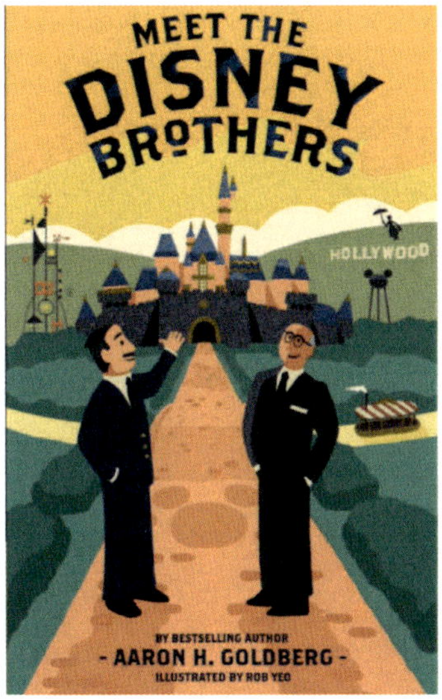

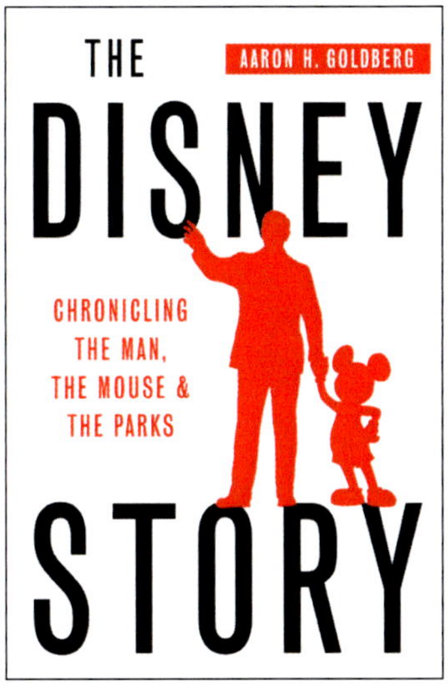

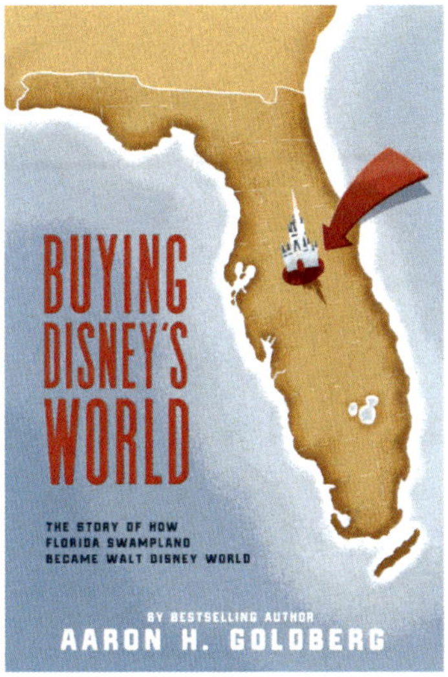

Made in the USA
Las Vegas, NV
24 June 2026

1aecde1f-30ae-4b09-90fe-c4eadce728a7R01